ERIC NEWBY was born in London in 1919 and was educated at St Paul's School. In 1938 he joined the four-masted Finnish barque *Moshulu* as an apprentice and sailed in the last Grain Race from Australia to Europe by way of Cape Horn. During the Second World War he served in the Black Watch and Special Boat Section, and was a prisoner-of-war from 1942 to 1945. After the war his world expanded still further – into the fashion business and book publishing. Whatever else he was doing, he always travelled on a grand scale, either under his own steam or as Travel Editor of the *Observer*. He was made CBE in 1994.

ALSO BY ERIC NEWBY

ERIC NEWBY

LOVE AND WAR IN THE APENNINES

PICADOR

in association with Collins

First published 1971 by Hodder and Stoughton

This edition published 1983 by Picador
an imprint of Macmillan Publishers Ltd
25 Eccleston Place, London SW1W 9NF
Basingstoke and Oxford
Associated companies throughout the world
www.macmillan.co.uk

In association with William Collins Sons & Co. Ltd

ISBN 0 330 28024 4

31 33 35 37 39 38 36 34 32

A CIP catalogue record for this book is available
from the British Library.

Printed and bound in Great Britain by
Mackays of Chatham plc, Chatham, Kent

To all those Italians who helped
me, and thousands like me, at
the risk of their lives, I dedicate
this book.

Preface

Anyone who reads this book is entitled to ask how anyone can remember events which happened twenty-eight years ago and, what is even more extraordinary and unbelievable, what happened on a particular day. It is, of course, impossible, except for some rare people who have the gift of total recall, which I do not possess.

The events described fall into three distinct periods: the one in which I was captured; the time I spent as a prisoner of war; and the third period when I was free after the Italian Armistice. I find no difficulty in remembering being captured. It is something, as most people who have been captured would agree, that is such a disagreeable experience that one remembers the circumstances for the rest of one's life. Neither does one forget what it was like to be a prisoner, although it is impossible to separate one day from another unless one keeps a journal, which I didn't.

The third period was the one which I really needed to remember in order to write this book, and I was able to do so because I kept a skeletal day-by-day diary, without naming people or places, and I used this record to write a detailed account of what happened while I was in a prison camp in Czechoslovakia in the spring of 1944 soon after I was recaptured. This, although I didn't think of it as such, was the first draft of the present book.

The reader may also ask another, equally sensible question. Why have I allowed such a long time to pass before writing it?

Not long after the war finished a minor flood of books about prison camps, escapes and life with the Resistance appeared. Some of them were so good—George Millar's *Horned Pigeon* and *Maquis* for instance—that I felt that a book about an escape that was nothing but a mass walk-out from a camp and my subsequent experiences, did not seem exciting enough to write about— I myself didn't even succeed in getting through the enemy line as so many people did. In fact I did not even attempt to. Nor did I join the Partisans. There were none to join at that time in the particular part of the Apennines in which I was hiding, anyway. Scarcely a help in producing an exciting book. I let the whole thing drop.

I finally decided to write the book because I felt that comparatively little had been written about the ordinary Italian people who helped prisoners of war at great personal risk and without thought of personal gain, purely out of kindness of heart. The sort of people one can still see today working in the fields as one whizzes down the Autostrada del Sole and on any mountain road in the Apennines. If only I had been able to speak the language better at that time perhaps their qualities would have emerged more clearly than they do now.

There are certain omissions and additions. In the Autumn of 1943 there were more prisoners of war in the part of the Apennines described in this book than actually appear in it. There have also been widespread changes in the names of people and places, and many characters are composite. As Belloc wrote in *Cautionary Tales for Children*:

> And is it true?
> It is not true.
> And if it were it wouldn't do.

If I have only succeeded in producing an inferior version of "Mademoiselle from Armentières", without the music and the song, than I can only apologise. I can't give the reader his money back. Those who are bored by descriptions of abortive cloak and dagger operations should skip the first chapter.

The peasants are the great sanctuary
of sanity, the country the last stronghold
of happiness. When they disappear
there is no hope for the race.
Virginia Woolf

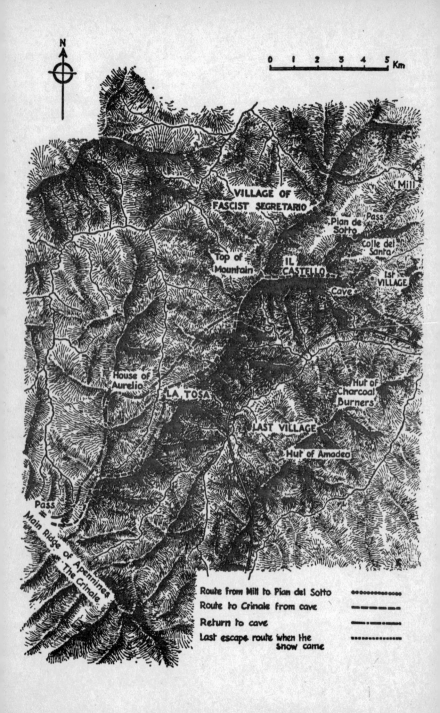

N

| 0 | 1 | 2 | 3 | 4 | 5 | Km |

VILLAGE OF
FASCIST SEGRETARIO

Mill

Pian de
Sotto

Pass

Colle del
Santa

Top of
Mountain

IL
CASTELLO

1st
VILLAGE

Cave

House of
Aurelio

LA TOSA

Hut of
Charcoal
Burners

LAST VILLAGE

Hut of Amadeo

Pass

Main Ridge of Apennines
The Crinale

Route from Mill to Pian del Sotto ●●●●●●●●●●●●●
Route to Crinale from cave − − − − − − −
Return to cave −·−·−·−·−
Last escape route when the ▪▪▪▪▪▪▪▪▪▪▪▪
      snow came

Contents

Chapter One

Operation Whynot

We were captured off the east coast of Sicily on the morning of the twelfth of August, 1942, about four miles out in the Bay of Catania. It was a beautiful morning. As the sun rose I could see Etna, a truncated cone with a plume of smoke over it like the quill of a pen stuck in a pewter inkpot, rising out of the haze to the north of where I was treading water.

There were five of us. Originally there had been seven, but one, a marine, had had to be left behind on the submarine and another, Sergeant Dunbar of the Argylls was missing, killed, wounded or captured, we none of us knew, lost among the coast defences in the dunes. We were all that remained of M Detachment of the Special Boat Section. Three officers, of whom I was one, Corporal Butler of the South Lancashire Regiment and Guardsman Duffy of the Coldstream, one of the smallest sub-units in the British Army, now about to be wiped out completely.

About eight o'clock we were picked up by some Sicilian fishermen who hauled us into their boat like a lot of half-dead fish. They were surprised. We were thankful, although we knew that we would now never make the rendezvous off Capo Campolato which had been fixed for the following night if we failed to reach the submarine by one o'clock on the morning of the twelfth.

I remember lying among the freshly caught fish in the bottom of the boat, some of them exotic, all displaying considerably greater liveliness than we did, and discussing with the others the possibility of taking it over and forcing the fishermen to head for Malta, 120 miles to the south, for the boat had a sail, as well as an engine. And if we had been in a war film made twenty years later this is what we undoubtedly would have done, but we had been in the water for nearly five hours and were very cold and could hardly stand.

Besides, the fishermen were kindly men. They thought that we were survivors from a torpedoed ship and they gave us what little wine and bread they had with them which amounted to a mouthful each. To them the war, as they made clear by various unequivocal gestures, was a misfortune which had brought misery to everyone and, as far as they were concerned, had seriously restricted their fishing. The idea of using violence against such people was unthinkable. And even if we had decided to try and take over the boat it would have been impossible to get away. It was one of a fleet of a dozen or so whose crews now brought them alongside so that they, too, could view this extraordinary haul. We were prisoners without, as yet, having admitted the fact to ourselves. It was too soon. Everything had happened too quickly.

On the afternoon of the tenth, immediately before we sailed from Malta, we had been given the bare, gruesome bones of what had been christened *Operation Whynot*. For the flesh we would have to rely on some last-minute aerial photographs of the target which were still in the darkroom and which we would have to study when we were submerged.

We were told that we were going to attack a German bomber airfield four miles south of Catania in Sicily which was expected to have between fifty and sixty J.U.88s on it on the night of the eleventh, and destroy as many of them as we could so that they would be out of action on the twelfth and thirteenth when a British convoy essential to Malta's survival would be within a hundred miles of the island but still beyond effective fighter cover from it. There would be no time for a preliminary reconnaissance. We had to land and go straight in and come out if we could. The beach was heavily defended and there was a lot of wire. It was not known if it was mined but it was thought highly probable. The whole thing sounded awful but at least it seemed important and worth doing. Irregular forces such as ours were not always employed in such ostensibly useful roles.

We travelled to Sicily in *Una*, one of the smaller submarines. Her commander, Pat Norman, was a charming and cheerful lieutenant of our own age.

I was already in the conning tower and we were just about to sail when a steward came running down the mole brandishing a piece of paper which, after having received permission to climb into the conning tower, he presented to me. It was a bill for an infinitesimal sum for drinks which I had ordered in the wardroom (our hosts, the Tenth Submarine Flotilla were so generous that it was almost impossible to buy them any). Apparently the others had already been presented with theirs while I was elsewhere. Actually, I had been attempting to dig down to my kit which had been buried when a large bomb had fallen that morning on the great impregnable-looking Vaubanesque fort in which we were billeted and destroyed my room.

No one, including Norman, had any money on them. Like me, none of them had thought that they might conceivably need money underwater.

"I'll pay you when I get back," I said, airily. "There's nothing to worry about. I'm attached to the Tenth Submarine Flotilla."

"That's what they all say, sir," he said, gloomily. "Military officers attached to the Tenth Submarine Flotilla. And then we never see them again, more often than not. I'm afraid I must ask you to give me a cheque, sir."

I told him with some relish that, if he wanted a cheque from me, he would have to shift some tons of masonry in order to find one.

"No need for that, sir," he said. "I've brought you a blank cheque. All you have to do is fill in the name and address of your bank and sign it."

Even then it seemed an evil omen.

As soon as we were submerged and clear of Sliema Creek, George Duncan, who was our C.O., gave us all the information about the larger operation of which *Whynot* was a minute part that his superiors had thought fit to give him. The rest he had picked up for himself, which he was very good at doing. Listening to him I was glad I was no longer a merchant seaman.

In a final attempt to save Malta from capitulation, a convoy of fourteen merchant ships was being fought through the Mediterranean from the west. One of them was a tanker, the only one that could be found that could attain the sixteen knots at which the ships were to steam. The safe arrival of this tanker was essential, for without it the island would be deprived of fuel.

The convoy had already passed through the Straits of Gibraltar the previous night and it was now somewhere south of the Balearics. The escort and covering forces were prodigious: two battleships, four carriers, one of which was going to fly its entire complement of Spitfires into Malta when it got within range, seven cruisers and twenty-five destroyers. Somewhere at the mouth of the Sicilian Channel the covering force would turn back and the remaining cruisers and destroyers would take the convoy through to Malta. Heavy losses were expected.

The enemy's preparations for the destruction of the convoy were on an even grander scale than the arrangements for protecting it. They had been following its movements with great interest ever since it had left the west coast of Scotland and they probably knew its destination (crates marked MALTA had been left conspicuously on the quayside at Glasgow while the ships were loading them for anyone interested to see but, mercifully, none of us knew this at the time). All the Sardinian and Sicilian airfields were crammed with bombers of the Second and Tenth German Air

Fleets, and that remarkable military jack-of-all-trades and master of most of them, Field-Marshal Kesselring, was in overall command of the air operations. There was also a force of Italian torpedo bombers, which was to play an important part in the operation, and large numbers of German and Italian submarines and motor torpedo boats had been deployed along the route.

The code name of the convoy was *Pedestal*. It was commanded by a rear-admiral, and the cruiser and destroyer force which had the truly awful task of taking the convoy through to Malta, by a vice-admiral. George didn't know their names but it was unimportant. I did not envy them; but I envied much less the men in the merchant ships. Besides, we had enough on our hands with our own piddling little *Whynot* to worry about them. By this time, one o'clock in the afternoon of the tenth, although none of us knew it, the carrier *Eagle* had already been sunk by an Italian submarine. And this was only the beginning.

It would be tedious to relate the details of the voyage. They were the same as any other for passengers in a submarine. The wardroom was so minute that apart from the times when I emerged to eat and discuss our plans, such as they were, and pore over the aerial photographs which had been taken from such an altitude that they needed an expert to interpret them and we soon gave up trying to do so, I spent the rest of the time lying on a mattress under the wardroom table, a place to which I had been relegated as the most junior officer of the party. I shared this humble couch with Socks, a dachshund, the property of Desmond Buchanan, an officer in the Grenadiers who was one of our party and who had persuaded Pat Norman to allow him to bring her with him because of the noise of the air-raids on Malta which were practically continuous. ("I wouldn't dream of leaving my little girl here. Her nerves are going to pieces.") From time to time Socks went off to other parts of the submarine, from which she returned bloated with food and with her low-slung chassis covered with oil, a good deal of which she imparted to me. But on the whole it was a cheerful journey and we laughed a lot, although most of it was the laughter of bravado. We all knew that we were embarked on the worst possible kind of operation, one that had been hastily conceived by someone a long way from the target, and one which we had not had the opportunity to think out in detail for ourselves. I felt like one of those rather ludicrous, ill-briefed agents who had been landed by night on Romney Marsh in the summer of 1940, all of whom had been captured and shot.

By four o'clock in the afternoon of the eleventh we were in the Bay of Catania, about a mile offshore, and Pat brought *Una* up to periscope depth so that we could have a look at the coast.

He got a bit of a shock when he did. He had come up in the midst of a fleet of Sicilian fishing boats and they swam into the eye of the periscope like oversize fish in an aquarium. Raising the periscope he was lucky not to have impaled one of them on the end of it. Nevertheless, with what I thought an excess of zeal, he insisted on giving each of us an opportunity to look at the coast which we did, hastily, before causing *Una* to sink to the bottom where she remained for the next five hours with everything shut off that might produce a detectable noise. It had not been a very successful reconnaissance; but there had been nothing to see anyway. With an immense sun glaring at us from behind a low-lying coast, the shore had appeared as nothing more than a thin, tremulous black line with a shimmering sea in front of it.

We surfaced at nine o'clock and the four folboats were brought up on to the casing through the torpedo hatch without their midship frames in position, the only way we could get them through it, and we carried out the final assembly.

It was not a very dark night, but after thirty-six hours in artificial light underwater it seemed terribly black until we became accustomed to it, when it seemed altogether too bright. To the north we could see the lights of Catania and to the west the landing lights of the airfield. Planes were coming in to land a couple of hundred feet above our heads, and when they were directly above us the noise was deafening. The wind was on-shore and there was a nasty swell running which made the launching of the canoes over the bulges difficult with the tanks blown, and the loading of them once they were in the water even more so. One canoe was so badly damaged getting it into the water that it had to be left behind, together with the marine who was going to travel in it. He was very disappointed at the time. How fortunate he was.

"Rather you than me, mate, but good luck anyway," were the last words addressed to me by a rating as he threw me the stern line; then we set off in arrowhead formation towards the shore, if three canoes can be said to constitute an arrowhead.

The water was extraordinarily phosphorescent. We might have been in a tropical sea and as we dipped the blades of the paddles it exploded into brilliant green and blue fire and as we lifted them out of it they shed what looked like drops of molten metal which vanished when they fell back into the water. At any other time these effects would have seemed beautiful; now they seemed an additional hazard. Surely to the sentries

17

patrolling the beach it must look as if there was a fire out at sea, and surely the crews of the bombers which were still coming in to land over our heads from dead astern must see it, just as surely as they must have already seen the submarine. Together with Corporal Butler of the South Lanca-shire Regiment, my companion at bow who was no doubt sharing these gloomy thoughts, I paddled towards the shore, trying to hearten myself with the prospect of the bacon and eggs which we had been promised if and when we returned on board.

After a few minutes we heard the boom of surf and soon we were on the outer edge of it. It was not very heavy, but we got out of the canoes as we knew how to without capsizing them, and swam in with them until our feet touched bottom and we could stand. It is better to arrive sopping wet on two feet on a hostile shore than to be capsized or thrown up on it dry but immobile in a sitting position, unless you are a secret agent who must immediately enter the market place and mingle with the crowds.

The beach, with the wind blowing over it and the surf beating on it, seemed the loneliest place in the world. The wire began about fifty feet from the water's edge. We carried the canoes up over the sand and put them down close to the entanglements without being blown to pieces. At least this part of the beach did not seem to be mined with anything that a man's weight would set off, or perhaps we were lucky, there was no way of knowing.

Now we attached the time pencils to the bombs, which were a mixture of plastic and thermite. (With the white cordtex fuses they looked like big black conkers on strings). This was something that could not safely be done on board a submarine costing a mint of money, because time pencils were rather erratic, and I always hoped that the workers in the factory in which they had been made had not got all mixed up and substituted a thin, thirty-second delay wire for a thicker, thirty-minute one, or simply painted the outside casing with the wrong colour paint, which was one of the methods of identifying them, mistakes that could quite easily happen after a pre-Christmas factory beano.

When the bombs were ready we buried the canoes upside down in the sand and obliterated our footprints, working upwards from the water's edge.

The wire entanglements were about twenty yards wide and they stretched away along the shore north and south as far as the eye could see. Behind them, there were two blockhouses about 150 yards apart. We had landed exactly half way between them. I felt as if I had survived the first round in a game of Russian roulette.

Now we began to cut a narrow swathe through the wire at a place where there appeared to be none of the more visible sorts of anti-personnel mines with which we were acquainted. Nevertheless, it was a disagreeable sensation. Only God and the enemy knew what was buried underfoot.

By the time we got to the other side it was ten o'clock. An hour had passed since we had left the submarine. We were already late, but it was difficult to see how we could have been any quicker. The earliest possible time at which we could arrive back at the submarine had been estimated to be eleven o'clock. The latest possible time, providing that *Una* had not been discovered, in which case she would have to submerge and leave us anyway, was one o'clock in the morning. If all went well it still seemed that we might make it by midnight, or earlier.

On the far side of the wire at the edge of the dunes, we came to a track which ran parallel with the shore and presumably linked all the blockhouses on this stretch of coast. Fortunately, it was deserted and we pressed on across it and pushed our way through a hedge of some kind of coarse vegetation which had probably been planted to stop the sand drifting inland. For the first time in my life I was in Europe.

Behind this windbreak there was a line of stunted pines and a low drystone wall with a sunken field on the other side of it. Coming from this field was an appalling noise which sounded like a body of men marching along a road and we crouched behind the wall for what seemed an age, waiting for them to pass, until we realised that it was only a horse that was munching grass.

Feeling very stupid we dropped down into the field and crossed it. The horse went on munching. It was a white horse. How I envied it. How silly the whole business seemed at this moment. It was a nice horse but at this moment it was an enemy horse. If it whinneyed or began to gallop around the field we might be discovered; but it did neither of these things. It simply went on eating its dinner.

On the far side of the field there was a high stone wall which, like the wire entanglements on the beach, seemed to be endless, and we pushed George up on to the top of it so that he could see what there was on the other side; but all that he could report was that the landing lights on the airfield had been put out. No more planes were coming in and everything seemed quiet. Our prospects began to seem quite good.

He hauled us up one by one, on to the top of the wall and we dropped down into what proved to be a farmyard full of dogs. Previously they must have been dozing, but the thump of our great boots as we landed on the cobbles brought them to life and they came at us barking and yelping furiously.

The farmhouse had been invisible from the top of the wall, hidden among trees, and now we had to pass the front door, but in spite of the din the dogs were making, no windows or doors were flung open and we made a dash for the far side of the yard where there was a gate which opened on to a dark lane, overshadowed by trees, which seemed to lead in the direction of the airfield. And as we went along it an engine, which sounded as if it was on a test bench, began to scream and sob, drowning the din the dogs were still making, and then died away, tried to start again, but failed.

After about a mile, the lane suddenly came to an end and we found ourselves in the workshop area of the airfield, among buildings with bright lights burning in them. One of them had a number of large wooden crates standing outside it, some of which had only recently been broken open. They contained aircraft engines. On as many of these as we dared expend them we stuck a bomb. It was a terrible waste of explosive; but if we failed on the airfield itself we wanted to leave something to be remembered by. Perhaps, unconsciously, in destroying the engines we were performing some primitive ritual of atonement.

We were now very close to the edge of the airfield and we were just about to split up into pairs and set off for our various targets, Butler's and my own being the bombers on the far side of it, more than half a mile away, when we ran straight into a body of men, one of whom shouted at us in Italian, demanding to know who we were. We said nothing but pressed on through them until the same man shouted at us again, this time more insistently—what sounded to me like "Eh! Eh! Eh!"—so insistently that George was forced to reply, using one of the phrases which we had all memorised, "*Camerati Tedeschi*", which we had been told meant "German Comrades".

It sounded even less convincing now, on enemy soil, coming from the mouth of a captain in the Black Watch who had been a sheep farmer in Dumfriesshire before the war, than it had when we had all practised it, and other Italian and German phrases, on one another in the submarine. And it must have sounded even more so to the Italian because he immediately took a pot shot at us with some sort of firearm. Fortunately it was not an automatic weapon, or perhaps it was on single rounds. If it had been he would probably have rubbed us out completely. Whatever it was, he only fired a single shot.

Then one of our party, I never knew who it was, fired back, a single round from a machine pistol.

The effect of the two shots was positively magical. Immediately the airfield was brightly lit by searchlights which were disposed around the perimeter—as if the man who had fired at us had his hand on the switches—and then pandemonium broke loose: lorries and trucks started up; Verey lights rose; the air was filled with the ghastly sounds of commands being issued in Italian and German; and there was the, to me, equally terrifying noise made by men in boots running on hard surfaces in step. It was difficult to repress the thought that we were expected.

I was not surprised. What had surprised me, had surprised us all, was that we had managed to land at all. This kind of operation had been successfully attempted so many times in the past and with such losses in aircraft to the enemy, that by now it was inconceivable that they would not be permanently on the qui vive, and on the very eve of a major action, doubly so. Probably the only reason we had got this far unchallenged was because not even the Germans could imagine that the sort of small party that had done such damage on their airfields in the past would be crazy enough to make a frontal assault on a target of this magnitude. We were lucky to have got over the wall into the farmyard. In this way we seemed to have avoided the official way in.

There were men all round us now but they were confused as to who was who, and afraid to open fire for fear of killing some of their own side. Fortunately the workshop area was one of the few parts of the place which were still comparatively dark, because it was masked by the buildings.

It was at this moment, with everyone milling around in the darkness as if they were playing Murder at a party, that a man loomed up in front of me speaking excitedly in German. There seemed no alternative but to shoot him before he shot me and I stuck my pistol hard against his ribs and was just about to press the trigger when he said in Lowland Scots "Don't shoot you stupid bastard, It's me!"

Then we dodged round the corner of one of the buildings and ran as hard as we could across a piece of brilliantly illuminated ground on which some clumps of bushes partly hid us from view, towards a wood, a hundred yards or so away.

As soon as we reached it we lay down and tried to make out what was happening. There was no need to use night glasses. With half a dozen searchlights playing on it, the airfield looked more or less as it must have done under the midday sun, except that now it was swarming with infantry who were being formed up to carry out a large-scale *battue*, and every moment more lorryloads were arriving. I felt like a pheasant looking out on the approaching beaters from the false security of a covert. Surprisingly, there seemed to be no guard dogs. I had expected

21

the place to be seething with them, as some of the Cretan airfields had been, according to those who had visited them.

And beyond the soldiers were the planes. I had never seen so many J.U.88s in my life.

"What I think we should do," George said, "is . . ."

"Fuck off," said a readily identifiable voice which was not that of an officer. "That's what we ought to do, fuck off, while there's still time."

The suggestion was so eminently sensible, and the person who made it so experienced in these matters, that it only remained to put it into practice. The operation was off for anyone who was not trying for a posthumous award of the Victoria Cross, and there would be no one left alive to write the citation if he was. There was now not a hope of crossing the airfield and reaching the planes, and even if one succeeded there would still be the guards to deal with. The thing to do now was to get out before we were cut off from the beach.

We moved back through the wood which was all lit up and reminded me vividly of Act Two, Scene One of *As You Like It*, the Forest of Arden in the Open Air Theatre in Regent's Park, until we came to an expanse of open heath in the middle of which stood a tall electric pylon, one of a long line which stretched away in the direction of Catania—strange things to find close to an airfield where one would have thought that they would have been a serious obstacle to flying; and we stuck a couple of bombs on it and piled the rest at the foot of it and set them going too. It was a puerile thing to do. The pylon would certainly be repaired in a couple of days.

It was now eleven-twenty. To get back to where we had started from we had to travel on a diagonal course across country, roughly south-east, and we set off very fast in single file until we reached a wood filled with dead and dying trees which had fallen across one another and dry branches which made a shattering noise when they broke underfoot. Beyond the wood there were some fields planted with lines of vines supported by wires at right angles to the direction in which we were travelling and beyond them there was a swamp with thousands of frogs croaking madly in it and in this we floundered miserably, and beyond the swamp were the dunes. It was midnight. Just as we reached the dunes we heard the sound of an approaching aircraft and immediately all the lights on the airfield went out and so did those to the north in Catania, sirens wailed and flak began to rise lazily in the air from around the perimeter. This was a solitary Wellington gallantly coming in to drop its bombs and create a diversion in order to help us, although what purpose this diversion was to serve when no one except ourselves could know where we would be at this particular time, or what stage the operation would have reached, had not been clear to any of us; but whether we liked it or not there had been no one on Malta who had known how to stop the diversion happening. It was something out of Kafka, immutable.

Our feelings were expressed by the man who said that we ought to fuck off.

"If they can send one Wellington to bomb the bloody airfield why not send six, knock shit out of it, even if they only get the runways, and save us getting our feet wet."

But although we were unappreciative, the arrival of the Wellington was very opportune and it coincided with the explosion of our own first lot of bombs which we had planted in the crates outside the workshops.

We were in among the coastal batteries now. It was a place in which to move warily. If you fell into one of the trenches which linked them you could easily break your neck. Fortunately they were deserted. Everyone was in the casemates and in spite of the din of the air raid we could hear the mumbling and rumbling of conversation inside. The occupants were the coastal gunners, and probably the infantry as well, who should have been manning the trenches and machine-gun emplacements; all of them prudently keeping their heads down.

It was here, among the trenches that we lost Sergeant Dunbar who had been bringing up the rear of the retreat. One moment he was with us, the next he was gone and it was not until some days later that we found out what had happened to him. He had trodden on what he thought was terra firma, but was really nothing but a camouflaged groundsheet which a number of Italian soldiers had erected over an open strongpoint so that they could play cards without showing a light (not all of them had taken refuge under concrete) and he had fallen through it on to their makeshift table and in the ensuing struggle had been wounded and overpowered. It was lucky for the rest of us that there seemed to be no communication between the defenders of the airfield and those on the coast who did not appear to have been alerted to what was going on at all.

By the time we reached the wire the Wellington had droned away and it had begun to rain. There was no time to waste if we were to get back to the submarine before it submerged, which it was due to do in just over three-quarters of an hour. But while we were trapped in the middle of the entanglement we saw a party of men walking along the beach on the seaward side of it and they saw us, too.

There were about a dozen of them and it was obvious that they had seen us, because when they were opposite us they stopped and, literally, put their heads together. The effect was both alarming and comical. We must have had the same effect on them, frozen in the attitudes in which they had discovered us, most of us hooked on the wire, some of us, although they could not see this, with the rings of Mill's grenades between our teeth, wondering whether to pull the pins and chuck them, or wait and see what happened. (How I prayed that the hothead who had returned the fire of the Italian outside the workshops would not do this. If he did we would never get off alive.) But they must have been as reluctant as we were to start any trouble, because, after what seemed an eternity, they turned round and went off southwards along the shore in the direction from which they had come, and no doubt they reported that they had seen nothing out of the ordinary in the course of what was probably a routine patrol. Both parties had had a very lucky escape.

Our route back to the beach had been so roundabout that when we finally emerged from the wire on the foreshore we were not sure whether the place where we had buried the canoes was to the north or south of us. I wondered why, if we had been travelling roughly south-east, as we all thought we had, we had not crossed the dark lane from the farm to the airfield or, failing that, had not seen the sunken field with the horse in it if the boats were now to the north of us. But as we were all reluctant to go in the same direction as the enemy, even an enemy as pusillanimous as they had been, we turned left, which was north, walking in the sea, so that we should be less visible from the blockhouses. And while we were splashing along the edge of the surf which was heavier now, the wind having freshened, there was a succession of glares and heavy thuds inland as the pylon charges and those in the haversacks, perhaps the whole lot of them, went up. It was now twelve-thirty on the morning of the twelfth. At home in a few hours, as George reminded us, grouse shooting would be beginning.

Luckily we were heading in the right direction and soon we found the canoes, or rather the place where we had cut the wire. It was fortunate that we had met the patrol where we did, otherwise they would have gone on and seen the hole in the wire and this would have been something that they could not possibly have ignored. They were going to have some difficulty in explaining why they hadn't seen it, anyway.

Now we dug up the canoes. What had been George's and Sergeant Dunbar's was in such bad shape, having been smashed against the side of the submarine while it was being launched, that we decided to abandon it and after we had punctured the flotation bags and had made an unsuccessful attempt to sink it, I took George into my canoe. We were now three men to a two-man canoe and we had some difficulty in getting into it once we were through the surf and when we did there was very little freeboard.

It was now a quarter to one and there were only fifteen minutes left before *Una* was due to submerge. We paddled the two canoes off on the back bearing, occasionally flashing a hooded torch which was a terribly risky thing to do and might have imperilled the submarine if there had been a patrol boat offshore; but we could think of nothing now beyond being picked up and saving our skins.

But we were not picked up. By the following year a homing device had been produced which was used successfully in the Far East and with which we would have been able to find her. As it was, in the rain and darkness, we never saw her. We must have gone out and beyond her, probably passing quite close, and then the north-east wind and the tidal stream, which was setting south-west, must have taken us down to leeward of her.

By three in the morning there was a nasty sea running and shortly afterwards my canoe filled with water and we had to abandon it; and although we tried to get the flotation bags out of the bow and stern, which would have been a great help in keeping us afloat, we were not able to do so. The other canoe, with Desmond and Duffy in it, was not in much better condition, and if any of us had tried to hold on to it in such weather it would have gone too.

It was very dark, the water was surprisingly cold and I was very frightened, more frightened than I had ever been. What upset me more than anything, quite irrationally, was the thought that if we drowned—which seemed more than probable—none of our people would ever know what had happened to us and why.

I had just succeeded in getting my boots off when I saw George swimming away into the darkness, and I knew immediately that he was doing so because he felt that he could not keep afloat much longer and did not want to be a burden to the rest of us. He was not a strong swimmer and he had no spare flesh on him to combat the cold.

I was the only one who saw this and I went after him and persuaded him to come back, after a fantastic conversation in the sea of which I shall never forget the gist but have completely forgotten the actual words which passed between us; all I can remember was that he was very calm and determined, just as Captain Oates must have been, walking out of that tent in the Antarctic; but eventually he swam back with me and Desmond insisted on getting out of his canoe and giving George his place, which was difficult to do but undoubtedly saved George's life.

Now we tried to swim shorewards to where we thought the mouth of the Simetto River ought to be. If we could only reach the right bank before dawn we might be able to lie up among the trees until nightfall and then make the rendezvous for the second night with the submarine, by Capo Campolato, six miles to the south. But although by first light the wind died away, we never reached the mouth of the river or the rendezvous. It was a pity because, at great risk, Pat brought *Una* back three nights running to wait for us although he and his crew having seen the explosions on the airfield and heard the shooting, were more or less convinced that we were captured or dead.

Of the fourteen merchant ships which took part in *Operation Pedestal*, five reached Malta, including the tanker *Ohio*, which was enough to save it. The remaining nine were all sunk, at least four of them by J.U.88s operating from Sicily on August the twelfth and thirteen. *Operation Whynot* is not one on which I look back with either pride or pleasure. The fishermen took us in to Catania where we were surrounded by a hastily assembled escort, and marched, presumably for the edification of the inhabitants, bootless and in the few clothes which remained to us—some of us were without trousers—up past palaces and convents, some of them like those on Malta and equally golden in the sunshine, to a more modern building in the centre of the city. Here we were subjected to a long, inexpert interrogation by unpleasant men in civilian clothes. We were still very sure of ourselves and Desmond made the kind of rude remarks about the Duce, whose photograph glowered down at us from the wall, which only Guards officers are really capable of making, and to such an extent that we were in danger of being badly beaten up, as we certainly would have been if we had been Italian prisoners insulting a portrait of Churchill.

The Italians were angry enough without being taunted. We had penetrated their coast defences and the Germans, whose aircraft had been in some danger, had already pointed this out to them. That we had failed completely to do what we had set out to do did nothing to appease them. It was now that we made a rather feeble attempt to escape from the window of a lavatory to which the guards had, rather stupidly, taken us *en masse*. What we would have all done in the middle of Catania with hardly any clothes on, none of us had stopped to think; we were too bemused.

We were given nothing to eat or drink, and all that morning we sat shivering in our damp underwear and shirts in a north-facing room; and George, who had not recovered from his immersion, became ill. Finally an Italian colonel arrived and cursed our hosts for keeping us in such a condition and we were issued with cotton trousers and shirts and cotton socks and canvas boots made from old rucksacks, which were very comfortable, and we were also given food. Later in the afternoon we were put in a lorry and taken to a fort with a moat round it in which the conducting officer told us, we were to be shot at dawn the following morning as saboteurs because we had not been wearing any sort of recognisable uniform when we were captured. Looking out of the window into the dry moat in which the firing party was going to operate, I remembered the innumerable books about first war spies that I had read at school which invariably ended with ghastly descriptions of their executions. Mostly they were cowardly spies whose legs gave way under them, so that they had to be carried, shrieking, to the place of execution and tied to stakes to prevent them sinking to the ground, and although I hoped that I wouldn't be like this, I wondered if I would be.

By this time George was very ill. He had a high temperature and lay on one of the grubby cots, semi-delirious. We hammered on the door and shouted to the sentries to bring a doctor, but of course none came.

Finally, sometime in the middle of the night (our watches had been taken away from us so we no longer knew what time it was), a young priest arrived, escorted by two soldiers, as we imagined to prepare us for the ordeal ahead; but, instead, he dismissed the sentries and knelt down by the side of George's bed and prayed for him.

The priest spoke a little English and before he left he told us that the Germans were even more angry about the Italians' decision to execute us without consulting them first, than they had been about the attack on the airfield, and that they had given orders that we were on no account to be shot but sent to Rome at once for further interrogation. Perhaps they never meant to shoot us but, all the same, we thought ourselves lucky.

The next day George was better, although still very weak, and later that day we left for Rome by train with a heavy escort of infantry under the command of an elderly *maggiore* who had with him an insufferably conceited and bloodthirsty *sotto-tenente* who had obviously been recently commissioned.

By now we were all very depressed but Desmond, who had a positively royal eye for the minutiae of military dress, had the pleasure of pointing out to the *sotto-tenente* that he had his spurs on the wrong feet.

"He is quite right," said the *maggiore* who was not enjoying his escort duty and appeared to dislike the *sotto-tenente* as much as we did. "Go, instantly and change them. You are a disgrace to your regiment."

At Rome station while being marched down the platform to the exit, we were able to pick up some of the ruinous and extensive baggage belonging to some very pretty peasant girls who had travelled up from the south on the same train. Happy to be given this assistance, for there were no porters even if they had known how to hire one, they trotted up the

27

platform beside us between the escorting lines of soldiers who had been given orders only to shoot or bayonet us if we tried to escape, with the residue of their possessions balanced on their noddles, while the *sotto-tenente* screeched at us to put their bags down and the *maggiore*, not wishing to make an exhibition of himself, disembarked from the carriage in a leisurely fashion. These were the last girls any of us spoke to for a long time.

In the city we were housed in barracks occupied by the *Cavalleria di Genova*, a regiment in Italy of similar status at that time to one or other of the regiments of the Household Cavalry in Britain. They still had their horses and the few officers and men who were about looked like ardent royalists. They certainly all knew about which was the right boot for the right spur, which was more than I did and, although they were not allowed to speak to us, their demeanour was friendly. They sent us magazines and newspapers and the food, which was provided by the officers' mess and brought to us by a white-jacketed mess waiter who had the air of a family retainer, was of an excellence to which none of us were accustomed in our own regiments, although there was not much of it.

After the first day we were all separated from one another and we began a period of unarduous solitary confinement in the course of which we contrived to communicate with one another by way of the mess waiter who carried our innocuous written messages from one room to another among the dishes. At intervals we were all interrogated, but never really expertly, by people from military intelligence. As we had been taught never to answer any questions whatsoever, however fatuous they might seem, we learned more from our interrogators than they did from us. It was interesting to find out how much they knew about our organisation. About some parts of it they knew more than I imagined they would; about others they seemed to know much less.

Once a day, but never together, we were let out to exercise on the pathway which surrounded the *manège*. Here "by chance", we met other "prisoners", an extraordinarily sleazy collection of renegades and traitors, most of them South African or Irish, dressed in various British uniforms, some in civilian clothes, who called us "old boy" and offered to fix us up with nights on the town and escape routes into the Vatican in exchange for information.

I enjoyed being alone. It was so long since I had been. From my room, high up under the eaves of the barracks, I used to watch a solitary, elegant officer taking a succession of chargers around the tan. He was a wonderful horseman, even I could tell this without knowing anything about horses. The days were poignantly beautiful. The leaves on the plane trees were golden. Here, in Rome, in late August, it was already autumn. I was nearly twenty-three and this was my first visit to Europe. Locked up, isolated in the centre of the city, I felt like the traitor Baillie-Stewart, "the Officer in the Tower", or, even less romantically, someone awaiting court martial for conduct scandalous and unbecoming, looking out across the Park in the years before the war.

After a few days we were dispersed, the officers to one camp, the men to another. We all survived the war and so did Socks, the dachshund. Pat, in accordance with Desmond's last wishes, took her to Beirut where she took up residence with Princess Aly Khan. And George recovered sufficiently within a few days to make one of the most cold-bloodedly successful escape attempts from the camp to which we were sent when he, in company with a number of others, marched out through the main gate disguised as Italian soldiers. Unfortunately, they were all re-captured soon afterwards.

Chapter Two

Grand illusion

A year later, on the seventh of September, 1943, the day before Italy went out of the war, I was taken to the prison hospital with a broken ankle, the result of an absurd accident in which I had fallen down an entire flight of the marble staircase which extended from the top of the building to the basement while wearing a pair of nailed boots which my parents had managed to send me by way of the Red Cross. The prison camp was on the outskirts of a large village in the Pianura Padana, the great plain through which the river Po flows on its way from the Cottian Alps to the sea. The nearest city was Parma on the Via Emilia, the Roman road which runs through the plain in an almost straight line from Milan to the Adriatic.

"That's right, knock the bloody place down," someone said, unsympathetically, as it shuddered under the impact. The doctor, who examined my ankle, who was also a prisoner, took much the same view. He couldn't do much, anyway, because he hadn't got any plaster of paris. It was, however, he said, "on order" and for the time being he did it up with some adhesive plaster which was a rather wobbly arrangement.

The only other occupant of the hospital was another officer who was suffering from a boil on his behind. He was the one who had proposed that we should dig a tunnel, the most dreary and unimaginative way of getting out of any prison, on which a number of us had been working for some months, and which we had only recently abandoned because events seemed to have rendered it unnecessary. The head of the shaft of this tunnel was in a bedroom on the *piano nobile* of the building, practically in mid-air, and the shaft went down through the middle of one of the solid brick piers which supported it and down into the cellars. When we reached mother earth, somewhere below the floor of the cellar, if ever, he had planned to construct a chamber, in which the spoil could be put into sacks and hauled to the surface, and from it the tunnel would be driven outwards under the wire. The shaft had a false lid, designed and made by a South African mining engineer. It was a marvellous piece of work—a great block of cement with tiles set in it that was so thick that when the carabinieri tapped the floor of the bedroom with hammers, which they sometimes did, the lid gave off the same sound as the rest of it. This lid was so heavy that special tools had had to be devised to lift it.

There were a lot of attempts at escape, some successful, some of them funny. One prisoner hid himself in a basket of dirty linen, destined for the nuns' laundry over the wall. We wondered what would have happened if they had actually unpacked him inside the convent. Some were very ingenious—two people had had themselves buried in the exercise field which was outside the main perimeter wire and was not guarded at night. They nearly got to Switzerland.*

No one from our camp ever reached Switzerland before the Italian Armistice in 1943. It was generally believed that two British prisoners of war had succeeded in getting there, but I have never met anyone who actually knew who they were or which camps they came from. It was very difficult to get out of a prison camp in Italy. Italian soldiers might be figures of fun to us, but some of them were extraordinarily observant and very suspicious and far better at guarding prisoners than the Germans were. It was also very difficult to travel in Italy if you did get out. The Italians are fascinated by minutiae of dress and the behaviour of their fellow men, perhaps to a greater degree than almost any other race in Europe, and the ingenious subterfuges and disguises which escaping prisoners of war habitually resorted to and which were often enough to take in the Germans: the documents, train tickets and ration cards, lovingly fabricated by the camp's staff of expert forgers; the suits made from dyed blankets; the desert boots cut down to look like shoes and the carefully bleached army shirts were hardly ever sufficiently genuine-looking to fool even the most myopic Italian ticket collector and get the owner past the barrier, let alone survive the scrutiny of the occupants of a compartment on an Italian train. The kind of going over to which an escaping Anglo-Saxon was subjected by other travellers was usually enough to finish him off unless he was a professional actor or spoke fluent Italian. And in Italy, before the Armistice, there were no members of the Resistance or railway employees of the Left, as there were in France, to help escaping prisoners out of the country along an organised route.

The building in which we were housed had originally been built as an orfanotrofio, an orphanage, with the help of money contributed by pilgrims to the shrine of the miraculous Madonna del Rosario who, in

*One of them was Captain Anthony, later Major-General, Dean Drummond, CB, DSO, MC and Bar, captured in North Africa in 1941 and escaped in 1942.

31

1628, had performed the first of a succession of miracles when, in answer to his prayers, she raised a man called Giovanni Pietro Ugalotti from his death bed.

The foundations had been laid back in 1928, but the work had proceeded so slowly that the war began before it could be completed, and it remained empty until the spring of 1943 when it became a prisoner of war camp for officers and a few other ranks who acted as orderlies.

It was a large, three-storeyed building with a sham classical façade, so unstable that if anyone jumped up and down on one of the upper floors, or even got out of bed heavily, it appeared to wobble like a jelly. To those of us who were lodged on one of these upper floors, it seemed so unstable that we were convinced that if any bombs fell in the immediate neighbourhood it would collapse.

Next door to the *orfanotrofio* was the *santuario* in which the miraculous *Madonna del Rosario* was enshrined, and on its walls there were large quantities of ex-votos contributed by those who had been cured of some bodily affliction or saved from disaster by divine intervention—crutches, pale wax replicas of various parts of the human body that had been restored to health, primitive paintings of ships sinking, houses and barns on fire, or being struck by lightning, motor cars and aeroplanes crashing and farm carts being overturned, from all of which, and many other more fantastic mishaps, the occupants were depicted as emerging or being ejected relatively unscathed.

Behind the *santuario*, and joined to it, there was a convent in which a body of nuns resided in complete seclusion from which they never emerged except in case of grave illness or when they were being conveyed to another house of their order. Otherwise, their nearest approach to contact with the outer world was when they participated in the masses celebrated in the *santuario*, at which times they could look out on the congregation in the body of the church unseen, hidden from view behind an iron grille.

All the laundry for the prisoners was done in the convent and from time to time we discovered little notes wrapped up in our clean sheets or tucked inside our shirts, which said that those who had washed them were praying for us and were calling down the blessings of the *Madonna del Rosario* on our unworthy heads.

Although we never saw them most of us liked having the nuns next door, and the *santuario*, too. The clanging of its bells broke the monotony of the long days, making the campanile sway with their violence and frightening the swallows, making them sweep in panic to the sky, until some prisoners who had migraine, or were atheists, or simply disliked bells or noise generally, used to put their heads out of the windows and scream, at the top of their voices, "I SAY, WOULD YOU MIND TERRIBLY TURNING IT IN?" And if by chance the bells did stop at that particular moment, "THANK YOU SO MUCH!" Or, if they knew a little Italian, "*GRAZIE TANTO!*"

In the centre of the village, which was called Fontanellato, out of sight of the prisoners in the camp, was the Rocca Sanvitale, a forbidding-looking fifteenth-century castle, isolated behind a water-filled moat. In the castle, until the war came, had lived the *Conte Giovanni*, the last of the Sanvitales, one of the most ancient and illustrious families in Italy, which, today, is extinct. The buildings which faced the castle had deep, shadowy arcades under which there were shops and cafés where farmers used to congregate on Saturday, which was market day; and in the street which led to the *santuario* and the *orfanotrofio*, there was a war memorial of the First World War, which for Italy had been much more bloody than the one she was at present engaged in, with a long list of dead on a plaque at the foot of it. This was more or less all we knew about Fontanellato. Apart from a senior officer who had been taken on a tour of the village for some reason, none of us had ever seen it. What I have written is the sum total of what he told us when he returned. It was rather like listening to a lecture by some medieval traveller and hearing him say, as he pointed to the map, "Here be dragons".

Living in such a grandiose-looking building we felt that we could scarcely be regarded as objects of compassion by the local inhabitants. Although some officers when they arrived at it from other camps complained about the overcrowding, which was severe, and the lack of privacy, which was complete, to me and most of my friends who had been brought here from a much more primitive camp, it seemed a luxurious place and we were very surprised to find that we were to sleep in beds instead of the double-tiered bunks to which we were accustomed.

When we first arrived, at the beginning of March, there was no space for exercise outdoors, apart from a small, wired-in compound behind the building in which we assembled twice a day to be counted, or more frequently if the Italians suspected that someone had escaped; but the Italian commandant, an old, regular *colonello*, allowed parties of prisoners to go for route marches in the surrounding countryside once a week under a general parole, which covered the period when we were actually outside the gates. Parole or not, we were heavily guarded during these excursions which always followed routes along unfrequented lanes far from any village.

We looked forward to these outings which were sometimes cancelled at the eleventh hour for unexplained reasons, or because the senior officers refused to come to terms on some piddling point of military etiquette which most of the people in the camp, being temporary soldiers, and almost none of the Italians, because there were only about two regular soldiers among them, were ever able to comprehend. As in every other prison camp, the most lively differences of opinion between the senior British officer and the *colonello* and his staff arose over the interpretation of the various clauses of the Geneva Convention, which governed the treatment of prisoners.

We marched at a tremendous rate, glad of the exercise and taking sadistic pleasure in exhausting our guards who were mostly small men with short legs. We marched along flat, dusty roads; past wheat fields; fields in which forests of Indian corn were growing and into which I longed to take flight; along the foot of high green embankments which protected the land from the torrents which at certain seasons poured down from the Apennines into the River Po; past huge fields of tomato plants and sugar beet, groves of poplars, endless rows of vines and great rambling farmhouses with farmyards full of cows and pigs and ducks and geese, and red-roofed barns with open doors in which we could just see great, mouth-watering Parmesan cheeses ripening in the semi-darkness. Where we went we saw very few people. Perhaps they were told to keep out of the way when we went past.

Looking at this burgeoning countryside in the spring and summer of 1943 it was difficult for the most optimistic of us to believe that Italy was in danger of collapsing through lack of food, although it was obvious that the Italian army was very badly fed. One had only to look at the exiguous rations which the soldiers who guarded us drew from their cookhouse. And here, so far as I could make out, there were no organisations as there were in Britain to make their life more supportable. No volunteer ladies dishing out fish and chips to them, and great squelchy, jam sandwiches, and cups of orange-coloured tea, and, saying "Hello" and asking where they came from, making them feel that they were doing something worthwhile which somebody cared about. They were like souls in limbo or a lot of untouchables in Hindu India, lost in the low-lying ground which no one ever visited, somewhere between the railway workshops and the cantonment.

By prison standards, the food in the *orfanotrofio* was good. The official rations were not abundant for non-manual workers, which is what we were, and without anything to augment them they had a lowering effect, especially in the previous camp where the British cooks had usually succeeded in making the worst of them—their version of *pasta al sugo* being particularly loathsome; to me it always smelt of dirty dish cloths.

But here, at Fontanellato, for the first time since I had been captured, there was a regular supply of Red Cross parcels and instead of the parcels being issued complete for us to make what we would of the contents, as had been done in other places, here all the cookable food was removed and prepared in the kitchens. This was much more civilised than keeping a lot of open tins under one's bed, as some of us had previously done (the Italians never allowed us to have unopened tins in case we hoarded them for an escape) and risking death by eating the contents of a tin of disgusting meat loaf that had been open for two or three days or, even worse, spending ages on all fours blowing away at a stove made from old tin cans, stoked up with bits of cardboard or, *in extremis*, pieces of bed board from the bottom of our bunks, as many had done in the past.

Drink and supplementary food were bought on the black market, which was even more extensive and better organised than it was in Britain, and a special float of Red Cross cigarettes was kept for this purpose and for the general corruption of the Italian camp staff, by responsible members of the British administration, ex-bank managers mostly, to whom this sort of thing was second nature.

Officially, we were allowed one tot of vermouth and one of wine each day by our administration, which was all that could be allowed if, in theory, everyone took their ration; but you could always buy other people's ration tickets with cigarettes or chocolate if you preferred drinking to smoking. Because of this there were some good parties and some rather awful ones too.

The very first lieutenant-colonel who was sent to us, previously we had scarcely anyone above the rank of captain, gave a memorable one.

"Well, good night gentlemen," he said when most of the drink was finished. "Time for bed."

He opened the door of a tall cupboard which stood against the wall and walked into it shutting the door behind him, presumably under the impression that he was entering his own room. By the time it had been forced open, which was difficult because his rather ample trousers had caught in it, he was fast asleep. He was a nice, high-spirited old man, much too old in years to have been captured fighting in the Western Desert.

The wines were strange, dark and repulsive with various chemical additives, what the Italians call *vini lavorati*, worked on, primitive harbingers of the more sophisticated, doctored wines which rarely contain any grapes at all and which have made the Italian wine industry

35

the byword that it is today; but like meths drinkers we enjoyed them better than no alcohol at all.

There was even a bar in which these concoctions were served, high up in a sort of minstrels' gallery above the chapel, which was used by the more staid prisoners to play bridge, and on Sundays for church services. We were forbidden by the Italians to look out of the windows of the bar which faced the road to the village, and if we did, the sentries in the watchtowers beyond the wire used to fire shots at us, some of which used to come whistling through the windows—the glass had been blown out long ago—and bury themselves in the walls and ceiling of the bar which had the same ecclesiastical decor as the chapel below. These bullet-holes gave the place a raffish appearance, like a middle-western saloon built by some renegade, gun-toting priest.

But in spite of these fusillades we still continued to risk our lives by putting our heads out of the windows, in order to be able to look at the girls of Fontanellato who, every evening when the weather was fine, used to promenade along the road in front of the *orfanotrofio*.

Some of my fellow prisoners had not spoken to a girl since they had been captured in 1940. Old or new prisoners, few of us had set eyes on girls like these for years and years. They were all shapes and sizes and colours and as they went past they laughed, as if enjoying some private joke, and tossed their heads impertinently in our directions. They all had long hair, short skirts and brown, bare legs and, as they swayed along the road, the high-heeled wooden sandals, which they all wore because there was very little shoe leather in Italy, clacked on the hard surface of the road. Some of them walked arm in arm with other girls carefully chosen for their inferior looks; some were so sure of themselves that they walked with girls who were their equals; others wobbled past in little flocks on bicycles, so slowly that they sometimes fell off uttering squeals of alarm—none was ever injured. There were scarcely ever any men with them. Presumably they were at the war.

The effect of these visions on the wretched Italian guards who were immured high up in their watchtowers, was as powerful as it was on us. Utterly distracted, they turned their backs on the *orfanotrofio* in order to look at them more closely, until some N.C.O., old enough and sour enough to be indifferent to women, screeched at them so loudly that they whirled round and, seeing us, discharged their rifles in the direction of the bar.

But not even the Italian Army in its most bellicose mood was able to stop us looking at the girls of Fontanellato, or the girls at us.

On one side of the *orfanotrofio* was the village cemetery in which the dead were stacked in recesses in the walls, one above the other, as if they had been put away carefully in some giant filing-cabinet marked "Pending" until the last Trump sounded. Every Sunday, wet or fine, what must have been almost the entire girl population of Fontanellato as well as large numbers from the surrounding country, used to make the long pilgrimage up the via Cimitero to the gates, ostensibly to mourn their loved ones, and completely outnumbering the real mourners who could be easily distinguished by their black garb. If all these girls had been visiting the graves of their own kith and kin then the cemetery would have had to have been at least five times the size it was. Like participants in a slow-motion film they crawled past the front of the *orfanotrofio*, past the exercise field which had been opened a month after our arrival, and in which all exercise ceased from the moment the first of them came into view, and turned left up the road to the cemetery. Few of them bothered to enter it. Sometimes they waved if they thought the guards were not watching, or they might simply twirl a scarf, and from behind the barbed wire in the field and from every upper window of the *orfanotrofio*, from which the occupants could also see on fine days, and equally unattainable, the peaks of the pre-Alps beyond Lake Garda, more than 150 kilometres away to the north, the prisoners cheered and waved at them.

But in spite of these distant encounters with girls we were not unduly troubled by the lusts of the flesh—perhaps it was something to do with the diet. As one of my friends said, after drawing on himself one or two random shots while craning out of one of the windows of the bar, "It isn't that one just wants to poke them. I'm not sure if I could do it any more, but it would be heaven just to be with them," which for him was a pretty profound remark.

It was fortunate that most of us felt as he did. Had we felt otherwise there was not much we could do about it except pull our puddings, and to perform the operation while lying cheek by jowl with twenty-six other people in a room which was illuminated by searchlights, required a degree of stealth which had deserted most of us since leaving school. Nevertheless, some of the more vigorous among us revived these ancient skills.

The lavatories—the *gabinetti*—were even more unsuitable than the dormitories for this purpose. They were of the kind in which you squatted over a dark hole in the floor and at unpredictable intervals a huge head of water like the Severn Bore came swirling up and filled your boots. It was hazardous enough using the *gabinetti* for the purpose for which they had been constructed without lingering in them, even to study the astonishing *graffiti* which can only have been produced by people who owned wellington boots. One officer made a fortune in cigarettes, which were the hard currency of the camp, salvaging valuable objects such as lighters, false teeth and wrist watches which their owners had dropped down the holes while occupying the *gabinetti* and which had gone round the bends in the pipes.

Even more difficult for the residents in the *orfanotrofio* was any kind of homosexual act. Whatever loves there were between prisoners could only be expressed by looks and words or perhaps a surreptitious pressure of the hand, otherwise they had to remain locked away within the hearts and minds of the lovers until they could be free or were moved to some more private place.*

Although they were outnumbered by officers drawn from the middle and lower classes who had had to be commissioned, just as they had been in the First War, because there were not enough members of the upper class to go round, it was the upper class which set the style in the *orfanotrofio*, just as they had done in the pre-war world outside; the sons and younger brothers of peers and Highland lairds, young merchant bankers, wine shippers and gentlemen jockeys who had ridden in the National, most of them concentrated in cavalry regiments, rifle regiments, one or two Highland regiments and the Brigade of Guards. These amateur soldiers, for they were mostly amateurs, and any professional soldiers who had the same sort of background (any others were soon made into figures of fun), made up the coteries of O.K. people who exercised power.

These people were very reluctant to consort with outsiders, but as the *orfanotrofio* was very overcrowded and it was almost impossible to summon up a coterie large enough to take over one of the bigger rooms which contained anything up to twenty-seven beds, and because these rooms were the most desirable because they were on the side of the building which faced away from the afternoon sun, and because not all coteries found other coteries agreeable to them for innumerable reasons which there is no space to go into here, the members always tried to ensure that the rest of the beds were occupied with what they regarded as more or less acceptable ballast, that is to say, or as they would have said if they had actually said it out loud, marginally O.K. people, the sort of people they were prepared to talk to and drink with while the war was on, and then would never see again. And this included a number of people whom they regarded as being downright common but who had the saving grace of being funny; and they took these comics on to the strength in

*For a remarkable book on this subject, set in the *orfanotrofio*, see *The Cage*, by Billany and Dowie, Longmans, 1949.

much the same way as their ancestors had employed jesters and dwarfs, to while away the tedious hours between breakfast, lunch and dinner. Everyone else they ignored completely, unless they owned something worth buying, or had some skill which they could make use of to increase their comfort. It was not that they consigned these unfortunates to outer darkness; they simply never invited them in out of it.

If I had not had marginally O.K. friends who had not abandoned me when we moved to the *orfanotrofio* from the camp in which we had previously been imprisoned I, too, would have become a dweller in darkness, which I did not want to be. I wanted the opportunity to observe the O.K. people at close quarters and some inner voice told me, quite correctly for once, that this was going to be my last chance ever to do so in the whole of my life.

Before the war I had rarely spoken to O.K. people, let alone known any well enough to talk to. Even at Sandhurst in 1940, where I was a member of the Infantry Wing in the Old Buildings, which were so much more elegant than the New Buildings, O.K. people had been rarities. They were accommodated in the hideous New Buildings, which were not really new at all but were newer than the old ones; or else they were members of something called The Royal Armoured Wing—I now forget where they lived—which had to do with armoured fighting vehicles and therefore with what was still called the Cavalry, which was nothing to do with the Royal Tank Regiment and still isn't, thirty years later.

When I was very young I sometimes used to see what I immediately recognised as midget versions of O.K. people in Children's Hairdressing on the first floor at Harrods, to which my mother, who had been a model girl at the store and had a nostalgia for the place, used to take me from Barnes to get my hair cut, where they exercised themselves on the rocking horses while waiting to be given the treatment and never let me have a go. I used to see them, too, wearing hand-made overcoats with velvet collars and long gaiters with hundreds of buttons down the sides, the sort of outfit which would have caused any un-O.K. child to have a fit of apoplexy in the mild spring weather in which they were dressed like this, being pushed up Sloane Street in huge, glossy machines known as Victoria carriages, which were short-wheelbase prams with curled up fronts, like seashells, in which they travelled sitting more or less upright with their backs to whoever was pushing them and, usually, with a dark blue blanket clipped over the front with their initials, or their parents' initials, embroidered on them, on their way to the Dell, a charming grassy depression on the far side of Rotten Row, in the Park. They were still being conveyed about in these carriages at an age when I had long forgotten what it was like to be in a push-chair, which was what I had had to make do with after my nanny had been shown the door.

The nurses who had the pushing of these little O.K. boys who sat, as it were, with their backs to the engines, were invariably bad-tempered looking and absolutely hideous. They wore pork-pie hats with badges on them, long, drab overcoats of putty-coloured gabardine or grey flannel, with lisle stockings to match, and clumpy great shoes; not like my very sexy suburban nanny who wore a uniform bought for her by my mother—who had not been a model girl for nothing—a blue denim dress in summertime with stiff white collar and cuffs and black silk stockings and high-heeled shoes, and whose head was swathed in some sort of dark blue veiling when she took me out for an airing, often to have assignations with what looked to me like very old men but were probably quite young ones, in a graveyard, not in fashionable S.W.1 but in S.W.13, keeping me quiet while she did whatever she did with them by giving me handfuls of Carrara marble chippings from the tombs to play with. (She was fired when my mother found me still playing with them in the bath.) If this nanny, of whom photographs still exist in an album, which enables me to remember more clearly than I would otherwise have been able to do what she looked like, had taken me to the Dell, the other nannies would have ignored her, not only because she was far too good looking to be a nanny, but because I was not an O.K. child.

Whatever else I may have envied them I certainly did not envy these little O.K. boys their nannies.

"Why is the sky blue, Nanny?" I heard one ask in the bell-like upperclass voice which I envied and always wished that I could emulate—mine sounded as if it emanated from my boots. To which he got the reply, "Ask no questions and you'll be told no lies, little Mr. Inquisitive."

And later when we were all a bit older, and I was on my way to or from the dentist, also in S.W.1, with my mother's "Help", I sometimes used to see a shambling crocodile of them, all wearing the strange-looking, tomato-coloured caps of a smart pre-prep school, which looked like the sort of caps that some Irish peasants still wear, being shepherded along the road by a number of brisk grown-ups, all wearing no-nonsense-from-you-expressions.

"Well-born they may be, Master Eric," the "Help" said stoutly, when they had shuffled past, "but most of them look half-barmy to me." And when the war came and I was on embarkation leave I saw them again in Harrods, in various splendid uniforms with their mothers and sisters and girl friends who all wore miniature replicas of their regimental badges picked out in diamonds, and again listened with awe to their loud, self-confident voices, usually we were ascending or descending together in one of the lifts, slightly cracked versions of the bell-like tones I had listened to with envy on the way to the Dell sixteen years before. But this was the first opportunity I had had to consort with them and study them at leisure and *en masse*.

In the camp the members of the coteries moved easily in a mysterious, almost Edwardian world and when they addressed one another they used nicknames, just as the Edwardians had been so fond of doing, which were completely unintelligible to anyone else, and they knew who was who so far down the scale of the aristocracy to a point at which one would have thought that any blue blood corpuscles would have been non-existent. They alone knew that "Bolo" Bastonby was the nephew of the Earl of Crake, that "Jamie" Stuart Ogilvie-Keir-Gordon was the youngest brother of the Master of Dunreeking and that "Feathers" Farthingdale was the third son of the Marquis of Stale by his second wife. No one outside these coteries had even heard of the holders of the titles, let alone "Bolo" Bastonby, "Jamie" Stuart Ogilvie-Keir-Gordon or "Feathers" Farthingdale.

One interesting thing I noticed about them, and this applied to almost all of them, was that they would not tolerate any criticism by outsiders of anyone whom they regarded as being "one of us", even though the person being criticised might be hundreds of miles away.

Down at the marginally O.K. end of the otherwise O.K room which I inhabited, there was an officer in a very grand regiment who was not completely accepted by the coterie because none of them knew anything about his family and because he had been commissioned from the ranks of the same regiment in peacetime, a rare thing and one that implied that he probably possessed gifts which, in such a regiment, might take him to the heights of his profession and one that most marginally O.K. and un-O.K. people in the *orfanotrofio* who knew about it, regarded as "a good thing" or "a good show". And because he was in such a grand regiment he was allowed more latitude than the average marginally O.K. resident. But one evening he went too far.

"I think Randolph Churchill's a shit," he said, in the course of a long, rambling, semi-drunken conversation about the past which had temporarily united the two ends of the room. And from the other end of it, like an echo that had somehow gone wrong, came a passionate *cri de coeur* from someone who—I happened to know, because he had himself told me so on a previous occasion—had never met Randolph Churchill in his life, and everyone else at his end of the room, some of whom did know Randolph Churchill well, knew it too.

"How dare you say that! Randolph's a personal friend of mine!" He spoke in exactly the same voice as one of the little boys in Children's Hairdressing in Harrods had when I tried to get a ride on the rocking horse which he had been astride ever since I arrived. "Go away!" he said to me. "It's *my* rocking horse!"

The next morning while we were out in the courtyard being counted by the Italians I asked Alastair why he had sprung to the defence of Randolph Churchill whom he had never met and might, for all he knew, be a shit.

"I don't care whether Randolph Churchill's a shit or the sun shines out of his arse," he said, "I just can't bear little men like that saying that kind of thing. Someone had to teach him a lesson. He had it coming to him."

The "little man" he was giving the lesson to was well over six feet tall.

Although some members of the coteries could be described, without irony, as being "cultivated", none by the wildest stretch of the imagination could be said to be "intellectual". The intellectuals in the camp, of whom there were not many, were most of them not even marginally O.K. One, who subsequently became a very successful leader of the Italian partisans, was regarded as being what they described as "Bolshie and odd"; not because he was not a good soldier, which they had to admit he was, but because every opinion that he held was completely at variance with their own—about the war and why it was being fought and why he was fighting it, and about the sort of Britain which would emerge as a result of it—and, most suspicious of all, he actually learned to read and write Italian while he was in the *orfanotrofio*.

On the whole they weren't great readers, although we had a large library made up of books brought from other camps which had originally been sent out by the Red Cross, books from the British library in Rome and books sent by next-of-kin which were handled by the Bodleian. Books even continued to arrive, minus their covers, after an extremely inept attempt by a then highly secretive section of the War Office (M.I.9), interested in encouraging us to escape, to send us money and maps hidden inside the boards, after which every book had its covers ripped off and had to be re-bound with cardboard from Red Cross parcel boxes before it could be read.

But although not great ones for a book, few coterie men would have dared to express themselves publicly as one late arrival did, as soon as he arrived at the camp.

"Since I've been captured I've been locked up alone for a bit and I've been thinkin'," he said. "I've decided to take up readin' and I've written to Mummy askin' her to send me the *Tatler* and the *Book of the Month*."

In all the time I was in the *orfanotrofio* I can scarcely remember a moment, except when we were eating or we were being counted, or the lights were out and we were supposed to be asleep, when the rattle of dice and the shuffling of pieces on a backgammon board could not be heard. Down below in the cellars where we ate our meals, those temporarily expatriate members of White's Club in captivity, who themselves formed a unique inner coterie, had a big table for baccarat, at which they played after the plates had been cleared away, for the kind of stakes to which they had been accustomed in St. James's Street before the war, using the letter cards which were intended to be sent to their next-of-kin as cheques which they sent to one another's bankers on settlement days. And later in the summer, when the exercise field, from which we all admired the girls of Fontanellato on their way to the cemetery, was opened some of them used to race corks, also for big stakes, down a minute rivulet which rose mysteriously from the earth at the top end of the field, flowed briskly for a while, and as mysteriously died away. Or else they would make a book on the running races which some lunatic organised between members of the various armies which were represented in the camp.

I ran the mile for the Eighth Army, because I needed the exercise and loathed football and basket ball. And because of the form I displayed, by the day of the meeting there was a lot of money on me, mostly placed by White's men who had been watching me during my early morning "gallops".

At the beginning of the last lap I knew that I would win. I put in a tremendous spurt and romped home. Unfortunately, I had miscounted the number of laps and there was one more to go. I finished third. I was disappointed, but not nearly so much as the little group of White's men, shoulder to shoulder, not as I have so often seen them on race courses since the war, dressed according to season or the grandeur of the event in morning coats and top hats or flannel-suited with squashy brown felt hats pulled down over their noses and always with big race glasses, philosophically marking their race cards before setting out once more for the paddock, but still shoulder to shoulder.

"You didn't pull it, Eric, did you?" one of them said as I went in to change.

At the time, only having been to a couple of trotting races, I wondered what on earth he meant.

The *orfanotrofio* was more like a public school than any other prison

43

camp I was ever in. If anybody can be said to have suffered in this place it was those people who had never been subjected to the hell of English preparatory and public school life; because although there was no bullying in the physical sense—canes had been taken away for the duration, and the twisting of arms was forbidden by the Geneva Convention—there was still plenty of scope for mental torment; and although the senior officer thought he ran the camp it was really run by people elected by the coteries, just like Pop at Eton, where so many of them had been.

This state of affairs continued until a very regular full colonel arrived who had not been at Eton but at Wellington and was so horrified by the lackadaisical, demilitarised state in which he found us all, that he immediately organised the camp on the lines of an infantry battalion, in companies with company commanders. Under him the *orfanotrofio* began to resemble the prison camp in Renoir's *Grande Illusion*. It had a commandant who was a regular *colonello* of the *ancien régime* who found himself in sympathy with our colonel, who came from the same sort of background as he did.

When one of the prisoners was found to be stealing food, a most awful crime in a prison camp where everyone started off with exactly the same amount however much more they managed to acquire by exchanging tobacco and cigarettes for it, and the problem arose of punishing him without the added and unthinkable indignity of handing him over to the Italians to keep in their cells, the *colonello* offered our colonel a small Italian infantry bivouac tent and a piece of parched ground in what was normally a zone that was out of bounds to us on which the sun shone all day, so that the offender could expiate his crime in solitary confinement and on a diet of bread and water provided by the British, from their rations, not by the Italians.

Some of the prisoners were very old prisoners indeed, not in age or seniority but because of the number of years they had been locked up. Most of the "old" prisoners had wonderful clothes which no one who had been captured later in the war could possibly emulate, things that had been sent to them before the Italians had instituted rigid sumptuary laws for prisoners of war in order to prevent anyone having anything which vaguely resembled civilian clothes. By some technicality those who already had these clothes were allowed to keep them, providing that the larger items bore the large red patches which were sewn on to everything we wore. They had pig's-whisker pullovers, scarves and stocks from the Burlington Arcade secured with gold pins, make-to-measure Viyella shirts, and corduroy trousers, and those who were members of the

Cherry-Pickers wore cherry-red trousers. Some of this gear had reached them by way of the Red Cross and neutral embassies, but not all of it. One officer had an elegant hacking coat which had been made for him while he was a prisoner, out of a horse blanket which he had rescued from his armoured car when it went up in flames near Sollum, and which he paid the Italian tailor for with cigarettes.

The one thing which united the prisoners in the *orfanotrofio* and which gave them, as it were, a "team spirit", was their attitude towards the "Itis". "Itis" in the abstract, because it was difficult for any but the most hidebound to actively dislike our "Itis", apart from one or two horrors who would have been horrors whatever their nationality, and we all loved the "Iti" girls—soldiers always make an exception for the women of the enemy, for otherwise they would feel themselves completely alone.

The *colonello* was generally conceded to be "all right", a "good chap" in spite of being an "Iti"; and most people liked one of the Italian officers because he smoked a pipe and was more English than many of the English. For most of the others and the wretched soldiery who guarded us, the privates and the N.C.O.s, with their miserable uniforms, ersatz boots, unmilitary behaviour and stupid bugle calls, we felt nothing but derision. What boobs they were, we thought. We used to talk about how we could have turned them into decent soldiers if only we were given the opportunity.

How arrogant we were. Most of us were in the *orfanotrofio* because we were military failures who had chosen not to hold out to the last round and the last man, or, at the last gasp, had been thankful to grasp the hand of a Sicilian fisherman and be hauled from the sea, as I had been. We were arrogant because this was the only way we could vent our spleen at being captured and, at the same time, keep up our spirits which were really very low. Deep down in all of us, prisoners isolated from the outside world and Italian *soldati*, far from home, subjected to a twentieth-century Temptation of St. Anthony and without the money to gratify it, firing volleys at us in fury because we laughed at them in front of girls who by rights should have been their girls, tormenting us all, reminding us constantly of something for which we felt that we would give up everything we had for one more chance to experience, something we ourselves talked about all the time, was the passionate desire to be free; but what did we mean by freedom? I thought I knew, and so did everyone else; but it meant so many different things to so many of us.

We were, in fact, as near to being really free as anyone can be. We were relieved of almost every sort of mundane pre-occupation that had afflicted us in the outside world. We had no money and were relieved of the necessity of making any. We had no decisions to make about anything, even about what we ate. We were certainly much more free than many of us would ever be again, either during the war or after it. And as prisoners we did not even suffer the disapprobation of society as we would have done if we had been locked up in our own country. To our own people we appeared as objects worthy of sympathy.

Chapter Three

Armistizio

The evening of the eighth of September was hot and sultry. The hospital was a room on the *piano nobile* immediately opposite the wooden huts in which the Italian guards lived and in which they kept the radio going full-blast.

At about a quarter to seven, while Michael and I were lying on our beds sweating, he on his stomach because of his boil, a programme of music was interrupted and someone began reading a message in a gloomy, subdued voice. It was to the effect that the Italian Government, recognising the impossibility of continuing the unequal struggle against overwhelming superior enemy forces, and in order to avoid further grave calamities to the nation, had requested an armistice of General Eisenhower and that the request had been granted. As a result, all hostilities between the Italian and Anglo-American forces would cease forthwith. Italian forces, however, would resist attacks from any other quarter, which could only mean Germans..

The voice we had been listening to was that of Marshal Badoglio who had been head of the Italian government since the fall of Mussolini on July the twenty-fifth. Although neither Michael nor I could speak Italian we both understood what was said because, like a lot of other prisoners, we had become quite proficient in the kind of clichés which the Italian Supreme Command employed in its bulletins, and this announcement was in the same idiom. What the Marshal didn't say in his speech was that what had been arranged was not an armistice but an unconditional surrender signed under an olive tree five days previously in Sicily, and that he had been forced to make the announcement this evening very much against his will, because Eisenhower had already done so an hour and a quarter earlier, and the B.B.C. forty-five minutes before that, in what was to prove one of the most lamentable scoops of the war (lamentable, because it gave the Germans valuable extra time in which to disarm the Italian forces before any Allied landings began).

Later that night, without having done anything to organise the resistance to the Germans which he had called on his soldiers to make,

Badoglio departed from Rome for the Adriatic coast, together with the King, from where they were taken by warship to Brindisi, leaving an apathetic and utterly disorganised nation in the lurch, a state in which the Italian people had long been accustomed to be left by their rulers and so-called allies. They were now left in an even deeper mess by the Anglo-Americans who had been stupid enough to inform the Germans of their intentions.

Badoglio's announcement provoked some mild cheers from various parts of the building and a more extravagant display of joy by the Italian guards outside our window which we watched a little sourly. We had seen and heard it all forty-five days before when Mussolini had been deposed. Then the Italians had hurled his picture out of the window, torn down Fascist insignia, defaced the notices on the gable-ends of their huts with their injunctions *Credere, Combattere* . . . and other similar nonsense, and shouted to us in Italian simplified for our benefit, "BENITO FINITO!" Now they shouted "ARMISTIZIO!"

The only difference Mussolini's departure had made to us was that the sentries no longer fired at the windows of the bar when we looked out of them, and our walks were cancelled. If anything, we had suffered a reduction rather than an increase in our amenities. What now roused us from our lethargy was the thought that when the Germans retreated northwards, as none of us doubted they would have to, they might carry us off with them over the Alpine Passes. "Like a lot of concubines," someone said on one of the innumerable occasions on which we had discussed the possibility.

Our friends gave us all the latest news when they came to see us later in the evening.

"The colonel called a parade in the hall," one said. "There's to be no fraternisation with the Itis and we've mounted our own sentries on the gate. A party's just gone off to recce the country round about in case the Germans come and we have to break out. If they do the *colonello* says he will fight, but there doesn't seem much chance of his having to. Airborne landings are expected at Rome and Milan, and sea landings at Genoa and Rimini. It's really a matter of holding out for twenty-four hours at the most until our people arrive. Anyway, we're getting your gear together and we've got two of the biggest parachutists in the camp organised to help Eric if we do have to get out."

"I wish the M.O. would hurry up and get some plaster of paris for my ankle," I said. "Then all I'd need would be a stick instead of a couple of bloody great parachutists."

"Pity you're both stuck here," said another. "Someone's done a big deal with the Itis, and the bar's doing terrific business. The ration's been abolished; but we've brought your mugs. You can have some more when you've finished."

Our drinking mugs were made from big tins which had originally contained powdered milk sent to us by the Canadian Red Cross, whose food parcels, together with those from Scotland, were easily the best. Each of these receptacles held more than a pint and they were now filled with a dark brownish liquid of a sort which neither Michael nor myself had ever seen before.

"I say, this is rather strong," Michael said after tasting it. "What do you think it is?"

"It's supposed to be Marsala, but the wine merchants in the camp say they've never tasted Marsala like this. And I've just met someone on the way here who was drinking it out of an enamelled jug and the enamel's coming off."

"Could you remember to put *all* my socks in my pack and my pullover and *The Tour of the Hebrides*," I said. "Otherwise, I mightn't finish it before we go home."

What we did not know, how could we, was that the Allies' dispositions were already made, and that none of their plans included the liberation of the occupants of the *orfanotrofio*. The assault convoys bound for Salerno were at sea and had already been sighted south of Capri. The Sixteenth Panzer Division which was in the area had already ordered a state of alarm, and its members were now engaged in disarming all Italian troops and taking over the coastal batteries. The only airborne operations which had been planned, a drop on Rome by the United States Eighty-Sixth Airborne Division, had already been cancelled after its deputy commander, who had arrived in the capital on the afternoon of the seventh on a secret visit, had found on the morning of the eighth that all the airfields were in German hands. It was he who told Badoglio that the main Allied landings were due to begin the following morning, the first that the Marshal or any of his staff had heard of it. They had been led to believe that no landings would take place until the twelfth. What difference it would have made no one will ever know, or care.

For the rest, the greater part of the British Eighth Army was committed in Southern Italy where it was fighting its way up through Calabria in order to link up with the troops which were to be landed at Salerno. There were not going to be any airborne landings at Milan or anywhere else and no seaborne ones at Rimini or Genoa either.

Chapter Four

The ninth of September

Late on the following morning an Italian bugler sounded three "g's", the alarm call which meant that the Germans were on their way to take over the *orfanotrofio*, and everyone began to move out of the building into the exercise field at the back. From the window of the hospital, of which I was now the only occupant, Michael's boil having burst during the night, brought to a head, perhaps, by the events of the previous day, there was no one to be seen on the road; only Italian soldiers setting up machine-guns and scurrying into slit trenches, reluctantly preparing to carry out the *colonello*'s order to defend the camp to the last round and the last man.

Looking at them I knew that they would not do so. By this, the fourth year of the war, too many personages too far from the scenes of the battles which they were trying to control, without themselves being under the necessity of firing a shot or of laying down their lives, had issued too many such orders to too many troops who invariably ended up by having to lay down their arms ignominiously, in order to save their skins. These Italian soldiers would have been mad to die in defence of an empty building, and they didn't.

With my pack on my shoulder I hopped through the deserted corridors towards the back door. On the way, amongst the debris on the floor, I found a little book with the Italian *tricolore* on the cover, entitled "*Say it in Italian*", or something similar, and I picked it up. By the time I reached the corner of the field where the rest of my company were, they were just beginning to move off through one of the several gaps which had been cut in the wire.

There, the two parachutists were waiting for me. They looked enormous in their camouflaged smocks, in which they must have been roasting, but without which any parachutist feels naked. They had been relieved of their packs so that they could help me.

They told me to take it easy and we went out through one of the gaps in the wire in the sweltering midday heat, and as soon as we were beyond it one of the British orderlies in the camp, a small, nut-brown man, a trooper in some cavalry reigment, came up and said, "It's all right. You got a horse! Name of Mora, quiet as a lamb." And there she was, standing with a stolid-looking Italian soldier in the shade of some vines, taking mouthfuls of grass, swishing her tail at the flies, looking contented and well-fed. She was a little horse.

The parachutists were delighted to have my weight off their shoulders. They hoisted me into the saddle, half-strangled by my pack strap which was twisted round my neck, and then the soldier led Mora forward, chewing a straw, happy to be seconded for this easy duty, free of the obligation to sell his life to no purpose, while the rest of the people in our company moved on ahead in the shade of the vines, picking great bunches of grapes and churning the earth into dust.

For me the journey was a nightmare. Although the country was dead flat it was intersected by irrigation ditches (the same ditches that the escapers who had had themselves buried in the field had spoken of with revulsion after they were re-captured). The last thing one wanted in such country was a horse. The last thing I wanted anywhere was a horse. All I knew about horses was derived from a couple of ruinous visits to some trotting races at Heliopolis. I had never been on a horse in my life and I was terrified of them. And every horse I met knew it too.

At the first ditch Mora stopped dead on the edge of it and refused to move backwards or forwards, more like a mule than a horse. Perhaps she was a mule. She took no notice of the blows which the Italian soldier was raining on her behind with a cudgel; and I was no help at all. Every time my damaged foot touched her it was agony.

We seemed destined to remain there for ever, but something happened to make her utter a terrific snorting, whinnying noise, rear up on her hind legs and come down with her front ones in the slime in the bottom of the ditch with a resounding splosh, which catapulted me over her head on to the far bank and hurt my ankle dreadfully.

"Bloody funny, that Iti must have struck a lighted cigarette up her chuff," someone said.

"One way of crossing the Rubicon," someone else said who had had a different sort of education. Everyone who witnessed it was cheered by this spectacular happening.

Then the parachutists picked me up and lugged me over a whole series of similar ditches while Mora, who had crossed them unencumbered, waited for me to catch up.

Finally, we emerged on to a narrow lane. In a field to one side of it men and women wearing wide-brimmed straw hats were harvesting wheat with sickles. They stopped work as the head of the column approached and looked alarmed, but when they realised that we were unarmed prisoners from the camp they smiled and waved to us.

Then a man in a striped city suit with square shoulders appeared and spoke to one of the Italian interpreters who was with us, and we halted in the shade of a grove of tall poplars. No one spoke and it was very cool and quiet. The only sound was the humming of bees and insects and the wind stirring the tops of the trees. High above them in a dark blue sky, small puffs of cloud floated, as if of a cannon that had been discharged at regular intervals. After some minutes we moved on again. None of us, except the interpreter and the more senior officers at the head of the column, knew what the man in the striped suit had said. None of us really cared. We were not yet used to the idea of freedom. Although we each one of us still felt that we were individuals, we were really a herd lacking any power to make useful decisions, and although we were in theory a battalion organised in companies of a hundred or so, any one of these companies could probably have been re-captured in this moment by two or three resolute Germans armed with Schmeissers. We were rather like one of those outings of lunatics which I had so often encountered in the Surrey pine woods when we had been training in the first summer of the war. And like many of them we were irrationally happy. Even I on my horse, or mule, of which I was terrified.

Then, suddenly, there was an awful roar and the Italian soldier was trying to drag Mora into a deep, watery ditch, and I clouted him over the head with his cudgel, of which I had relieved him, harder than I needed to in revenge for his having stuck a lighted cigarette end up Mora's backside, as a Messerschmidt 110 skimmed overhead, two hundred feet above us, silvery, like a flying fish in the sun. It was gone before we had time to hide ourselves, and then it didn't seem to matter much whether the pilot had seen us or not.

With so many stops and starts it took us until early afternoon to reach our destination, some fields on the far bank of one of the torrents which roared down from the Apennines at certain seasons, now with hardly any water in it at all. Here, below one of the steep, grassy embankments, we lay down under the vines and waited, dozing and discussing the various rumours that came to us, no one seemed to know from where: that the Germans had arrived at the *orfanotrofio* with tanks, that they were looting, were drunk, were smashing everything, had gone away for good, had gone away and were coming back the next day to round us up.

What had actually happened was that some lorryloads of Germans, probably *feldgendarmen*, military policemen, had arrived at the camp, had fired a few rounds in the air, the Italian soldiers had capitulated instantly, the *colonello* had been arrested, and the Germans had taken him away as a souvenir of their visit. Later he was sent to a concentration camp in Germany where he suffered such privations that he died soon after he returned to Italy at the end of the war. He was an honourable, gallant but rather stupid man—honour being as much use in dealing with Germans in war time as a peashooter would be to a prehistoric man attempting to destroy a mammoth. The only looting was being done by the inhabitants of the village. It was lucky for us that they were.

Then the colonel sent for me. After a lot of frenzied hopping I found him hidden away behind a line of vines, together with his staff.

"I'm afraid you'll have to get under cover," he said. "We may have to move at any time and I can't ask the chaps who have been helping you up to now to jeopardise their own chances of getting away in order to save you. Bad luck, but there it is. We've arranged with a farmer in that house over there to let you hide in his hay, but if the Germans find you he won't know anything about you being there. If they do come it will be every man for himself, anyway."

At the farm I said goodbye to the Italian soldier. If I had been a horse lover I would have said goodbye to Mora too. I gave him one of my six packets of cigarettes and we shook hands.

"*Vado a casa,*" he said. "I am going home." Then he got into the saddle and set off southwards along a line of vines, away from the colonel and the prisoners and the camp, a squat, rectangular figure. I wonder whether he made it. I expect he did. He was an invisible sort of man who blended well with the landscape. If I had had any sense I would have got up behind him and ridden pillion.

The farmer was a large, red-faced man with a roman nose. He was like a bucolic emperor, but his florid appearance belied his character which was shy and retiring. I was glad of this because I was not capable of making any sort of conversation. All I knew was a number of words—*buono, male, oggi, domani, bello, brutto* and some sentence which had stuck in my memory from the official communiques, *Due velivoli sono stati abbattuti,* two aeroplanes have been shot down, *Un piroscafo è stato colato a picco,* a steamer has been sent to the bottom, not much use in everyday conversation.

He helped me up a couple of steep ladders to a big loft where I lay deep in the hay with a bottle of water to slake my thirst, sneezing and with streaming eyes, wishing that I was in England where, for me, the hay fever season would have been over, and soaking the only two handkerchiefs I had with me.

Through a large opening in one of the walls of the loft, I looked out over a vast sea of vegetation to an infinitely distant horizon, from the surface of which, as if the lower parts of them were engulfed by it, rose red-roofed farmhouses, the tall campaniles of churches and dark groves of poplars. Much closer, a couple of hundred yards away, occasional movements among the vines betrayed the presence of scouts posted by the colonel, who were somewhat out of practice, otherwise there was no sign that there were more than five hundred prisoners hidden among them.

From away to the south, where the Via Emilia ran through the plain, came the solid roar of transport on the move. From somewhere closer came the pooping sound of motor cycles. They would probably be German B.M.W.s with sidecars, carrying three men armed with grenades and machine pistols. A few of these units could pick the lot of us up. They were probably using one of the minor roads which we had sometimes got to on our walks which ran roughly parallel with the Via Emilia from Piacenza to Parma and they were probably doing this because there was so much traffic on the main road. I wondered which way they were going, coming in from the north or pulling out across the river. The Italian Area General was said to have telephoned the *colonello* just before we left and told him that there was fighting in Milan where American parachutists had landed, and that there had been seaborne landings at La Spezia on the west coast. I didn't believe any of this; but I still clung to the irrational belief that everything would be all right if only we could see the night through.

When it grew dark the farmer, whose name was Merli, came up the ladder and signed to me to come down. I was glad to get out of the *fienile*, the loft, although my hay fever had gone at last.

His wife was dark and pale and slight. The two children were beautiful, miniature editions of their mother. They were all curious about my uniform, the whipcord trousers, the battle-dress jacket with the polished brass pips, my silk muffler and my one beautiful new boot (the other was in my pack). Like everyone else, I was wearing my best clothes, wanting to appear decent when our own troops arrived. She fed me on *pasta asciutta*, and what she called *grana*, what I called Parmesan. It was nothing like the cheese of that name I had eaten in England. Afterwards she gave me a piece to eat. It had hard, salty nodules in it, the curd which broke into small pieces when the cheese was made. And her husband gave me some frothy, purple wine to drink, called *lambrusco*, which was very refreshing.

Then one of the Italian interpreters appeared, the elegant,

pipe-smoking *capitano* who spoke excellent English. The news he brought was not altogether good.

"The Germans are coming in from the north," he said, "and in great strength. But they may have left it too late. There's been a big Allied landing at Salerno, south of Naples. We'll know better what to do tomorrow."

While we were sitting on chairs in the yard talking about the place where he lived, an extraordinary great vehicle, which in the moonlight looked as big as a barn, came charging round a corner belching sparks and smoke and disappeared.

"What on earth was that?" I asked him.

"That was the steam tram that goes from Busseto to Parma by way of Ponte Taro," he said. "I'm surprised it's out on such a night as this."

I found it strange sitting with someone who up to a few hours before had been an official enemy. Like the soldier who had been put in charge of Mora, the *capitano* had been lucky to have been given the job of looking after us instead of being called upon to make a last stand at the *orfanotrofio*. I asked him how long he thought it would be. He said a week at the most. I noticed how the time from liberation was rapidly receding.

"Now go and sleep," he said. "The farmer has put some sacks in the cowshed for you."

Then he went off, into a dark mist which had risen. It hung just above the ground so that his head and shoulders emerged above it and the lower part of his body was invisible as he walked away. It was a weird sight. The moon was sinking, shedding an unearthly reddish tinge on the misty plain. Against the dark line of the Apennines Verey lights rose at intervals. From time to time there were explosions at the foot of the hills as if dumps were being blown. On the Via Emilia the traffic roared. Altogether, it was a thoroughly macabre night.

Chapter Five

Interlude in an *Ospedale*

The next morning, after a slow start, things began to happen with increased rapidity. It was as if a piece of an old film in which the actors emerge from vehicles, zoom into buildings with incredible speed, and miraculously appear at a window sixteen storeys up within seconds, had been interpolated in a modern one in which the characters move at a normal rate.

Around eleven o'clock an Italian doctor arrived in a Fiat 500. He was an enormous, shambling man with grizzled hair, like a bear and one of the ugliest men I had seen for a long time.

He examined my ankle, which was rather painful after the strains to which it had been subjected, raised his shoulders, made a noise which sounded like *urgh* and went off to have a conference with the *capitano*.

"The doctor says you must go to hospital," the *capitano* said, when they emerged from their conclave.

"But that means I shall be captured again," I said.

"You'll be taken anyway if you don't. Apparently things are not going too well at Salerno and we're six hundred kilometres north of it. Everything's going to break up here, anyway. Unless you can walk you won't stand a chance. The doctor can get you into a hospital in Fontanellato. No one will think of looking for you there."

While he was speaking, the forerunners of an army of women, girls and small boys began to arrive at the farm on foot and on bicycles; the same girls, or the same sort of girls I had seen on the road outside the camp, except that now they were wearing their working clothes. I felt less bold now that we were at close quarters and there was no wire between us, and so did they, and all we managed were some nervous smiles.

They all carried baskets and panniers filled with civilian clothing, wine, bread, cheese, fruit, eggs and tinned food and cigarettes which they had saved from the *orfanotrofio* after the Germans had left and all at once the farm became a depot for the prisoners hidden behind the embankment.

I found myself a mechanic's jacket and a pair of dark blue cotton trousers and a shirt, filled my pack with the food and cigarettes that were being pressed upon me from every side, and once again climbed the ladder to the loft where I changed into them, chucking my uniform down from the window into the yard from which it was instantly taken away.

While I was doing this I noticed a bold, good-looking girl. She was different from the others. They were all brown or black haired; but she was an ash blonde with blue eyes and she was very slim which made her seem taller than she was. She looked more like a Scandinavian than an Italian to me, but with more fire. Whatever she was she smiled at me.

Then the doctor arrived. For the last time I descended the ladder and said goodbye to the farmer and his wife who cried. They were the first people in the whole district to take the risk of helping us. Then I hopped across the yard to the Fiat.

As I was getting into it the girl came up and leant over the top of the open door.

"I vill com to see you in the *ospedale*," she said, in fractured English. She had a deep middle-European voice. "Wonce I have seen you in the *orfanotrofio* and you vaved and the *soldati* went pom pom. Ve vill have lessons in languages," she said. "Your language and my language." And she smiled again. Then someone shut the door and we drove away.

"If iu uont tu enter dhe steiscen iu mast haev e plaetfom tikit," Wanda said. "*Se vuole entrare nella stazione deve avere un biglietto.*"

I was lying in a bed in the *Ospedale Peracchi* on the outskirts of Fontanellato, only a few hundred yards from the *orfanotrofio*. I had now been free for three days. It seemed much longer. Wanda was seated on a chair which one of the *suore*, the nuns who were also expert nurses, had placed in a corner of the room, as far away from me as possible. Equally discreetly, the door had been left wide open. Both of us were armed with phrase books, she with a large Italian/English version, I with the English/Italian booklet which I had salvaged on my way out of the *orfanotrofio*. With their help we were making heavy weather of one another's languages, and it was not fair of her to change subjects like this.

Up to now we had been reading useful phrases to one another from the chapters on "Trams and Buses". "Last stop. *Ool ghet aut!*" "*Kwah-lee ow-toh-bus vann-oh ah Toh-reen-oh*? Which buses go to Turin?" I ruffled through the pages of my book which was so small that it looked as if it had been printed for a midget, until I found a section headed "At the Station—*Alla Stazione*", and said, "*Oh per-soh eel mee-oh beel-yet-oh*. I have lost my ticket." To which she replied, severely, "Iu haev misleid iur tikit. Iu caant continiu iur geerni anless iu ricaver it. *Lei ha smarrito il suo biglietto. Non può proseguire il suo viaggio se non lo trova.*"

"*Nohn vawr-ray-ee cohn-teen-u-ar loh.* I don't want to continue it," I said. I enunciated this, and all the other phrases, with such painstaking slowness that I sounded like a run-down gramophone.

"*Iu hev mist dhe train. È partito il treno,*" she said, triumphantly, like one of the White's men in the orphanage putting down a natural at baccarat.

"*Grahts-ee-ay. Lay ay stah-toh jehn-tee-lay.* Thank you very much. Most kind of you."

"*Rieli nathing,*" she said, airily. "*Ai em ounli tu glaed if ai kaen help iu. Proprio nulla, per me è un vero piacere poterla aiutare.*"

She shut her book and looked at me with an air of despair which, to me, was very beautiful.

"*Hurrock,*" she said (this is what my name sounded like on her lips).

"You will never learn *italiano* like this. You spik and then you forget. First you must learn *la grammatica.* I have learned English *grammatica,* so also must you learn Italian. And you must learn *presto,* queekly, queekly. Here, you see, I have written for you a *grammatica* with *aggettivi, come se dice?*"

"Adjectives! Adjectives! *Che lingua!* Also auxeiliary verbs and verbs, *regolari* and *irregolari.* You will learn all these, please, by tomorrow."

"I can't learn all this by tomorrow."

"You *vill,*" she said, "or I shall not kom more. I shall teach to someonels. The *superiora* says I can kom ven I vish. If you vont me to kom you must vork."

She consulted her book. "*Hueer dheers e uil dheers e ui. Proverbio. Dove c'è la volonta c'è la via.*"

"Where there's a will there's a way," I said. "That's a proverb. I want you to come to see me more than anything."

"Then learn your *grammatica,*" she said, consulting her superior phrase book. "*Far presto!* Luk slipi!"

When the doctor drove me to the hospital he made me sit next to him in the front seat. It seemed insanely risky, but the lanes through which we whizzed were as empty as the fields on either side. It was midday, *mezzogiorno,* and everyone, friend and foe, was under cover, eating their dinners and sheltering from the gigantic sun. Behind us a long plume of dust rose from the road and spread out across the countryside as dense as a smokescreen laid by a destroyer.

At the hospital we were expected. As soon as I got out of the car in the forecourt, two astonishingly powerful women wearing black habits and starched white head-dresses, whom I took to be nuns, came running down the steps towards me, flung my arms round their shoulders, just as the two parachutists had done, and rushed me into the building under a dilapidated iron and glass canopy, like the ones outside old cinemas, with the words *Ospedale Peracchi* above it, through a pair of mahogany doors, down a dim corridor in which there was a bust of Signor Peracchi, the benefactor, after whom the hospital had been named, and into a hall in which they paused for breath. To me they seemed tough enough to be members of one of those German parachute units whom everyone at the time believed had dropped, dressed as nuns, in the Low Countries, in 1940.

While we stood there a number of very old men and women of a sort who would now, in the ruthless jargon of our time, be called "geriatrics", emerged from the room in which they had been eating their midday meal. In their hands, unheeded, they held crusts of bread, glasses of wine and bowls of *pasta*. They mumbled excitedly at the sight of this unexpected apparition, and their eyes lit up with pleasure. But it was not for long. They were shepherded back into their dining hall and the two *suore* picked me up again and whizzed me up a flight of stairs and into a small room on the top floor of the building, as if they were a couple of express messengers delivering a large parcel. And once we were safely in the room they began to unwrap me, just like a parcel. There was no false modesty about these women. In a minute they had stripped off my newly acquired clothes, inserted me into a pair of English pyjamas looted from the *orfanotrofio*, and put me to bed.

Then the doctor appeared, huge, authoritative and uncommunicative, and put my foot in plaster of paris, and I was given a bowl of the same *pasta* that the old people below had been eating, while various *suore* clucked sympathetically, saying *poveretto* and *poverino*—words that even I could understand—and then they all went away and after a while I fell asleep in heavenly, clean sheets, like a great cosseted baby.

I woke at four. The venetian blinds were down and the room was in darkness. I got out of bed, hauled on the webbing strap which raised the one over the window which faced the road, and looked out on it. I half expected it to be swarming with Germans; but apart from a small boy who was grubbing about in a ditch, and a girl with black hair done up in a yellow handkerchief who went creaking past on a bicycle, there was no one in sight. The heat was terrific.

By sticking my head out of the window I could see the whole of the front of the hospital, the peeling stucco, the mouldering canopy over the door and the little forecourt, now in shadow, with its iron seats under the trees on which ancient men and women sat placidly or slept and one or two idiots lolled, just as I remembered them on our early morning walks from the *orfanotrofio* under guard, before the sun had got too hot for them to sit there. Then I had imagined the inside of the building to be a mixture of nineteenth-century workhouse and madhouse, and I had looked at the occupants with feelings of pity and horror; but now that I was inside it and had seen it for myself it seemed a clean and friendly refuge from a crumbling world.

Then the *superiora*, the head of the hospital appeared, a middle-aged woman with a gentle, resolute face. She wore a more elaborate head-dress than the two *suore* who had rushed me into the building and a big bunch of shiny keys and an ebony and silver crucifix swung from her black belt. She was carrying a large tray loaded with tea things and bread and butter, ginger biscuits and raspberry jam; everything except the bread and butter looted from the *orfanotrofio*. She was a more elderly version of the Gaoler's Daughter in *The Wind in the Willows*, visiting Toad in his dungeon with a great trayload of tea and buttered toast.

I tried to thank her, partly in French, partly with the few Italian words I knew, but they got mixed up with bits of school Latin, and then I ran out of words completely and looked at her in despair, and she smiled and went out of the room and came back with the girl I had met in the farmyard that morning.

She was wearing a white, open-necked shirt and a blue cotton skirt. She was brown, she was slim, she had good legs, she had ash blonde hair and blue eyes and she had a fine nose. When she smiled she looked saucy, and when she didn't she looked serious. She was all right.

She began to speak with the rich, faulty, slow English of which I have already tried to give some inkling, and which it would be tedious to continue.

"You have not forgotten me?" she said. (I would have had to have been peculiarly gormless to have done so in the five hours which had elapsed since I had last seen her.)

I assured her that I had not done so.

"Your friends are well. They are now all dressed in clothes the people have given them. Some have already gone away across the Via Emilia. Some are in the farms, most of them are still in the fields. You must stay here until your foot is strong enough to walk on. Yesterday when the Germans came, everyone from the village was in the *orfanotrofio*. We were stealing the things you left behind. *Che robe!* What things you left behind you! I was with my father. We had just come out and we met them on the road. They fired, only in the air, but we did not know this. I lay on the road. My father had many packets of cigarettes and he jumped into a ditch to hide, but it was full of water. He held them up like this, above his head, and kept them dry. Then we ran away. My father spoiled his suit, but he is very pleased with his cigarettes."

"My mother has made an *apfelstrudel* for you," she went on. "In my country we call them *struklji*. We are not Italian. We are Slovenes. You can eat it after your dinner. Tonight you have chicken. The *superiora* told me. Be kind to her and do what she says. Now I must go. I have to take food to your friends."

I asked her when she would come again.

"I will come tomorrow, if the *superiora* allows. If you want I will teach you Italian. It will be useful for you, and you can teach me English. I speak badly. My name is Wanda." She picked up her basket. At the door she paused.

"You know," she said, "You are the only one in this part of the building who is not *incinta*. You know what is *incinta*?" She puffed out her stomach and banged it with both hands, like a drum. "You are in the *sala di maternità* and tonight a baby will be born."

When they had gone I laughed out loud. For a year I had slept on a straw mattress with lumps in it, or on bare boards; the company of women had been a dream and I had thought constantly of food, the gnawing hunger of the bored and the unemployed, and I had longed to be alone, to have a room of my own and to be free. Then, suddenly, everything had come at once, freedom, at least of a sort, a wonderful clean bed, delicious food and a beautiful girl to talk to who had a name like a heroine in an Oppenheim novel. Perhaps it was all a dream, or worse, perhaps I had gone mad.

These reveries were interrupted by a huge droning. I got to the window and looked out. Three J.U.52 transport planes were beating over the village like great, dark birds, and as they passed overhead they let fall what seemed to be huge swarms of white butterflies which slowly fluttered earthwards, shimmering in the evening sun.

A few minutes later the *ospedale*'s male nurse and, apart from the gardener, the only man employed in it, puffed up the stairs to my room bearing one of the leaflets which the gardener had retrieved from the road outside. He was a fat old thing with a red face and a large, bushy moustache. He reminded me of Tenniel's drawing of the Walrus, but without the tusks. His name, he told me, was Giulio.

The leaflet was printed on a single sheet of paper. *Il Governo ha tradito l'Italia* . . . the text began and it continued in the same vein. Anyone reading it could be in no doubt either about the Germans' feelings or their intentions. They were very angry about being betrayed;

they were going to fight, and God help anyone who got in their way.

"*Molto male*," Giulio said, with gloomy relish, speaking in tele-graphese to make it simpler for me to understand, which he punctuated with puffing noises, the sort of sounds which I imagined a real walrus might make, surfacing by an ice-floe in some Arctic sea.

"PFF! *Roma kaputt*, PFF! *Tedeschi in tutta L'Emilia*, PFF! *Una disgrazia per l'Italia. Una disgrazia per lei, Tenente*, PFF! *Kaputt.*" He was just like the Walrus. It was as if he was saying "I weep for you. I deeply sympathise, Oyster, but somebody is going to eat you up."

Later that evening fearful groans and cries began to issue from the ward next to my room, which was only normally employed for "difficult" cases. Powerfully affected by other people's pains—I invariably faint away during performances of *King Lear, Coriolanus*, any Greek tragedy worthy of the name, and in any film in the course of which operating theatres and torture chambers form part of the *mise en scène*—and never having heard the sounds of a confinement at first hand, I lay on my bed listening to them in terror as they rose to ever greater heights. If this was an ordinary childbirth what on earth could a "difficult" one sound like, I wondered. Finally, in the early hours of the morning they ceased and were replaced by the powerful roarings of a baby. Only then did I go to sleep.

Every afternoon Wanda visited me in the *ospedale*. We sat together in the back garden, hidden from the outside world by one of the projecting wings of the building and a hedge, under the benevolent but constant chaperonage of the *superiora* and her attendant *suore* who were never far away. Centuries of invasion of their country by foreign soldiery, and the concomitant outrages which had been inflicted on them had made the members of female religious orders particularly adept in protecting not only their own virtues, but that of those temporarily committed to their charge.

She used to tell me the latest news about my friends. How some people had already set off towards the line; others were thinking of going to Switzerland; how one officer whose identity I never discovered had been hidden in the *castello* of a local *principessa* who had been so impressed by his girlish face that she had the brilliant idea of dressing him as a young woman of fashion and putting him on a train to Switzerland. This she had done but, unfortunately, he looked so desirable on the train that some soldiers had "interfered" with him, as the *News of the World* used to put it, and discovered the truth, although one of them got punched hard on the nose in the process of doing so.

Wanda herself was in favour of my going to Switzerland—she had none of my optimism about the Allies' capacity to advance rapidly up Italy—crossing from somewhere near the head of the Val d'Aosta with a party which was being organised by the pipe-smoking interpreter; but I hated the idea of going to Switzerland and perhaps spending the winter not imprisoned but interned which seemed to me the same thing, perhaps locked up in a hotel on the shores of some drab Swiss lake, watching the rain beating down into it. Her other plan, which seemed more cheerful and sensible than going to Switzerland, was that I should become gardener's boy at the castle of that same *principessa* who had sent the transvestite officer on his last journey.

In the garden we worked away, teaching one another our respective languages. After our initial, disastrous, but diverting attempt to do it with phrase books, we went back to the beginnings. Wanda made me start at the bottom, conjugating verbs and struggling with pronouns. Fortunately for me she already had a sound knowledge of grammar and was far ahead.

I concentrated on teaching her new words, the way to pronounce the ones she already knew and some colloquial expressions. But as the days went by, listening to her, I found myself increasingly reluctant to destroy her rich, inimitable idiom, and her strangely melancholy accent which to me was a triple distillation of the essence of middle Europe. It seemed monstrous to graft on to this vigorous stem my own diluted version of English, originally learned in a London suburb and further watered down by school teachers and the B.B.C.

"*Questo è un sasso*. Dis is a ston," she would say, picking up a piece of gravel from one of the paths. "I strait it avay," throwing it over her shoulder. She also employed a remarkable word of her own invention "to squitch". This could be used to describe any kind of operation from corking a bottle of wine to mending a piece of complicated machinery. "You just squitch it in," she said, as I tried to replace the winder which had come off her dilapidated wrist-watch.

It would have been tedious if we had confined ourselves to studying one another's languages; but, as well, we had long, rambling conversations about our lives. She told me about her family. They were Yugoslavs, Slovenes from the Carso, the great, windswept limestone plateau which extends inland from the Gulf of Trieste at the head of the Adriatic towards Ljubljana, territory which had been ceded to Italy after the dismemberment of the Austro-Hungarian Empire in 1919. Her father had been a schoolmaster in a Slovene village in the Carso called Stanjel until the provisions of the peace treaty moved the Italian frontier with Slovenia twenty-five miles inland from the Adriatic, when it was re-named San Daniele del Carso by the Italians. Much later, in the early thirties, Mussolini decided to break down the strong nationalistic spirit which still existed in those parts of Slovenia which had been ceded to Italy. He forbade the use of the Slovene language and Slovenian teachers were deported to Italy. Among them was Wanda's father. He was of the same age as the *colonello* at the *orfanotrofio* but his background was entirely different. He scarcely knew any Italian at all, his second language being German, the official language of the Empire (he had served in the Austrian Army in the First World War) but now he was sent to Fontanellato to teach in the school there where, for some years knowing little of the language, he experienced great difficulty in correcting his pupils' essays. He was a liberal of the old sort and detested Fascists and Fascism. Wanda told me that her family had never been allowed to return to their country and that her mother cried very often when she thought of her home, although the local people at Fontanellato, who had originally called them *Tedeschi*, Germans, were now very friendly. She herself was an accountant and she worked in the *Banca d' Agricoltura* in the village.

When Wanda was not at the *ospedale* she was either working at the bank or else taking supplies to the other prisoners in the surrounding country. Fortunately, the weather was still good. Meanwhile, I got on with the "prep" which she had set me; but without her I found the garden a rather creepy, shut-away place. Occasionally a low-flying German aircraft roared overhead; almost equally loud were the roars of out-patients who were having their teeth extracted without the aid of pain-killers, by Giulio who not only acted as *infirmiere* but also stood in as a dental surgeon in urgent cases in the absence of the real dentist who only visited Fontanellato once a week.

I had another companion in the garden. A little mongoloid child called Maria. She was olive-skinned and had a squat, pear-shaped body, a thick almost non-existent neck, a very large head, low brows, a vestigial nose and pig-tails. In fact just as Giulio looked like the Walrus, to me, Maria resembled the picture of Rebecca, the little girl who was always slamming doors, the one on whom the bust of Abraham had fallen and laid her out, in Belloc's *Cautionary Tales for Children*. Having done little else for the past year but read, I found that I had a tendency to make such literary comparisons; but it was one which I felt I ought to curb, otherwise the little world I inhabited would be entirely populated with figures of fiction—the *superiora* as the Gaoler's Daughter, Guilio as the Walrus, Maria as Rebecca Offendort, the daughter of a wealthy Banker who lived in Palace Green, Bayswater, and so on.

Looking at Maria it was difficult to guess her age; in fact she was nine but looked older. She was loosed on me every morning at eleven o'clock by the *suore* who were glad to have her off their hands for an hour. She used to enjoy being with me because I didn't tease her as some of the nastier inmates and one of the older *suore* did; I liked having her with me, providing that she didn't hurt me too much. For Maria was immensely strong. She used to creep up behind me, seize one of my fingers in a powerful lock and bend it back until, unless I freed it, she would have broken it like a rotten stick.

Once she almost succeeded in throttling me with one of her pig-tails which she wound round my neck in much the same way as Indian thugs used the handkerchief to strangle their victims. Sometimes she tried to bite me or gnaw off one of my ears; but mostly she was affectionate and when she was she used to plonk herself in my lap like a five hundred pound bomb, and together we used to look through old copies of *La Domenica del Corriere*, a magazine which always had highly coloured and skilfully executed illustrations on its covers, pictures of British battleship sinking, *Bersaglieri* performing terrific feats of valour with shells bursting all round them, and more domestic incidents, some of them macabre—one depicted a cloister full of nuns being attacked by a hungry lion which had escaped from a zoo during an air raid. Maria liked this picture very much. She used to look at the lion and make wuffing noises like a little dog; perhaps she identified the *suora* it was beginning to consume as the one who used to tease her when she thought that no one was looking.

Every day the news got worse. On the twelfth of September Radio Roma broadcast the news that Mussolini had been rescued by German parachutists. The station was now in the hands of the Germans, and temporarily at least, it seemed more reliable and less euphoric than the B.B.C. which, according to Wanda who had heard it, had actually broadcast on the same day the sound of the bells of St. Paul's ringing out in rejoicing at the invasion of Italy.

On the thirteenth and fourteenth the news from Salerno was really awful. Rome announced that the Germans were launching massive counter-attacks on the beachhead, and this was confirmed by the B.B.C. By the sixteenth the news was better. The counter-attack seemed to have lost its steam; but on that day an order was broadcast that all Italian officers, N.C.O.s and men were to present themselves forthwith in uniforms at the nearest German headquarters. No one but a lunatic would have obeyed such an order, and, in fact scarcely anyone did; but what was more serious was another announcement to the effect that anyone sheltering or feeding prisoners of war would be dealt with under martial law, and I had visions of the *superiora* going before a firing squad as Nurse Cavell had done. It was obvious that I could not stay in the *ospedale* any longer and, for the first time I realised what Wanda had been trying to din into me, that a knowledge of Italian was going to be essential if I was to avoid being recaptured.

On or about the sixteenth the *Gazzetta di Parma*, Italy's oldest newspaper, which had enjoyed a very brief period of editorial freedom after the Armistice, before once again being muzzled, published a statement by the Commandant of the S.S. in Parma. Full of gruesome bonhomie, he conveyed his felicitations to the population and especially to members of the Fascist organisations, and then went on to speak of a new period of prosperity in store for the Italian people. Next to this absolutely crazy announcement there was a notice to the effect that a curfew was imposed on the inhabitants of the entire Province from ten p.m. onwards, and that anyone who disregarded it was liable to be shot.

Chapter Six

Back to Nature

The next day, the seventeenth of September, while we were having what was to be our last language lesson together, I told Wanda that I must leave the *ospedale*.

"You are right," she said. "If you had not suggested it yourself I was going to tell you. I am worried for you but I am much more worried for the *superiora*. There are Germans everywhere now. But it will have to be tomorrow. My father and the doctor will arrange something. They are great friends."

I was worried for everyone who was helping me. All I had to lose was my freedom; their lives were in danger. I was particularly worried about Wanda and all the other women and girls quartering the country round about on their bicycles bringing food every day to the prisoners who were still hiding among the vines wondering, like me, what was the best thing to do.

Our relationship had changed a great deal since we had first met. It had progressed far beyond the stage of giving one another language lessons. I had begun by thinking her a very good-looking girl and being flattered that she should take any notice of me. Then I had begun to admire her courage and determination; now I was in love with her.

These feelings were not entirely one-sided. Now, when we were alone together, we sat as close as we dared to one another on the seat in the garden, knowing that we were under observation by one or other of the *suore* but on several occasions I managed to kiss Wanda in one of the dark corridors on the way back to my room.

Early the next morning I received a visit from the *superiora*. She was in tears. Apparently the Germans had discovered that I was in the hospital, and a guard was already posted outside my door.

'What is to become of you?" she wailed.

I told her not to worry. If I was recaptured I would be protected by the Geneva Convention and she had done everything she could. I was sure she would not be punished for taking in an injured man whatever his nationality was; but when I got out of bed and opened the door to go to the *gabinetto*, there were two *carabinieri* sitting on chairs in the corridor armed with carbines, the tools of their trade; heavy-jowled, big-behinded brutes, rustic oafs, but none the nicer for being so.

"Eh! Eh!" they both screeched, uttering the depressing, minatory epithet that I had first heard what now seemed a lifetime ago on the airfield in Sicily and that I knew so well from being guarded by Italians and had hoped never to hear again, at the same time waving me back into my room. Just like all the other *carabinieri* I had ever encountered, these two seemed incapable of performing the simplest task—in this case guarding an unarmed, partly incapacitated man—except in pairs; but it was and still is a rule of the service that each *carabiniere* must have a mate who goes everywhere with him.

"*Devo andare al gabinetto.*"

"*È vietato!*"

What a gormless pair they were! How could they forbid anyone to go to the lavatory in a hospital? They must have thought they were guarding someone in a cell in some filthy provincial gaol, which is what I was probably destined for.

"*Perchè?*"

"*È proibito.*"

It seemed a waste of time to ask them who could possibly have issued such an ordinance.

"*Ho mal di stomaco*," I said.

Immediately, their attitude changed completely. They roared with laughter.

"Ho-Ho!" they went, slapping their great thighs. Like certain coprophilous German soldiers to whom the mere mention of excreta and, or bottoms, was sufficient to lay them on their backs helpless with mirth, they thought this very funny; but they let me go.

When I emerged they told me, laying their hands on the places where those organs should have been, that it broke their hearts, but that the *feldgendarmerie*, who were more or less the equivalent of our own, to me, odious military police, had given orders that they were to guard me closely until arrangements could be made to send me to Germany; and that if I tried to escape they would, reluctantly and with tears in their eyes, be forced to shoot me, or themselves risk being shot by the *feldgendarmerie*.

I was at some pains to try to appear sympathetic to them in their dilemma; but I had no tears to waste on these men. I was as impressed by their lamentations as a condemned criminal by the executioner, who not only wants to carry out the execution but at the same time wants to be loved by his victim. Nothing would have pleased me more at this moment than to be certain that they would both be shot.

With my lunch, which was brought to me on a tray by one of the more forbidding-looking *suore*, who had been specially selected for this dangerous mission by the *superiora* in order to discourage the *carabinieri* from rooting amongst its contents, came a message, hidden under an almost redhot dish. It was unsigned but I recognised the style. "Get out!" it read, in English. "Tonight, 22.00, if not Germany tomorrow, 06.00. Go east 500 *metri* across fields until you reach a very little street, then torn right and go on 500 *metri* until you reach a bigger street. Wait there! Don't worry about clothes and shoes."

These were less ambiguous orders than most of those which I had been accustomed to receive during the last few years and, what was best, they left the method of executing the escape to the discretion of the person who was going to carry them out. They had, in fact, been drafted by Wanda's father who had not been an officer in the Austrian Army for nothing, and she had rendered them into English.

They were not difficult to carry out. At 21.57, after having eaten a formidable last dinner at 19.30, I opened the door of my room for the tenth time that afternoon and uttered the magic words. *Ho mal di stomaco* to the solitary *carabiniere* on duty. They no longer stirred him to mirth, or his companion either, when he was on duty. After a few hours spent in a dark corridor sitting on a pair of chairs of a hardness which only the Roman Catholic church could devise, outside a labour ward from which awful sounds came from time to time, they had decided to each do stints of two hours on guard, while the one off duty sat below in the entrance hall. Whichever one of them was on duty now ignored me completely.

As soon as I had hopped into the *gabinetto* I locked the door, and after a short interval began to make various groaning and grunting noises which I hoped were appropriate, having practised them already that afternoon on nine previous visits, at the same time hoisting myself with some difficulty through the high, narrow window which I had already opened, and slid with surprising ease, down a convenient drainpipe, bootless and in my pyjamas, like someone leaving a burning house in an early Keystone film, to land with a great clonk on my plastered foot on the path below.

There was no need to worry about making a noise. The croaking of innumerable frogs, and the chirping of crickets were deafening; but I was no less apprehensive for that. Wishing that I had with me the crutches I had used in the *ospedale*, I rushed across the path and crashed through a hedge into a large field of stubble, over which an enormous moon was just rising. It was horribly bright and, as I began to cross it, I heard violent banging noises from the interior of the *ospedale*, which must have been the *carabiniere* hammering on the door of the *gabinetto*. I set off across the stubble at a terrific rate, which was extraordinarily painful with one bare foot, like walking on nails, so fast that I failed to see a large, concealed ditch, an upstream continuation of one which Mora had catapulted me over eleven days before, and into which I plunged up to my waist in black slime. The 500 metres to the very little street where I was to 'torn' to the right seemed longer than I had imagined they would, but eventually I reached a rutted track which led away to the north, and there was no doubt that this was it.

I followed it for a quarter of a mile or so, past a farmhouse with a yard full of savage, barking dogs, until I reached a place where three roads met. There, at the junction, I found a motor car with two men hovering impatiently about it. One of them was the doctor, the other was someone whom I had never met before, a man with grey hair *en brosse*, whom the doctor addressed as *Maestro*. It was Wanda's father.

"You are late," he said in Italian with more than a hint of severity, just as I imagined he did to the boys and girls in his class. He had the same high forehead and the same stubborn expression which I had seen on her face when she had been trying to make me work harder at my Italian, except that he looked as if he wore it permanently. I would have liked to have asked him how his daughter was but this was not the right moment, exposed in the moonlight at a treeless crossroads, with a hue and cry beginning less than half a mile away.

"I'm sorry," I said. It sounded feeble and for a moment I thought of adding some flippant, mock-heroic remark about having had to go to the lavatory on the way, but I was not yet sufficiently good at the language, and if I had I would probably have found myself being bent over the bonnet of the Fiat and being given "six of the best" with a Slovene cane for impertinence.

"Well, get in!" said the doctor. "Don't stand there!" He sounded just like a doctor who has been called out in the middle of the night to minister to some trivial complaint which, in effect, he had. Neither of them commented on my extraordinary appearance, wearing nothing but pyjamas and covered in filth.

As I got into the back of the car I noticed for the first time that the door panel had a Red Cross painted on it. This at least partly explained how the Doctor was able to drive about the countryside during the curfew without being riddled with bullets. But now, if we were stopped and I was found travelling with these rather severe-looking middle-aged men who addressed one another formally as *maestro* and *dottore*, who, as Wanda had told me, first became friends because of their longstanding mutual distaste for Fascism, there was little doubt that they would be shot.

We set off at a terrific rate on a road which had all the qualities necessary to produce a fatal accident; narrow, winding and raised above the surrounding country on an embankment with deep ditches on either side. It was an eerie night, remarkably like that of the ninth of September. The moon, which was like a huge rusty coin, had barely risen above the level of the vines and long, tattered streamers of mist floated above the fields. Apart from ourselves there was not a living soul to be seen. It was as if, suddenly, we had become the only inhabitants of the *pianura*. The black-out and the curfew had done their work too well. We were extremely conspicuous, simply by being in it.

We crossed a little bridge over a stream which flowed between high, grass-grown embankments with a farm standing alone like a guardhouse beside it, and roared through a hamlet which the *maestro* said was called Cannetolo and then followed a winding road which eventually crossed the torrent on the banks of which, according to the doctor, further downstream, we had taken refuge. We must have been heading almost due south now because sometimes I could see the Apennines ahead of us, black against the night sky and far off. I wondered where we were going, but I contented myself with asking the *maestro* the names of some of the places through which we passed, names which I immediately forgot.

At a sharp bend in the road we crossed an irrigation canal by a bridge, and after a bit we came to a junction with a signpost pointing right to a place called Soragna, and left to Fidenza, a town on the *Via Emilia*, which itself must have been quite close because the noise of the traffic on it was very loud now, and I could distinguish the peculiar whining sound that the treads of the cross-country tyres of army vehicles make on a hard surface. Here we turned northwards, away from the main road.

We must have covered five miles, still without seeing anybody, when we reached a village which seemed to be about the same size as Fontanellato, with a large castle and a church with a campanile looming up in the middle of it.

"Soragna," said the *maestro*, informatively. "*Il castello del Principe*," and then, suddenly and urgently, "*carabinieri!* Get down!"

There were two figures in the road in front of us and one of them was waving us to a halt with a torch. One side of the bottom of the little car was occupied by the doctor's bag and as I tried to squeeze myself down head first behind the seat my huge feet, one a soggy mass of plaster of paris, the other bare, rose in the air to occupy the position in which my head had been previously, until the *maestro* got hold of both of them and forced them down, at the same time putting a blanket over me. He managed to finish performing these operations just as the car came to a stop.

Upside down in the back, I could hear the doctor opening the side window and I could see the glare of the *carabinieri*'s torch through the blanket when he shone it into the car. Then I heard a voice say,

"*Ah! È lei, dottore! Da dove viene?*" The tone was friendly enough but just verging on being suspicious. The man was obviously curious.

"*Da Fidenza. Ho avuto un caso di emergenza, uno scolaro del Maestro Skof con la polmonite.*"

"*È adesso?*"

"*Vado a casa.*"

"*Avanti! Avanti!*" said the voice, "*buona notte!*"

Beyond the village we left the main road, such as it was, and entered a labyrinth of small lanes in which I was once more allowed to come to the surface. The country was much lonelier now; the air was colder and there was low-lying fog which was dense in places.

We drove for some time along a road on top of a dyke, the biggest I had yet seen, high above the tops of the trees which grew in the low ground on either side. Then we turned off it down a sort of ramp and followed a long, straight, ride through plantations of poplars for about three miles until, finally, in the middle of one of them at a place where a million frogs all seemed to be croaking at once, we stopped. Here the doctor handed me my pack which had somehow been rescued from the *orfanotrofio*, together with my boots, without which I would be done for. Luckily neither my pack nor my boots had been in my room; the *superiora* had thought them too dirty. The only things they hadn't been able to salvage were the clothes in which I had arrived at the *ospedale*, which had been in a cupboard in my room.

Now Wanda's father gave me a complete change of clothes which included a black jacket and striped trousers of the sort that bank managers wore, which were obviously his best, and told me to put them on. I felt a pig taking them from him but there was no time to argue, and I had no choice anyway, and he and the doctor both waited impatiently while I stripped off my pyjamas, which they stowed away under one of the seats of the car. He also gave me a knife; but, as he said, it was intended for cutting food and not a weapon of offence. And the doctor gave me a small bottle.

"You may need this," he said grimly. "There are many mosquitoes. Put it on your face and hands." He spoke very slowly and simply so that I could take in what he said. "At noon tomorrow a man will come here. He will whistle three times, as if he was whistling to his dog, like this." At this point he gave a rather muted imitation of what it would sound like.

"Has he got a dog?" I asked.

"No," he glared at me in the moonlight, angry at such an irrelevance. "This man is about forty-five," he went on, "and he has a big moustache. You can call him Giovanni. If it is safe he may take you to his house. I will fetch you tomorrow night. There is enough food and water in your pack to last you until he comes, but don't use it all because he may not come, and neither may I. Don't drink the water in the ditches. If anything happens to either of us," he indicated the *maestro* who stood like a sawn-off monolith in the moonlight, "you will hear from his daughter. If anything happens to her someone else will come. We are going to try to get you into the castle at Soragna, or else to Switzerland. You have had a long journey tonight—I'm sorry we had to go all that way round, but you are still not more than twenty kilometres from the hospital."

I have a good sense of direction and this did not surprise me. Then they shook hands with me. It was not my idea to shake hands, but I was pleased when they offered them. To tell the truth, I was becoming fed up with their more than Anglo-Saxon phlegm. Then they got into the car and the doctor drove up the track until he found a place wide enough to turn the car. I didn't want to go to Switzerland, but this did not seem the right time to say so.

As he passed me on the way back, the car lurching in the pot-holes, I remembered to ask him where I was, which was something that would be important to me if they failed to return and if Giovanni, the man with the moustache and no dog, also failed to appear.

"You are about six hundred metres from the Po," he said, "and about twenty-five kilometres upstream from the bridges at Casalmaggiore. The nearest village is in that direction." He pointed into the wood. "Don't go to it." "One thing," he said, just as he was moving off, "whatever you do, if we don't come back, don't try to cross the Po. Make for the mountains."

When they were gone I went down into the wood. The moon was shining between the boles of the trees, even more rusty-looking and decrepit than it had been, but powerful enough to lay bare the lack of amenity. Apart from being very lonely, which was why I was in the wood, it was very cold; very wet, because it was irrigated by a network of shallow ditches, and incredibly noisy—by comparison the croaking of the frogs outside the *ospedale* had been a mere gurgling, but even the racket these frogs made was not loud enought to drown the noise of the gigantic mosquitoes which, mad for human blood, dived on me with a high-pitched screaming sound, remarkably like that made by the Stukas when they used to come howling down out of the late afternoon sun to bomb the harbour at Tobruk. There the navy, primed with Plymouth gin, used to blaze away with Lewis guns from which the cooling jackets had been removed in order to make them more handy for a quick right and left. Here, my only defence against these monsters, was a bottle of oil of citronella; but I was past caring. The alarms and excursions of the evening had worn me down. One place was as good as another to me at this moment, so I laid out the blanket which the *maestro* had given me, got into my sleeping-bag, which after my boots was my most treasured possession, rubbed my arms, hands and face with oil of citronella, put my head in my pack to shield it from the mosquitoes, and fell asleep.

Chapter Seven

Down by the riverside

When I woke and pulled the pack off my head it was already light, but there was a dense fog and it was very quiet. It was like being wrapped in cotton wool. The frogs had stopped croaking and the mosquitoes had gone. The air was cold but I was glad that it was. After having slept with my head in the pack I had a splitting headache and a horrible mouth; otherwise, apart from one or two giant mosquito bites on my neck, I was unscathed.

I stayed in my sleeping-bag until the fog began to turn yellow in the light of the rising sun. Then I got up, cleaned my teeth, rolled up the sleeping-bag, which was very wet, put on my left boot and set off through the wood, parallel to the track, in what I imagined must be the direction of the river. My other foot was a soggy amalgam of mud and plaster, but I no longer cared. It didn't hurt anymore. The rough treatment which it had received ever since I had injured it seemed to have done it good.

After about twenty minutes I emerged on the edge of a dried-out backwater of the river. The banks were loose shingle and the bottom was filled with big, round stones which I found difficult to cross. The far bank was covered with a dense growth of what looked to me like dwarf acacia trees, in which I lost myself in a maze of sheep runs which led nowhere. It was a creepy place full of dung, but after blundering about in it for a bit I suddenly came out on the right bank of the river.

It was a marvellous, unforgettable sight, especially for someone like myself who had seen nothing for a year except walls, barbed wire and, at the best, a rather humdrum domestic country. I was on an inside curve of a big bend of the river. Here it was about 250 yards wide. Although it was low, it was running strongly. The water was the colour of milky coffee, and in places it erupted and formed whirlpools which whirled for a time before they collapsed, and on its surface there were gouts of foam, like clotted cream which the current seized on and swept away. The fog was going now, rolling away upstream to the west in a series of giant billows, all golden in the sun. Downstream was the dried-out channel I had just crossed, with a deep pool in a sort of bay at the mouth of it, from which a long spur of stone embankment curved away. It was unfinished, and on top of it there were piles of fascines that looked like sausage rolls filled with stones, and the remains of the workmen's fires, although no work seemed to have been done on the embankment for some time. Behind it there was a plantation of willows in which the saplings had been cut down to make the fascines. On both banks there were diamond-shaped navigational marks painted red and white, and in midstream there were buoys at which the current was pulling so hard that some of them were almost under water.

As the fog dispersed the river was revealed with dark woods of poplar looming up on either side of it, between which it flowed as if through a series of canyons. The landscape was scarcely European, the river was too powerful-looking to be Italian, although it might conceivably have been Russian. It was a river of the New World painted by a romantic artist of the nineteenth-century. Swifts dipped over the water, a great heron beat its way slowly up a backwater between a wooded island and the shore, snowy white little egrets stood motionless in the shallows, and on the far bank a flock of sheep were grazing at the foot of a big, grass-covered dyke, similar to the one from which we had come down into the wood the night before, but which here formed a salient at the water's edge from which it ran away inland on either side; and from behind it, from the invisible chimneys of an invisible village, thin columns of bluish smoke rose into the windless air. Upstream, on the right bank of the river there was a huge fishing net in a circular frame, like an upturned umbrella and behind it, half-hidden among the trees, there was a flimsy hut on stilts.

Soon the sun was hot and I decided to swim. It was a crazy thing to do, but there was no one about. I crossed over to the pool at the mouth of the backwater, took off my clothes and plunged in. It was icy. Perhaps it seemed colder than it was because I was rather thin. Then I dressed, ate some food from my pack and hobbled back to the wood.

The plaster of paris was like a great lump of chewed nougat, and I cut it off, using the knife that the *maestro* had given me. Then I lay down under the trees to wait for Giovanni.

It was deliciously cool there. The sun beat down on the tops of the poplars, but they were so close together that it only succeeded here and there in sending down long shafts of dappled light into the green, damp shadow of the wood. Their slender trunks soared upwards like columns and the intervals between them were dim, green aisles. It was like being in a cathedral that had been engulfed by the sea. Then I fell asleep.

I was awakened by someone tugging at my arm. Standing over me there was a man with a big brown moustache, and with a thick head of hair which was just beginning to go grey above the ears.

"You sleep too strongly," he said. "I have been whistling for ten minutes and I am tired of it. I am called Giovanni. I have brought you a picnic," he said. He called it *una merenda*. "We shall eat it by the river. Then later we shall go to my house."

He was dressed in an old suit of snuff-coloured velveteen and over his shoulder he had a sack which presumably contained the *merenda*. He was a powerful-looking man, above five feet eight but with a chest like a barrel and a long scar down one side of his nose. He walked with a limp. We went back towards the river, more or less by the route which I had followed before. My ankle now hurt abominably, but at least it stood up to being used just as well without the plaster.

Eventually we reached the bank of the dry backwater that I had already crossed, but farther upstream. Here, beyond the shadow of the trees, the light was incandescent; the stones so hot that I felt they might explode. On the far side there was a path through the dwarf trees, and after following it for a bit we came out in a small clearing behind the hut I had seen earlier which stood high above the embankment on a little forest of piles.

"My house in the country," Giovanni said. He went up a ladder to it and unlocked the door. Inside there was a room about eight feet square with a bunk on one side, some cooking pots, a fishing rod, a pair of decayed rubber waders, and that was about all.

"*C'è ura d'mangar*." "Time to eat," he said. He spoke the dialect which here, on the river bank, sounded even deeper and more mysterious than it had at the farm on the first night that I was free. I told him I couldn't understand it and he said that, in future, he would speak Italian, and very slowly.

We sat outside in the shade and ate a delicious meal, the best of its kind that I could remember. Everything was home-made.

"*È nostrano*," he said, whenever he offered me anything. No wonder he had brought a sack. We ate a delicious, thick soup full of vegetables and *pasta* that was made in the shape of sea shells which he ladled from a pot; and we ate *polenta*, a sort of solidified yellow porridge made from maize, which he sliced with a piece of wire; wonderful hard white bread, made from something called *pasta dura* and with it slices of *culatello*, a kind of

77

unsmoked ham from part of the pig's behind that was cut so thinly that it was almost transparent which, he said, was a local speciality; and there was another sort called *spalla*, made from the shoulder which he said was the sort that Verdi preferred; but I thought the *culatello* was the best.

"It's good, the *culatello*," he said, relapsing into the dialect and offering me more.

We drank *lambrusco* from a black bottle which held two litres. The cork was similar to a champagne cork but without the metal cap with the maker's name on it, and it was prevented from blowing out of the mouth of the bottle by strong thread which was lashed down over the top of it and round the lip. The Italian word for cork was *turacciolo* but he called it *bouchon* in the dialect which seemed to have a lot of French words in it. The wine was deep purple and it seethed in the glasses with its own natural gas. The same wine the farmer had given me on that first night. And then we ate cheese that had been maturing for two years in one of his barns.

Afterwards we lay on our stomachs on the grass on the slope of the embankment, looking out over the top of it across the river, and he told me about his life. It took a long time; because he found Italian difficult.

Before the war he had been one of the men employed on the river in rowing boats to shift the leading marks and buoys for the barges which went up to Mantova, which had to be done constantly because the bed of the stream was always changing. It was a hard way of earning a living which he had combined with that of being a fisherman. His wife had died in childbirth in 1937. Until six months ago he had been in the navy with some special force rather like the one I had been captured with, training on a lonely part of the west coast, when somebody had dropped a snatch block on his foot and he had been invalided out. Now he lived with his mother and with his father who had been both fisherman and farmer, in a house near the dyke. He was anti-German, anti-Mussolini, anti-King and anti-Badoglio who, he considered, had betrayed Italy and then left it in the soup.

"From now on I'm Communist," he said. I would have liked to have talked to him more about this, but that was all he would say and I was really content to leave it at that. The war seemed far away. It might never have happened. Looking out on this dream-like landscape it was difficult to believe that a few miles away *feldgendarmen* and *carabinieri* were after one's blood. And they might be even closer.

Occasionally, far off, I could hear a train rumbling across some bridge, whistling mournfully. Otherwise, there were no sounds, not even the barking of a dog to disturb the silence of that long, golden afternoon, during which I sometimes dozed and sometimes listened to Giovanni as he droned on, with lots of careful explanation, about his beloved river, while the river itself slid past like molten metal. About how powerful it was, how many mouths it had on the Adriatic, some dying, others already dead, as every year the silt extended further and further, sixty metres and more a year, out to sea—a lighthouse which had been built a hundred and fifty metres from the sea in 1882, twenty years later was more than three kilometres inland. This was one of the reasons for the great floods with which the valley was afflicted.

Even when it was in normal flood in October or November the wood in which I had slept would be deep under water, and from the main dyke beyond it to the one on the other bank where it ran away from the salient where the village was, at least three kilometres would be like an inland sea.

"That's the time when I take down my little hut," he said, "otherwise it would end up in the Adriatic."

In winter it was bitterly cold here and there were terrible fogs—there was fog about seventy days a year—which obliterated everything. Down near the mouth of the river, in the delta were the *valli*, vast enclosures of brackish water, separated by dykes. In winter these shallows were invaded by clouds of migrant duck and wild geese and men like Giovanni, who was mad for shooting, waited, shivering, for the flights at dawn and dusk, or else stalked them, using punts. The *valli* were also the hunting grounds of men called *fiocinini*, fish poachers, who took eels by night from under the noses of the keepers of the *valli*. On dark, stormy nights in November millions of eels were on the move in the river valley, all travelling eastwards on the first stage of their journey to the Sargasso Sea where, in the depths of the Atlantic, they would beget their young; a journey from which only the new-born eels returned.

"No one knows what happens to those that make the journey," Giovanni said, "but some don't go at all and they become as fat as eunuchs."

Of those that did make the journey, thousands and thousands were caught in the great eel traps at Comacchio in the *valli*. Once thirty-four tons of eels were taken there in a single night, and to celebrate the catch a mortar was fired and wine distributed. And he spoke about the other fish that inhabited the river; carp, pike, fish called *cavadane* and *pescegatto* and the big sturgeon that sometimes came up it. Finally, aroused by so much talk of fish, he showed me how the big net worked which I had seen from further downstream that morning, which was what he called a *bilancione* because it was operated by counterbalance weights. He let fly some tackle and the net lowered itself into the water like a giant, prehistoric bird fishing and then, when he hauled on a rope, it rose again.

By this time the sun was setting. The air was becoming chilly and there was a mistiness in the woods far off up and down stream.

"*Anduma a cà*," said Giovanni. "Let's go home." He threw the remains of the picnic, which was not much, into the river, put the pot which had contained the soup back into his sack, locked up his hut and set off through the trees. It was one of the best days I could ever remember, and I hated the thought that it was almost at an end.

But at the house, when we got to it, there was disastrous news, brought by Wanda whose bicycle I recognised propped against the wall outside, and who had cycled twenty kilometres to do so.

Early that morning before it was light and while everyone was still in bed, a mixed force of Germans and Fascists had descended on the neighbourhood of Fontanellato and surrounded the house of a farmer called Baruffini in which they found several prisoners. Then they beat the surrounding fields in which a number of others were sleeping under the vines. Altogether their total bag was thirteen. But worst of all one of the prisoners had been mad enough to keep a day-to-day journal of all his doings in clear, which gave the names of a number of people who had helped him and which he had not even had the presence of mind to hide or destroy when he was taken. As a result of this, further arrests had been made and more were thought to be imminent.*

The other news was not good but it was less tragic. At the same time as all this was going on, the Germans had requisitioned the *castello*, in which Wanda had succeeded in arranging that I should be taken on as the gardener's boy, in order to turn it into a military headquarters, it was said, for Field-Marshal Kesselring who seemed to dog my footsteps. I was lucky to have got out of the *ospedale* when I did. Once the castle became a headquarters for someone as important as Kesselring, all the roads for miles around would have blocks on them.

"Pity you didn't go there before," Wanda said. "No one would think the gardener's boy in a German headquarters could be English." It would certainly have been a joke if I had already been installed in the *castello* and had been taken over by the Germans, with the rest of the staff, to help look after the Field-Marshal.

The last piece of information she brought concerned the *carabinieri* at the hospital. They had been saved from severe punishment by an extra-ordinary circumstance. On the night that I escaped from it another

*Some of these unfortunate people were taken to Germany, including Signor Baruffini, who died in Buchenwald, and other members of his family.

British prisoner had been brought to it suffering from some serious complaint and they had simply substituted him for me.

There was now no question of my remaining in this house or any other for a moment, let alone in a *castello*, and as soon as it grew sufficiently dark Giovanni and his father, who was an older fascimile of himself, set off with a hand-cart loaded with planks and other materials to construct an underground hiding place for me until arrangements could be made to get me out of the area altogether, leaving me alone with Wanda in the middle of a big plantation of maize which grew at some distance from the house.

"I know you never wanted to, but you won't be able to go to Switzerland now, perhaps you never will," she said. She spoke in Italian. "And none of us may be able to help you anymore. We may not be here to do so. No one, except the people who have got it now, know how many names that stupid wrote down in his little book. The doctor could be in it and so could my father."

And so could she. My blood ran cold at the thought of it.

"Look," I said in English. This was no time for language lessons. "You must give up trying to help me, all of you. If I'm caught all that will happen is that I'll be sent to Germany and be put in another camp; but if any of you are caught helping me you're quite likely to be shot. It just isn't worth it. I'm protected by the Geneva Convention. They won't shoot me. And my ankle's fine now. I can look after myself."

"I don't know anything about your Geneva Convention," she said, "but I know more about Fascists than you do and if they take you and send you to Germany, you may be there for years and years the way things are going and you may never come back. What we're going to try and do is get you to the mountains tomorrow, and when things have quietened down a bit I'll try and take you down closer to the line myself."

I tried to argue with her and for the first time since I had known her she became very angry.

"You're a stupid young man," she said, "almost as stupid as the one who kept a little book with all his stupid thoughts in it and all those names, and if we'd known he was doing that he would have been killed I can tell you. It's a pity we didn't know. Do you really think the doctor and my father are helping you just because they like the colour of your eyes? It's because this is the only way at the moment in which they can do anything against the Fascists. They really hate them, those two old men. Much more than I do."

"And what about you?" I said. "Is that the only reason why you've done what you have?"

She took my hands in the darkness and held them. "Oh, Hurruck," she said, "when I said that you were stupid I didn't really meant it. Stupid in Italian, *stupido*, is a very rude word which gives great offence, as I told you when you were in the *ospedale* and a word that you just never use to an Italian; but it is an expression that I have learned from you who always tell me that to call someone stupid, 'don't be so stupid', is what you always say to one another in England, is just another expression like '*luk slipi*'; but now you really are being Italian stupid to say such a thing to me." By now she was crying with vexation.

"I'm sorry," I said. "It was a silly thing to say." She let go of my hands.

"Sorry! That's all you English ever are. Sorry to have troubled you! Even," she said, "if they go through a door in front of you that's all they say. Sorry! Why do they go through it first if they know they're going to be sorry afterwards? It's a word like stupid. It doesn't mean anything. When you and your friends say 'sorry' I feel like hitting you!" And she began to cry even harder.

There was nothing I could say and if I did say anything it would be all wrong. I put my arms round her and held her close to me among the tall maize for a long time until Giovanni and his father came back to take me to my hiding place.

"I must go now," she said, "because of the curfew; but wherever you go, whatever happens, I'll see you again. Never forget it."

The hole they had dug for me was in a small plantation of poplars far enough from their farm for them to be able to deny any knowledge of it if it was discovered. In fact, the land in which they had dug it was the property of an enthusiastic Fascist, as both Giovanni and his father told me with relish.

The hole was the size and shape of a grave, although slightly shallower, and I wondered how they had managed to dig it in such a short time. It was too dark to see much of their handiwork, but Giovanni told me that they had taken all the soil from the excavation away in their cart and put it elsewhere and that before digging the hole they had carefully dug under the grass and rolled it back like a carpet so that they could use it to cover the planks when I was inside.

"You had better ease yourself before you get in," the father said. "You will not be able to come out until we fetch you and we don't know when that will be."

I did not much fancy being entombed in this fashion but this was not the moment to say so and after I had "eased myself", as he put it, I lowered myself into the trench, the bottom of which they had lined with sacks and they handed me down my sack, a blanket, a bottle of wine and one of water, some bread and cheese, a watch and some matches so that I could tell the time, and a large tin can for future easements.

Just as they finished doing this it began to rain. Then they covered the hole with the planks, which were stout enough not to give under the weight of anyone who stood on them, and I could hear some earth which they had kept back for the purpose thudding down on top of them and then the sound of the turf being replaced. It was like being buried alive. I sat up while they were doing this. Lying down I would have felt too much like a corpse. I wondered if I could get the lid off unaided if I had to.

"The airhole's here," I heard Giovanni say just above my head when they had finished. "You won't lack for air. We'll be back tomorrow, but if anything happens so that we can't come, don't leave until tomorrow night when it's dark. You should be able to lift one of the boards off if you have to. Then make for the foothills. They begin about twenty-five kilometres to the south across the Via Emilia. There are two poplar trees standing in the middle of the field you came across from the house; get them in line and that's south. You have the map the signorina gave you!" (Wanda had given me the only map of the area she had been able to lay her hands on, one that she had torn out of a bus timetable. It was little more than a diagram, but it was better than nothing.)

"Keep well to the east of Fidenza," he went on. "Only travel at night, and across country. You should be able to make the hills before dawn. Try and cross the Ceno near Serravalle. By the third night you should be well into the mountains and then you can try travelling by day. Good luck!"

Then they both went away and I could hear the rain on the roof of my shelter but infinitely remote, as a worm might, and I felt water trickling down the airhole and down my neck, but then it stopped and it was as silent as the tomb and as dark. .

Nevertheless I slept well for most of the night but the next morning was intolerably long and I began to be very uncomfortable. The hole was deep enough for me to lie in or sit up in, but it was very narrow and the only way I could move my arms was to raise them above my head so I must have looked like Lazarus, and easements were very difficult; but finally, at about one o'clock in the afternoon, I heard voices overhead and the sound of spades being used, and then the planks were taken off and I received a shower of earth on my head, and although I was dazzled by the light, I could just make out Giovanni and his father looking down at me.

"Time to go," Giovanni said. I handed up my belongings to him, everything with the exception of the sacks and the bottles and the tin which he told me to leave where they were, and then he knelt down and gave me a hand and hauled me out because I was too stiff to get out by myself. It was a pale, colourless day, with a horrible glare in the sky, stronger to me because I had been underground.

"You had a good long rest," he said. "The doctor's waiting over there just beyond the trees. We'll fill this in and clear up—I'd like to leave it open so that that bastard would have to explain it to his friends, but it's too risky. Now get going!"

There was no time to thank them properly. I just remembered to give Giovanni back his pocket watch. They had the cartload of earth and they were already shovelling it back into the hole and I never saw them again.*

I stumbled away to where the Fiat was standing beyond the trees on a rough track.

"Get in!" the doctor said as soon as I reached it, which were about the only words he ever seemed to address to me. "We can talk later!"

"I don't think you ought to be . . ." I began to say, but he cut me short.

"IN THE NAME OF GOD, GET IN!" he said. "This place is swarming with Germans. It's like Potsdam." I got in. There was nothing else to do.

I was not the only passenger. In the back seat of the little car there was a very small, toothless old man, wrapped in a moth-eaten cloak, a garment which is called a *tabar* in this part of the world, and with an equally moth-eaten hat to match. Both had once been black, now they were green with age. What he was, guide, someone whom the doctor had recruited to lend verisimilitude to the outing, or simply an old man of the mountains on the way back to them from a black-market expedition I was unable to discover because, during the entire journey, he never uttered a word. He simply sat there in the back with a heavily laden rucksack on his knees, either completely ignoring the doctor when he addressed some remark to him in his dialect, or else uttering what was either a mindless chuckle or something provoked by the workings of a powerful and possibly diabolical intelligence. Whatever he was, the old man was certainly less conspicuous than I was, bolt-upright in the front seat in which I had been put in case, as the doctor said, I had to get out and run for it, absurdly English-looking in spite of my civilian clothes.

Eventually we arrived at the junction of the minor road, on which we had been travelling, with the Via Emilia. Blocking the entrance to it there was a German soldier, probably a military policeman, on a motor cycle. He had his back to us and was watching the main road on which a convoy was moving south towards the front. Knowing what sort of man the

---

*Giovanni was killed with a partisan group in the Apennines some time in the early spring of 1945. Both his parents died the previous year.

doctor was, I was afraid that he might hoot imperiously at him to get out of the way but fortunately he simply switched off the engine and waited for the man to go, which presently he did when a gap occurred in the interminable procession of vehicles, roaring away on his machine in pursuit of them, and we followed him.

Soon we overtook the front part of the convoy and the doctor drove boldly past it on the wrong side of the road, the only part of it available to him, the Via Emilia being narrow and some of the armoured vehicles, the tanks particularly, being enormous. It was a good thing that there were no vehicles coming in the other direction. They must have been halted because of the convoy, because all the time we were on the road we did not meet anything coming in the other direction.

"Sixteenth Panzer Division," the doctor said. "Reinforcements." How he could know this I could not imagine. There were no insignia on the vehicles to proclaim that they were part of Sixteenth Panzer Division, but he said it with such authority that I wouldn't have dreamed of questioning what he said. He was not a man given to making idle remarks.

I was paralysed by the thought of what would happen if he was stopped, if only for having the impertinence to pass part of a German Panzer Division on the move when all other civilian vehicles had been halted in order to allow it to monopolise the road; and I was temporarily hypnotised by the sheer proximity of the enemy in such strength and numbers. I had only to stretch out my right hand through the open window as we went sedately past them to touch their tanks, which were of a sort and size that I had not even seen in diagrams; their self-propelled guns which I recognised; their half-tracked vehicles with anti-aircraft guns at the ready which looked a little like great chariots; and the lorries full of tough-looking Panzer Grenadiers, all ready to peel out of them if the convoy was attacked from the air, who looked down at our tiny vehicle with the red crosses painted on the sides and on the roof, which were making this journey possible, with a complete lack of curiosity, just as our own soldiers would have done in similar circumstances, which I found extremely comforting. Less disinterested were a lot of grumpy-looking officers up in front in a large, open Mercedes, one of them wearing the red tabs of a general on the lapels of his leather coat, who all glared at us as they probably would have done if we had passed them in a Fiat 500, a Mercedes-load of important businessmen, on the autobahn between Ulm and Stuttgart in the years before the war, and, just as I would have then, I had an insane temptation to thumb my nose at them.

Soon, mercifully, we outdistanced the convoy, passed a castle among trees, crossed a wide river with more shingle than water in it by a long bridge, the approaches to which were flanked by allegorical statuary, and after crossing another, shorter bridge, entered the city of Parma, in the centre of which, or what looked like the centre to me, the doctor's motor car broke down under the eyes of Garibaldi, a large statue of whom stood in the *piazza*.

Fortunately it was half past one in the afternoon, according to a large, elaborate clock on the face of a building in the square and the city was in the grip of the siesta. Apart from a couple of German *feldgendarmen* with metal plaques on their chests who were obviously there to direct the convoy on its way when it arrived, and whose presence in the *piazza* was probably enough to cause its depopulation, the place was deserted.

Quite soon the reinforcements for Sixteenth Panzer Division, or whatever they were, began to rumble through it and once again I felt myself the cynosure; while the doctor fiddled with the engine which was fuelled with methane gas, I pretended to help him with my head buried in the engine—as far as anyone can bury his head in the engine of a Fiat 500—and the old man sat in the back cackling with laughter as if he was enjoying some private and incommunicable joke. "Heh! Heh! Heh!"

Eventually the engine started and the rest of the journey to the mountains was without incident.

Chapter Eight

Haven in a storm

"The Baruffas will look after you," the doctor said, "until we can find a place deeper in the mountains. This is a safe house, although it's on the road, but stay away from the windows and don't go outside. I'll be back in a few days," he said, "and if you want me to I'll bring Wanda." And he smiled one of his rare smiles.

"I do want you to," I said.

We shook hands. I heard him reverse the Fiat out of the farmyard on to the road and drive off. Two days later the Fascists came for him while he was asleep in his bed.

Apart from the slow ticking of a long case-clock, it was very quiet in the kitchen now and sad after all the joking and drinking. The fire which had been stirred up when we arrived had died down.

"You must go," Signor Baruffa said as soon as the doctor's car was out of earshot. He was not smiling anymore. His wife was not smiling either. She began washing the glasses from which we had been drinking strong, dark wine.

I couldn't believe him.

"Why? You said . . ."

"I'm afraid. *Ho paura.*" Literally what he said was, "I have fear." In the three weeks since Italy had collapsed it was an expression I had already heard many times.

"Of what are you afraid?"

In the *pianura*, which was alive with enemies of all sorts, everyone had *paura* and with good reason. Here, in the heart of the Apennines on the road to nowhere, it seemed absurd.

"I am afraid of the Germans. I am afraid of the Fascists. I am afraid of spies. I am afraid of my neighbours, and I am afraid of having my house burned over my head and of being shot if you are found here. My wife is also afraid. Now go!"

"But where shall I go?"

"I cannot tell you where to go. Only go!"

"You *must* tell me!"

"Then go to Zanoni!" It sounded like an imprecation. "Zanoni is poor. He has nothing to lose. His house is not like this, by the road. It is up the valley, above the mill. It will only take you an hour. Now go, and do not tell Zanoni that I sent you!"

I went. There was nothing else to do. Neither of them came to the door. As I crossed the threshold there was a long rumble of thunder immediately overhead, a blinding flash of lightning, an apocalyptic wind bent the trees in the yard, and it began to rain heavily. In all my life I had never felt so utterly abandoned and alone.

There was no difficulty in finding the way. The valley was narrow and a stream ran down through it and under a bridge on the road where the Baruffas' farm was, and from the house a path climbed high along the right side of the valley past abandoned terrace fields with mounds of pale stones standing in them, paler still under the lightning, which the people who had cultivated the land had weeded from the earth by hand.

Soon, both the stream and the far side of the valley were invisible, blotted out by the rain which was clouting down, while the thunder boomed and rolled overhead and long barbs of lightning plunged earthwards. There was nowhere to shelter from them but mercifully after a while they ceased and were replaced by sheet lightning which I hoped was less dangerous.

The path was surfaced with long cobbles and the stones were spattered with the dung of sheep and cows and what was more likely to be the dung of mules than horses in such a mountainous place. Some of it was fresh, all of it was now being washed away by the torrents of water which had turned the steeper parts of the path, which were in steps, into a series of waterfalls in which I slipped and fell on all fours, swearing monotonously. Although I did not know it then, this path was the main road to two villages higher up the mountainside, and at any other time I would have almost certainly have met other people on it. I was, in fact, lucky without appreciating my luck. This was the last occasion while I was in Italy that I ever used such a public path. From now on, whenever I travelled anywhere, unguided, it was always by more unfrequented tracks or through the woods.

After I had been climbing for about three-quarters of an hour, the path descended the side of the valley to the place where the mill was. The stream was in full spate. It came boiling down over the rocks and under a little hump-backed bridge and surged against the draw-gate which shut off the water from the leat. The mill-house was a tall, narrow building with a steep-pitched roof and it had rusty iron shutters clamped tight over the windows as if for ever, and a rusty iron door. Looking at this sinister building it was difficult to know on such an evening whether it was inhabited or not; but no smoke came from the chimney and no dog barked. The only sounds that could be heard above the thunder, the howling of the wind and the roar of the water, was the furious rattling of a loose paddle on the mill-wheel and the clanking and groaning of the wheel itself as it moved a little, backwards and forwards on its bearings.

By now, although it was only five o'clock it was almost dark. To the right of the bridge a steep track led away uphill towards a clump of trees beyond which I could just make out some low buildings. This I thought must be *casa* Zanoni and I squelched up the track towards it.

The house itself was more like an Irish dun than a house, a stone fort built against a rock on the hillside. It was so small that the cowshed, which had a hay loft over it, seemed bigger than the house itself and the cowshed was not large. Every few seconds the house and its outbuildings were illuminated by the lightning so that they looked as if they were coated with silver.

They were roofed with stone slabs and down towards the eaves these great tiles had rocks on top of them, rocks to stop the wind ripping them off. Smoke and sparks were streaming from the chimney of the house which had a cowl on it made from four little piles of stones with a flat piece laid on top of them, so that it looked like a shrine on a mountain with an offering burning in it. Apart from the smoke and sparks the house was as shut up and uninhabited-looking as the mill, but when I got closer I could hear, deep inside it, the sound of a dog barking.

The door of the cowshed was closed but through cracks and holes in it, faint pinpricks of light shone out into the yard in which the mire was boiling under the weight of the rain. I stood on the threshold and said, "*Permesso, non c'è nessuno?*"—"Excuse me, is there not no one?"—using one of the useful, colloquial, ungrammatical phrases which Wanda had taught me, the sort that everyone used in this part of Italy, and which were so important to me now, and a voice said "*Avanti!*"

I pushed open the door and went in. There was a sweet warm smell of fodder and cows and the light of a lantern was casting huge, distorted shadows of the animals, which I could not yet see, on the whitewashed wall in front of me. It was like Plato's Myth of the Cave. There was the sound of milk spurting into a pail; and now that the door had closed behind me, much more faintly, there was the noise of the storm.

Then the milking stopped and I heard a stool being pulled back over the stone floor and a small man appeared from behind one of the great, looming beasts which were to the left of the doorway. He had a small, dark moustache, wispy hair all over the place, a week's bristle on his face and although, as he told me later, he was only thirty-two, to me, ten years younger, he looked almost old enough to be my father.

He was wearing a suit of what had originally been thick brown corduroy, but it had been repaired so many times with so many different sorts of stuff, old pieces of woollen and cotton cloth in faded reds and blues and greens, and bits of ancient printed material, the kind of thing you see in museums, that it was more like a patchwork quilt with a little bit of corduroy sewn on to it here and there. But how I envied him his suit at this moment. It might be decayed but at least it was warm and dry. In the Sunday best black and white striped trousers, a cotton shirt and the thin black jacket that Wanda's father had given me, all soaked through, I felt as if I had just been fished out of an icy river.

"Signor Zanoni?" I said.

"Yes, I am Zanoni. Who are you?"

"My name is Enrico." This was the nearest anyone in the country had so far been able to get to my Christian name. My surname was beyond them. Nevertheless, I gave it and then spelt it out phonetically in Italian. "Newby—*ENNE A DOPPIO V BER IPSILON*."

"*NEVBU*," he said, "*Che nome strano!*" He raised the lantern above his head and shone the light into my face. "And what are you, Signor Nevbu, a *Tedesco*?"

He took me for a German deserter from the Wehrmacht of whom there were now said to be a considerable number who had prematurely left their units at the Armistice under the mistaken impression that the war was practically over. What an appropriate word for a German *Tedesco* was. It made me think of some great creature with an armoured shell, a sort of semi-human tank of which the carapace was a living part, the sort of machine that Hieronymous Bosch might have produced if he had been asked to design a fighting vehicle. What I was probably thinking of was a *testudo*.

I told him what I was and where I had come from.

"Now tell me who sent you here," he said, as soon as I had finished.

I told him this, too. I didn't feel that I owed the Baruffas anything; but I didn't tell him why they had sent me to him. There was no need.

"I know why," he said. "It's because old Baruffa has *paura*; but that's all very well, I have *paura*, too."

I wanted to make an end of it one way or the other.

"Signor Zanoni," I said, using one of my small store of stock phrases, "*Posso dormire nel vostro fienile?*" "Can I sleep in your hayloft?"

"Did anyone see you on the road coming here?" he said.

I told him that I had seen no one and that I was as sure as I could be that no one had seen me.

There was a long pause before he answered, which seemed an age.

"No," he said, finally, "you can't."

I knew now that I was done for. I had no food and very little money to buy any, about 100 lire which, at that time, was something like thirty shillings, and I was in no position to go shopping. The only clothes I had, apart from a pullover in the sack which I was carrying, were the ones I stood up in and everything in the sack, including my sleeping-bag was sopping wet, too. Even if I could find another house in the darkness it would be dangerous to knock on the door without knowing who the occupants were. Yet a night on the mountainside in this sort of weather would probably finish me off.

"No, you can't sleep in my hay," he said after another equally long pause. "You might set it on fire and where would I be then? But you can sleep in my house in a bed, and you will, too, but before we go in I have to finish with Bella." And he went back to milking her.

I shall never forget the moment when Signor Zanoni led me through the boiling slush in the yard and into the kitchen. It was more like a cavern than any room I had ever been in. One wall of it was part of the mountain, a great, smooth, shiny protruding rock which had been partly hollowed out to form the fireplace, itself a cave within a cave, as black as the outside of the copper pot which was suspended over the fire on a long chain, and the other three walls were made of rough blocks of undressed stone, some of them boulders, which heightened the illusion that this was an excavation rather than a room. In it the hot embers of the fire gave everything a reddish tinge and lamps hung on hooks on the walls which were nothing more than iron dishes filled with oil in which the wicks floated, the sort of lamps the Etruscans might have used while digging their tombs.

On one side of the fireplace there was a niche in the rock with a seat in it which was occupied by the oldest woman I had ever seen. Everything about her was black, except for her face which was so wrinkled—and the wrinkles were so regular and so close together—that they were like the contours of a steep-sided valley on a large-scale map. She wore black felt shoes, thick black stockings, some kind of long black garment the sleeves of which concealed her hands, and a sort of black coif or hood which hid her hair from view, if indeed she had any. And when I was taken forward to be introduced to her, which was the first thing that was done, I found that even her eyes were invisible, hidden behind a pair of thick pebble glasses in wire frames which pressed against her eyeballs, so that the water in them had turned to steam in the heat of the fire. I spoke to her and her lips moved but no sound came from them. It might have been a welcome that she was trying to utter, or it could have been a prayer.

Then I was made to take off my wet clothes behind a high-backed wooden settee and I was given a big brown blanket to wrap myself in. Signora Zanoni made me sit down at a table and I was given *gnocchi* to eat, *pasta* made with potatoes and flavoured with tomatoes, and some rough red wine to drink, and she encouraged me to eat more, while three small children peeped out at me from behind her skirt like mice, and I was made to drink more wine by her husband. Later I was taken up a staircase that was like a ladder to a bedroom on the upper floor of the house where I exchanged the blanket for a long, hand-knitted vest which smelt of sheep and reached down below my knees.

The bed was high and white and ghostly-looking in the light of the single candle, and there was a great hump in the middle of it that looked very strange to me.

"It's the priest (the *prete*)," said Signor Zanoni. "You'll be warm enough when he gets out of it." What he said sounded almost obscene on the lips of a man like this, but then his wife peeled back the sheet and blankets for a moment, long enough to remove from it a strange contrivance, something that I had never seen before, or even heard of—an iron pot full of hot coals from the fire on a wooden base with a framework of laths over it to stop the bedding coming in contact with the pot and catching fire. This was the priest, a dangerous apparatus which, in its time, they told me later, had burned down many houses.

Then they went away and I climbed up into the bed and burrowed down into it between the rough, white sheets. It was the best bed I have ever slept in before or since. It was as warm and soft as a woman and almost equally alive. I was almost tempted to talk to it but instead I fell asleep laughing with sheer joy while the thunder rolled and the rain beat down on the roof overhead. At this moment, about seven o'clock on the night of the twenty-fifth of September, 1943, there could have been few people in the whole of Fortress Europe more contented or fortunate than I was.

The next morning when I woke the rain was still pelting down. The cows in the *stalla* were like a lot of fog-horns, the hens were making disgruntled noises in the yard and I could hear faint movements in the kitchen as if whoever was there was trying to make as little noise as possible. The shutters were closed and I got out of bed to open them and when I was back in it I found that by sitting up I could look down into a little orchard in which there were some battered old apple trees with their branches bowed down by the rain and the weight of fruit on them, and with a lot of windfalls from the storm at the foot of them.

There was nothing else to see. The valley up which I had climbed the previous afternoon, and the hills on either side of it, were still hidden in mist and cloud. Before coming to Italy I had never imagined that the countryside could ever be so dreary-looking. This sodden landscape reminded me of a wet Sunday morning on holiday as a child in Devonshire long before the war, when I had looked out of the window in despair, wondering what I should do all day, but then discovered a lot of old bound copies of the *Strand Magazine*, and spent the rest of the day lying on a broken-down horsehair sofa in the billiard room happily reading instalments of Sherlock Holmes.

This, too, was a Sunday and it was raining even harder than it had been that day in Devonshire, but there the resemblance ended. Then my only worry had been that I might be bored. Now I knew that in an hour or two I would probably be out on the hillside again on my way to try to find somewhere to spend tonight, and it would be the same the next night and the night after that, but for the moment I had the pleasure of being in this marvellous, deep, warm old bed. The huge feather mattress was so soft that its edges curled up under my weight and enveloped me so that I looked rather like a hot dog, and under the bed there was a large chamberpot, a *vaso da notte*.

Besides the bed the only other items of furniture were a chair and an old wooden chest with an iron lock on which stood the candlestick and snuffer with which I had been preceded up the stairs to bed. On one white-washed wall, hanging from a rail, carefully preserved from dust under layers of newspapers, were the family's best clothes. Signor Zanoni's black suit for weddings and funerals and days of *festa* and his best corduroy suit which was also beginning to show signs of wear, the signora's best dress and coat and the children's clothes—one of them had a velvet tam o'shanter as big as a soup plate. To one side of the bed there was a crucifix and above it there was a large, sombre framed photograph, taken long ago, of a heavily moustached young man and a solemn looking young woman who bore such a resemblance to the signora that she must have been either her grandmother or her great-grandmother.

I wondered where on earth everyone else could be sleeping in such a small house. After all there were six of them and the room I was in was obviously the one used by the signor and signora. I wondered where the old lady slept. It seemed impossible that she could be got up such a steep flight of stairs; and although I knew there must be other rooms, I felt guilty about all the discomfort and disturbance that I was causing them.

Above my head the roof was supported by the roughly shaped trunk of a chestnut tree a foot and a half thick, and smaller transverse beams of the same wood formed a framework of immense strength, all of them a uniform deep chocolate brown without a single wormhole to be seen. Whoever had made it had intended it to last forever.

I had scarcely got back into bed after emptying the *vaso da notte* out of the window, the sound of which I hoped was deadened by the rain and which seemed the best plan, when the door opened without warning and Signor Zanoni came in his socks to fetch the family's Sunday clothes. He was a different man from the previous evening. He had shaved and his hair was sleeked down with water.

"Today is a holiday," he said, "but you, Enrico, must remain in the room until the evening. Usually on Sunday mornings we go down to the village and my wife goes to mass with the children, but to go with them and come back takes two hours and a half and the weather is too bad today. But people always visit the houses on their way back up the mountain after mass—it is the custom here—and who knows, one of them might like to have 1800 lire for denouncing you. And even if they didn't everyone up there would know by this afternoon that you're here and someone else might want the money, so don't make a sound if we have visitors."

Eighteen hundred lire was the price which the newly arisen Fascist Republic Party, known as the *Repubblichini*, had placed on the head of every escaped allied prisoner of war. Eighteen hundred lire was about twenty-five pounds, a lot of money in Italy in 1943. Sufficient to make a poor man think seriously about taking up prisoner-of-war hunting as a profession.

"You know the song," Signor Zanoni said:

> *"Se potessi avere mille lire al mese*
> *Senza esagerare sarei certo di trovare tutta*
> *la felicità."**

"But at the moment you won't find many people who will give you away," he said. "These mountains are full of our own deserters. Most of the Party members are too frightened of what will happen to them when the Allies arrive to bother about chasing prisoners of war. And some of them are hiding their own sons and grandsons, anyway. Everyone's waiting to see what's going to happen. If your people arrive soon, then all

*Which roughly translated, means: If you could only have a thousand lire a month, without a word of a lie you would be certain to find real happiness.

the Fascists will be waving your flags and telling them how much they helped prisoners of war. When it's all over no one will be able to prove that they didn't. If the Allies don't come then we shall have the *milizia* up here. Then watch out. We shall all be *KAPUTT!*" He ran the edge of his hand across his throat.

The Fascist Militia, a vile body if ever there was one, had been disbanded when Mussolini fell in July but it had been re-formed on the fifteenth of September. From what Wanda had told me it now had among its members even more odious elements of the population than it had previously.

"The people I'm afraid of with you here," he went on, "are the *Guardie Forestali.* It's not that they're bad men, most of them are all right, but they work for the Government and anyone who works for the Government in Italy is afraid for his pension. I would be the same. If they're told to look out for strangers, and you can be sure they have been, you can be sure they will. And they're not like the *carabinieri* who are much too lazy to come up here unless someone orders them to. They like street corners best, the *carabinieri* and they don't like to get their uniforms dirty. But the *guardie* are another sort of thing. You never know where they are. They just appear. And they know how to move in the mountains."

He took the clothes off the hooks, the signora's dress, the little suits belonging to the three boys and his own best corduroys. It left nothing but his wife's coat, his black suit and the velvet tam o'shanter. I thought of my own too ample wardrobe before the war, and that of my parents. I was a long way from home in every sense.

"I must go now," he said. "If you have need of it, Enrico, there is a *vaso da notte* under the bed."

A little later the signora brought me a bowl of milky coffee with some bread to dip in it. She was sorry that the bread was a bit stale, but the oven was outside in the yard and she hadn't been able to bake because of the heavy rain. The coffee was made from roasted acorns but the milk was straight from the cow and with the dry bread in it, it was delicious.

During the morning I could hear the church bells ringing out in the valley. The people of Fontanellato would be going to mass in the *santuario*, and I wondered if Wanda would be among them. At midday the signora returned with some thick soup and some thinly sliced ham of which she was proud. "This ham was never smoked over a fire or cooked," she said. It was kept hanging high up in a loft where the fresh air could circulate around it. It was the air alone that matured it. This part of the Apennines was good for ripening hams, the *stagionatura*, she called it.

She was a handsome woman, but very thin and drawn, and I knew that with three small children in the house and an aged aunt, for that was what the wrinkled lady with the pebble spectacles was, she could not afford to feed me, and that although I had been reprieved until the next morning, I would have to go away then to some more remote place where I could at least work for my keep, which would be impossible here. After what Signor Zanoni had told me the *paura* of the Baruffas seemed more reasonable, although it was difficult to understand why they had waited until the doctor had left to tell me that they didn't want to help me. Perhaps they were afraid of him. I knew that I was, and of the *maestro*, too.

Down below in the kitchen the children played games which sometimes ended in tears and their getting the rough edge of the signora's tongue. Several times during the day the dog barked, and I heard the door open and the bandying about of lots of *permessos* and *avantis* and then the long rumble of voices speaking the dialect. All day it rained and rained. It was like being in the Ark. Only towards evening it finally stopped and shafts of sombre light broke through the leaden clouds that were moving away towards the west.

All day I thought about what it had been like to be a prisoner, and I thought about the most incredible thing of all, something that I had no right to do in the circumstances, that in the course of the last fifteen days of freedom which had already began to have a dreamlike, insubstantial quality about them, I had managed to fall in love.

Chapter Nine

Appointment at the Pian del Sotto

Standing under the apple trees in the orchard next morning with Signor Zanoni and looking down the valley, it was difficult to believe that the last two days of wind, rain, thunder and lightning had ever been. The sun was a huge orb of melted butter shining out of a cloudless sky on to a world that seemed reborn after having recently surfaced from the deluge. Everything was dripping wet, every blade of grass and every leaf sparkled with drops of moisture, the air was filled with the sweet smell of damp vegetation and little shining rivulets of water were purling down through the terraced fields to join the river below.

And there were more birds than I had seen in Italy before: blackbirds, bands of chaffinches and jays were the only sorts I could put a name to, but there were many others and the air was filled with their songs and chattering, and from the deep woods on the other side of the valley came the call of a solitary cuckoo. It was spring after winter with nothing to remind one that autumn was already here.

Out beyond the end of our valley to the south-east, a series of long outlying ridges, dark against the sun, ran up towards the main ridge of the Apennines which was somewhere out of sight to the right. Although it was only a couple of hours after sunrise it was already hot, and from the invisible valleys between them mist was rising like steam from a series of giant baths. And beyond the furthest of these ridges there was the outline of a fantastic mountain that was like the profile of a whale rising from the sea, its head a huge, vertical cliff.

"Bismantova," said Signor Zanoni. "Dante wrote about it in the *Purgatorio*."

"I never read the *Purgatorio*," I said, apologetically. "Not even in English."

"Neither did I," he said. "I was told about it at school. How he climbed it. He was a poet so they told me. I never got far enough at school to read the *Purgatorio*. I only got to grade two. It's time to go, Enrico," he said. "Are you still sure you want to?"

"I'm sure," I said. "It's for the best, really."

I had said goodbye to the rest of the family in the house; to the signora who had cried into her apron; to the children who were no longer at all afraid of me and with whom I had played games the previous evening and who had ended up by pinching and pummelling me until they had been told to "*Stai bravo!*" and "*Stai zitto!*"—be good! and be quiet!—and allow me to talk about England which was what their parents enjoyed most; and I had said goodbye to the old aunt sitting in her niche by the fire, which at this hour of the morning was nothing but a heap of warm ashes, and had received her silent farewell which could also have been a benediction.

It was that previous evening, when the last visitor had gone home and I went downstairs, that Signor Zanoni told me that they wanted me to stay with them, and it was then that I told them what I thought was the best thing to do.

I said that someone might come for me during the next few days but that I wasn't sure and I didn't know when it would be. I didn't mention the doctor or the *maestro*. I said that I couldn't just sit all day indoors and do nothing, and that I couldn't go on expecting help and give nothing in return, and I told them that I had no money, which to all intents was true. What I wanted to find was a place where I could work in exchange for my keep. I could help with sheep, cut wood, look after pigs or do any other kind of farm work, providing that it was unskilled; but wherever I worked the place would have to be lonely, which was why I couldn't stay with them. Here, it would never be possible to work out of doors close to a path which was filled with traffic at all times of day.

It took me a long time to say all this in Italian but eventually I succeeded in making them understand.

"*Dunque*," Signor Zanoni said after a long while in which he said nothing but was thinking. "*Dunque*. There's Giovanni. No! . . . There's Pasquale. No! . . . There's Andrea. No! He won't do . . ."

He was enumerating them on his fingers, and one by one rejecting them. He was like another of Belloc's characters in the *Cautionary Tales*, The Lord High Chamberlain, "the Kindest and the Best of Men", selecting somebody to be attendant on His Majesty; but finding no one suitable—". . . and William Coutts has got the flu . . . and Billy Higgs would never do," and so on.

Finally, the signora said, "What about Luigi?"

Like most men he didn't like his wife to come up with ideas he felt he ought to have had himself.

"Luigi!" he said grumpily. "Why Luigi?" And then, after a bit, "Well, he might do. Old Luigi, he might. It's solitary enough, the Pian del Sotto, and Luigi always liked getting something for nothing, or next to nothing, and he's very honest. A good man. Yes, Luigi might do."

"He's a hard man though, Luigi is," he said to me. "He has to be to get a living from that land, but he's done well. His place is on the Pian del Sotto. It's very high and the land's very poor, more stones than earth, and he never has enough help, or didn't have. I haven't seen him since . . . I don't know when. It must be a couple of years now. He never comes down this way. He goes down the other valley. If you really want to we can go and see him tomorrow; but if he takes you on he'll work you hard for what you get and that won't be much."

I told him that I enjoyed hard work and that as long as I had a roof over my head that was enough for me. This was the kind of thing I had said at interviews for jobs before the war and later when being interviewed by senior officers in the army. I had a fatal aptitude for being good at interviews, the results of which I inevitably regretted subsequently, as much as the interviewers. I was doing the same thing again now. I never seemed to learn anything by experience.

I picked up my pack, the contents of which were now dry, having been by the fire for two nights, and followed Signor Zanoni out of the orchard and down to the left bank of the stream by a path that was so overgrown and overhung by bushes that it would have been invisible to me, where we crossed it by four big stepping stones. Then we scrambled up the bank through the undergrowth, and after he had made sure that there was no one about we crossed the track which led up from the hump-backed bridge and entered the wood, the one from which the cuckoo had called but which was now silent.

I asked him if anyone lived in the mill.

"Not any more," he said. "The man who owns it uses it sometimes. I don't know much about him though. He lives somewhere down in the main valley. All I know is he grinds flour well; but whenever you come back here keep clear of it. It's on the way up to . . . (he named a village but I didn't catch it), and that's the track to it, as well as to the Pian del Sotto and like the road past my house a lot of people use it. That's why we're going up now by a way that no one ever uses. Try and remember it. You may find it useful one day."

He was wearing his old patchwork suit and from a metal clip on the belt under his jacket he took a billhook and began to cut a way up through the brambles between the trees. They were mostly oaks and some sort of thorn-bearing tree which I had never seen before. The oaks were not like

English oaks. The trunks were mostly small enough to encircle with two hands and few of them were more than twenty feet high. Perhaps if they had been thinned they would have done better, or perhaps they were just small by nature.

"This was a path once," he said, "but now it's all grown in."

There was no doubt about this. I followed close behind him as he hacked away, getting very wet. Although this side of the valley faced north the sun was still low enough at this time of day to shine into it, but as we climbed further round the hill it shone only on the upper branches and finally it disappeared completely, leaving us in shadow. There were no birds, no signs of animal life at all. The forest, it was too big to be called a wood, was a cold, damp place, and I longed to get out of it into the sunlight again but at least we were leaving a path behind us where there had not been one for years.

After what must have been half an hour of steady climbing we reached what seemed to be the top where there were trees that looked like small beeches and at last we came out in a clearing in which a dilapidated hut stood, a primitive construction made of turf and branches. Here, the trees had been cut down over a wide area and the place was a waste land filled with sharp stumps, nettles and weeds except in some places where there were big black circles on the ground.

"*Carbonari*," Signor Zanoni said. "This year they're burning charcoal much further in towards the main ridge. With things as they are they won't be anxious to go down into Tuscany before they have to. That's where this lot come from—the Maremma. They'll probably work very late. Some of them may stay up here and sit out the winter if they can find a place to live in."

"What are they like, the *carbonari*?"

"Very strange people, some of them," he said. "Especially those from the Maremma. They live their own lives and they speak their own language. Hardly anyone on this side of the mountains can understand them."

By now the miraculous promise of the early morning had passed. There were clouds coming in from the south-west and the sun was not yet high enough to reach into the clearing. It was a cold, sad place.

Once again we entered the forest and after a short while came out on the edge of it.

"*Colle del Santo*," Signor Zanoni said. "It's not far now, only about twenty minutes from here if you use the track. It'll take us a bit longer."

We were on a little pass, the meeting place of two tracks which crossed one another diagonally and we were between the two lower arms of the crossing. The track on the right was the one from the mill which we had by-passed by coming up through the forest. It continued over the pass and downhill into the head of another valley on our left and then through meadows to a small village of stone houses, larger versions of Signor Zanoni's, huddled together on the mountainside below a wooded ridge from which long, bare screes poured down towards it. Along this track a man was urging two heavily laden pack-mules towards the village under a sky that was now cold and threatening.

The other track wound up around the edge of the wood to our left and continued straight up the mountain beyond the crossing between two long hedgerows of bramble, and this was the one we took. In spite of being near a village this windswept pass with a splintered, dying chestnut tree on one side of it and a little shrine with a worn carving of some saint on the other, from which it took its name, had a very remote feeling about it.

We went up the outside of one of the hedges which was high enough and thick enough to hide us from anyone who might be using the path itself and after forcing our way up through another wood we came out on the edge of it, in a little promontory of trees, the only part of it which had been able to raise itself above the relative shelter of the slope on which it grew. We were on the edge of an inclined plateau about half a mile long and between three and four hundred yards wide, in which the fields swept down at a crazy angle to a cliff formed by an enormous landslide which appeared to be still going on. Apart from some root crops there was nothing growing. The harvest had already taken place and the rest of the fields were nothing but expanses of stubble and stones, although some of the less rocky ones had been ploughed. Some looked as if they had never been cultivated at all. Towards the northern end of the plateau, which was completely exposed to all the winds of heaven, except those from the west from which it was sheltered by the bulk of the mountain which was covered with forest and which soared above it, stood a great, bleak farmhouse, faced with grey cement and with so many storeys under its red-tiled roof that it looked like some rural skyscraper.

"Pian del Sotto," Signor Zanoni said. "We're nearly a thousand metres here."

If this was Pian del Sotto I wondered what the upper one was like. I asked him.

"There isn't one," he said. "This is the highest anything will grow. Higher up there's nothing but sheep, and then only part of the year. Wait here, I'll go and see old Luigi," he said.

He went on alone towards the house, where I heard him being

welcomed by a furious dog, while I stood at the edge of the wood with the wind moaning through the trees, waiting for whatever was going to happen next. It was certainly a lonely place. Far below, beyond the end of the landslip, were the fields full of grass and clover that I had seen from the Colle del Santo and I could just see the stone roofs of the houses in the village. Here, we were almost as high as the ridge under which it stood and now, for the first time, I could see part of the main ridge of the Apennines running down along the borders of Tuscany, with long slanting lines of rain in the sky above it as if someone had been scribbling with a black pencil on a sheet of grey paper.

I was becoming cold now and I was more tired than I had expected to be after such a comparatively short journey. I was not as fit as my occasional bursts of activity in the *orfanotrofio* had led me to believe but my ankle seemed completely mended. At least I could run if necessary.

I heard a window open somewhere in the house and then an awful scream as if someone was being murdered, "ARMAAAHNDOOOO!" was what it sounded like, sufficient in a place such as this to make my blood, already chilled by the keening wind, turn to ice. What on earth was going on inside this forbidding-looking building? Had the occupants done away with Signor Zanoni? Perhaps they were all in-bred and mad as hatters.

Almost immediately afterwards Signor Zanoni appeared in front of the house and signalled me to come and as I got to the door where he was waiting, a huge brute of a dog tethered to a running wire which gave it more scope for attacking intruders than it would have had on a chain alone, leapt out at me from where it had been lying in wait, snapping and snarling, longing for nothing better than to be at my throat.

"What was that noise I heard after you went to the house?" I said as soon as we were out of range of it. "It wasn't the dog."

"Noise?" he said. "Oh, that was Agata, Luigi's wife, calling Armando, the boy who works for them. She's a good woman Agata, but she's got a terribly strong voice."

"It's not going to be easy," he went on. "They've just heard that anyone who helps prisoners of war will be sentenced to death."

"I never heard that. Is it true?" I said.

"I told them. I had to. It would not have been right to do otherwise."

"Then you knew?"

"It was announced four days ago. I heard it down in the village. Luigi has a radio but it doesn't work very well. None of them up here go anywhere, except on Sundays, and yesterday it was raining so much that they all stayed at home."

102

"Did your wife know?"

"Yes, she knew."

If they knew then the doctor must have known and Wanda and her father must have known, and Giovanni and his father and mother, and the Baruffas. All of a sudden everything seemed much less simple than it had done.

"Mind you," he said, "I don't think they would dare do it, shoot people I mean, and neither do any of these people here. The Government, or what is supposed to be the Government, would have to shoot hundreds, perhaps thousands, I don't know how many, but, all the same it's making them think. It's making me think; that's why the people here haven't decided about you yet. They want to see you first."

I said that I didn't think it was right to ask them to take me now that I knew about the death penalty.

"Then there's only one thing you can do, Enrico," he said, "and that's come back with me. It's quite simple, really."

"Let's go in," I said.

There were five people in the kitchen, two men and three women: the farmer, a tallish, erect, thin man who, to me, looked exactly like Company Sergeant-Major Clegg of the Grenadier Guards, the one who used to scream at us outside the Old Buildings at Sandhurst; his wife, who was about the same age as he was, fiftyish, who had a pale face with a front tooth missing; and two young women, one with short, black hair, who was obviously the daughter, thin and slight like her mother, the other a big, powerful girl, an Amazon with long auburn hair to her shoulders. The other man was a stocky, muscular youth with dark, greasy hair, carefully combed. All of them were wearing working clothes and big, mountain boots. The girls were washing up in a stone sink, the signora was stirring up the fire which had only recently been lit, and her husband was sitting at the table on which there was a bottle of wine and two half-charged glasses. There was a feeling in the air as if a lot of talking had been done. The farmer had his hat on, as did Signor Zanoni.

I was introduced to the company in a general way, no names were exchanged, and there was a good deal of rather remote *buon giorno*ing, and when this was over I was invited to sit down at the table and I was given a glass of wine, which was extraordinarily acid, and some very good bread and some slices of sausage. Then they began to talk, or rather Signor Zanoni and the farmer began to talk, in a dialect that was so deep that I could make nothing of it, with the wife throwing in an occasional sentence, or a word, from the fireplace where she stood with her arms folded tightly across the place where her bosom would have been if she

103

had had one. Up to now the only time I had heard the mountain dialect had been a muffled version of it, coming up through the floor of Signor Zanoni's bedroom. Hearing it unfiltered and close to I found it equally incomprehensible.

As no one in the room took the slightest notice of me while my fate was being decided, I was able to look around me. It was long and high and the walls and ceiling, which had once been white, were now the colour of old ivory. At the far end of it a window looked out over the plateau to the ridge above the village. There was a fireplace with a high shelf over it, crowded with the sort of objects which end up over fireplaces, in this case a cast-iron coffee grinder, some dried bulbs, a piece of palm leaf left over from some bygone Sunday, a number of curled-up picture postcards and a book with the title *Lunario Barba-Nera* in archaic type.

On the right of the fireplace was the sink at which the girls were working; close to it there was a cast-iron stove with a silver-painted stovepipe rising from it which vanished into the wall just under the ceiling, and behind me, where I sat facing the fireplace there was a tall, dark cupboard and a chest on short legs with a removable table-top, a piece of furniture known as a *madia*, in which the flour which was used to make the *pasta* was kept, a piece of furniture which every house I had been to in the *pianura* and the mountains possessed. And on a box under the window there was a dilapidated radio set with wires sprouting from it, which must have been the one that had not given the information about people who helped prisoners of war being shot.

After what seemed an eternity the conversation rumbled noisily to a close, rather like a train of goods wagons coming to rest in a marshalling yard. It was the signora who was responsible for these effects, with her deafening interjections. Pound for pound she was the noisiest woman I had ever met. It was she who had uttered the bloodcurdling call to the boy Armando, to bring him in from whatever he was doing, to attend the family council.

Now her husband was filling Signor Zanoni's glass from a fresh bottle, at the same time looking at me as he poured it, with the air of someone who was about to acquire a slave. Watching him performing this difficult feat, I felt that something had been concluded.

"Luigi is of the opinion that if you want to stay here it is all right," Signor Zanoni said at last. "And so is Signora Agata, as long as things stay as quiet as they are. There's a lot of work to be done in the fields and they will be glad to have you, but they can't pay you anything. They'll give you your food and a bed. When you're working outside you will have to keep away from the path to the house, always. You're sure to be seen by someone wherever you're working, but if anyone asks who you are they'll say that you're someone from Genoa, a fisherman who's been bombed, and isn't quite right in the head. If anyone does speak to you act as if you're stupid and pretend that you're deaf and dumb. You'll have to keep your sack of stuff up in the woods above the house in the daytime, in case you have to run for it. Dig a hole and cover it up so that when it rains it won't get wet. If you have to escape at night there's a way out over the roof of the *stalla* from the second floor. They'll show it to you. If you need me at any time, one of them will bring me a message. And I'll arrange with the Baruffas so that when your friends come for you they'll send them to me. Now they'll show you where your room is and they'll give you some clothes to work in. The ones you have won't last more than a day or two in the fields and they don't look right."

The room to which Agata's daughter, Rita, the thinner of the two girls, escorted me was high up under the eaves of the building and we climbed up to it by a series of steep and flimsy staircases. In it there was a window at floor level which faced north and by kneeling down it was possible to look out along the track which led to the farm. I found this out while I was helping her to make the bed up. It was a very dilapidated bed but the bedding was very clean. And I was glad when she provided me with a *vaso da notte*, which may seem an unimportant detail, but released me from the necessity of descending all those stairs in the middle of the night and having to face that revolting dog in the yard.

When I got back to the kitchen Armando, the black-haired boy, and Dolores, the big girl, had disappeared and Signor Zanoni was about to leave. I had changed into the working clothes which Agata had given me and they looked a hundred years old. Signor Zanoni's working suit was composed of shreds and patches; but, at least, it covered his nakedness completely. Luigi's was made up of dozens and dozens of holes connected by pieces of black velveteen that was so tough that I wondered how the holes had appeared in it in the first place. It looked like a nineteenth-century poacher's suit in which the occupant had been caught in the cross fire from several gamekeepers' shot-guns. Nevertheless, I was delighted with it. Wearing it I felt that I was a part of the scenery.

I accompanied Signor Zanoni to the door and as soon as we got to it the dog began baying for blood.

"That's a brute of a dog," Signor Zanoni said (*Un cane proprio brutto*, was how he actually described it). "Keep out of its way, it's starving. I'd shoot it if it was mine, or else I'd feed it. Everything's kept very short here; but I've told them that if they want you to work they must give you enough to eat. They're not mean, but they're all used to doing without much. And I've told them that it's no good them speaking *dialetto* to you because you won't understand."

"Don't forget us," he said. "We won't forget you."

I shook his hand and watched this small, kindly, resourceful man as he walked along the path that led down to the Pian del Sotto.

"Come with me," a voice said. It was Luigi. It was the first time he had spoken to me, apart from wishing me *buon giorno*. I followed him round to the back of the house where the fields swept uphill to the edge of the woods in all their stoniness. Many of them could scarcely be called stones. They were rocks and boulders which had come rolling down off the mountain. It was like looking out on a parable.

"I want those fields cleared of stones," he said, quite casually. "All of them. I should start with that one up there. The others will help you with the big ones, when they've finished what they're doing, in a week or two. There's a cart over there," he indicated a vehicle with solid wooden wheels and sides made from the plaited stems of osiers. It looked like a primitive chariot.

"What shall I do with them," I said, "when I've put them in the cart, the stones?"

"You can do what you like with them," he said, "as long as they don't stop on my land."

Then he looked at me, and seeing that I was genuinely puzzled, he gave me the same kind of foxy grin that Sergeant-Major Clegg used to when he announced to us that there would be no weekend leave.

"You can throw them over the cliff," he said. "You can start now."

And he went back into the house.

Chapter Ten

Life on the Pian del Sotto

So life went on at the Pian del Sotto with Luigi, Signora Agata his wife, Rita the daughter, Dolores the help, Armando the ploughboy and me. Work started in the open when the sun rose or, if it was not visible, which was often, when it was deemed to have risen, about six, and stopped when it had gone down behind the mountains and the plateau was in deep shadow, which was probably about five-thirty. Perhaps it was earlier or later, there were no clocks in the house and no one had a watch as far as I could see. None of them would have been much the wiser if they had owned watches, as the strange vagaries of official war time in Italy which were as complicated as our own in Britain, ensured that no one knew what time it really was, and were incomprehensible to country people who never took any notice of it anyway.

I only know that it was still always dark outside when Agata used to climb up to the landing below my room and shriek up the shaft of the staircase to my room like a banshee *"EEENNNRIIICO! E L'OOORA!"* ("IT IS THE HOUR!") which never failed to make me leap from my bed in terror, believing that the Germans had come, the *milizia* were at the door, the house was on fire or the dog had broken its chain, or that all these things which I feared most had happened at once. Then I used to light my candle, struggle into my dank clothes, sometimes putting a foot through a hole in the trousers or an arm through a gap in the elbow of the jacket, wrestle with my boots which I prudently kept under the bed, and stumble down the dark staircases and outside into the yard with the *vaso da notte* in one hand, its contents slopping about, still more than half asleep, but hearing Agata's awful cries as she woke the other members of the household who were asleep in other parts of the labyrinthine building—*"DOLLORESSS! ... ARMAAANDO! ... REEETA! ... E L'OOORA!"*

The only one she never had to call was Luigi. He was already up.

In the yard where the dog, Nero, although it didn't answer to this name, or any other, was lying in wait for me, I used to hurl the contents of the *vaso da notte* in its direction, giving myself a mark if I scored a hit. Then, if it was not raining—if it was I skipped the next part of the programme—I went behind the house into the yard where a pipe delivered a jet of water from a perennial spring on the mountain side into a large stone trough which looked like the bath of some Roman senator, and under this I used to put my head and wake up with a jolt and then clean my teeth with the water which was so icy that it made them ache (at the Pian del Sotto I always woke with a taste in my mouth as if I had drunk too much the night before, which was something I never had the opportunity of doing), and finished up by rinsing my *vaso da notte* and secreting it under a disused barrel, to save myself the trouble of climbing all those stairs again, in order to put it under the bed.

Back in the house Luigi was already sitting at the table, wearing a black velveteen suit, a newer version of the one he had given me, and a felt hat, which he wore both in and out of the house. Luigi was always neat. He might have been about to set off for a weekly market, rather than to muck out pigsties and cowsheds or any other of the dirty jobs he would certainly be doing in the first hours of the morning. To my greeting, while his wife banged grumpily about the stove, as well she might having already been up for an hour or more milking the cows, he would answer, invariably; "There's a lot to do today," as if on all the preceding ones there hadn't been.

"*CAFFÈ*?" Agata would say, as if there was some choice, and plonked down before me a bowl of unsweetened acorn coffee—the sugar ration was practically non-existent and if there had been some way of getting one for me it wouldn't have been wasted in coffee. But although it was made with acorns the milk was fresh and the bread, which was stale, tasted much better than newly baked bread in it.

While I was drinking the *caffè latte*, very slowly so as to make it last as long as possible, the others came drifting in one by one, as sleepy as I had been before my visit to the trough: the girls finishing their dressing as they came, with thick, pendulous lower lips which looked as if they had been biting them in their sleep, which gave them a sullen look, both dressed in black pullovers, short dark skirts over which they were tying their aprons and white, home-knitted socks which they turned down over their mountain boots when they eventually put them on. They stood together in front of a small mirror which hung on the wall with pins in their mouths, combing their hair, barging one another out of the way to have a better view, and then trying it up in scarves, so that they looked like a couple of female pirates.

The last to appear was Armando, wearing a thick, sleeveless white

108

pullover which still had the natural grease of the animal in it and smelt like it, just as the enormous garment I had put on that night at Signor Zanoni's had done. Under it he wore a shirt, and beneath that a vest of the same make as the pullover. Armando had an enormous stomach for a boy of his age, and an equally large bottom. Why he had not been called up was a mystery. Perhaps he had been a soldier and had run away at the Armistice. He never offered any information about himself and neither did any of the others. It seemed better not to ask; but altogether he was an unforgettable-looking character. His trousers were supported with the utmost difficulty by a broad, low-slung leather belt, of the sort with which, a little later in life, I could imagine him beating his wife, and his trousers always had the flies gaping wide open. He wore very rural boots with wooden soles and bright yellow uppers which reached half-way up his bulging calves. I had never seen anyone with so many natural protuberances. As soon as he sat down at the table he invariably put his head on the table and at once fell fast asleep again and only woke when one of the girls pulled his hair and shouted CAFFÈ! in his ear. They enjoyed doing this.

While they were all slurping away at their *caffè latte* Luigi used to announce what each of them was to do that day. None of them appeared to pay the slightest attention to what he said; but they used to do what he told them all the same. The only one he never addressed himself to was me. There was no need. I knew what my job was on the Pian del Sotto. It had been laid down for me that first afternoon.

By the time he had finished telling them it was time to start. I went out to where I had left my prehistoric cart the previous evening, empty, and in the part of the field where I had been filling it. This was how I arranged it because the more boring and repetitive the job, the more imperative it is to develop some kind of theory about it in order to stop oneself going mad; and I had found that there was nothing I disliked more than starting off in the early morning by hauling a cartload of stones down to the cliff; throwing them over it and then dragging the cart up to the place where I was working, except pulling the empty cart up from the cliff edge, having thrown the stones over it the previous night, or, something I had never tried because I knew I would hate it, leaving the loaded cart on the edge of the cliff and throwing the stones over it first thing the next morning.

The truth was that the only thing I really enjoyed was the moment when I let the stones go down over the cliff, and sometimes I used to have crazy dreams about returning after the war when I had made a fortune, and employing people to fill carts with stones so that I could empty them over the cliff.

I had also developed theories about how the stones should be harvested. At first I began by throwing them straight into the cart and every so often, when I had cleared a few square feet of ground, I used to pull it after me on to a nice, fresh, stone-filled part; but after a while I got tired of doing this and I started making heaps of stones over a wider area and then making several journeys in succession with the cart to the cliff, but then I got fed up with spending so much time doing the same job—first making endless mounds of stones and then making endless journeys to the cliff edge—so I reverted to chucking them straight into the cart.

It was not so much that I was bored, though I was bored, and could understand why people doing repetitive jobs either strike or perform them very slowly—at least my stones were not of a uniform size and shape and I did know why I was picking them up. What really worried me was that I was sure that there must be one way of doing this job which was more labour-saving than any of the others. I could have asked Luigi or Armando what they thought was the best way, but it seemed a stupid question to ask.

One thing I knew was that it was impossible to fill the cart completely and still pull it. I had done this the first time and had then had to partially unload it. Probably the best way of resolving the whole problem would have been to have left the cart out of it altogether, and done nothing but make heaps of stones until there were no more left, or I got too old to pick them up, and then persuade Luigi to harness the bullocks to some bigger vehicle of which there were various sorts in the yard, and with the help of the others, load the stones into it; but as I could see no possibility of being allowed to have a bigger cart and the use of the bullocks, except in the case of the largest boulders, I carried on in my own, primitive fashion.

The actual stones, to the removal of which, after a few days, my entire life seemed to have been dedicated, were almost white on the outside where they had been exposed to the wind and sun and dark and damp underneath. They were all of shapes, and varied in size between the sort of stone with which I imagined David had slain Goliath, about as big as a tangerine orange, and red boulders which were embedded in the earth from which I was supposed to excavate them, using a long-handled instrument called a *vanga*, a sort of spade which had a small projection on it above the blade with which one pressed it into the earth. Some of these boulders were so large that when I had dug round them I found that, like icebergs, the greater part of their bulk was below the surface, and these I abandoned. How Luigi, or anyone else, had managed to cultivate land with so many rocks on it in previous years remained a mystery to me until the day after the first heavy rain fell, when I found that a piece of ground which I had cleared completely was again full of stones. Some had fallen from the mountain side and some which had been buried under the soil, had come up overnight, like giant mushrooms, to which they bore a certain resemblance.

When the cart was just sufficiently full of stones that I could still move it without rupturing myself, I used to heave it down to the edge of the cliff, a distance which could be anything up to three hundred yards, let down the back of the cart, lift the handles and tip it up, allowing the stones to roll down over the edge and listen to them as they landed with a satisfying crash at the bottom of what, I imagined, must be someone else's property.

The first time I did this the cart got out of control and nearly followed the stones over the edge with me clinging to it. I was glad that nobody had seen this happen, at least I thought that nobody had seen it, until I got back to the kitchen that evening, when Luigi was sitting at the head of the table with his hat on the back of his head.

"You watch that cart," he said. "It's a good cart. If that goes you'll have to carry them down in your hands."

On those parts of the Pian del Sotto which were relatively stoneless Armando had already begun to plough, using a very ancient-looking wooden plough with iron blades, which was drawn by two bullocks called Stella and Bionda. They were tough, corpulent, greyish-white animals with short necks and legs. When Armando talked to the bullocks, which he did constantly, telling them to stop or start or turn or simply urging them on, and at the same time walloping them with a long stick, for he was a rather brutal boy, the air was filled with his cries: "*OLAAA!* . . . *STELLAA!* . . . *OLAAA!* . . . *BIONDAA!* . . . *LEIII!* . . . *LEIII!* . . . *PORCA LA MISERIA!* . . . *LEIII!* . . . *DAIII!* . . . *DAIII LA* . . ."

The only thing that ever changed were the oaths—what were known as *bestemmia*—he interjected between these exhortations, most of them involving the defiling in various disagreeable ways of the Father, the Son, the Holy Ghost, the Virgin and the Host, or all of them together. Sometimes they were so terrible that I would not have been a bit surprised if the Almighty had got tired of being baited in this way and had hurled down a great thunderbolt from wherever he resided and obliterated Armando, a sitting target, exposed on the Pian del Sotto. But at least Armando's *bestemmia* was more varied than that of his counterparts in Australia where I had been in the year before the war, sitting astride their tractors ploughing their thousand-acre fields, monotonously chanting the only oath they knew, "fuck, fuck, fuck!"

111

In fact most of the time the Pian del Sotto was a thoroughly noisy place. It was not surprising. Unless you employ a messenger who does nothing else but run to and fro between them, or they possess some kind of signalling apparatus, any communication between the occupants of a piece of land half a mile long, most of whom are widely dispersed over it and the remainder of whom are hidden away in a congery of buildings all of which have walls at least two feet thick, and none of whom are disposed to give up what they are doing in order to speak to one another, is bound to involve a good deal of shouting.

On the Pian del Sotto, where no one seemed to know where any particular instrument was at any particular moment, the house was, of necessity, a sort of telephone exchange with Agata, who rarely emerged from it except to milk the cows and bake the bread, the switchboard operator in charge, either demanding information herself or relaying the demands of others, constantly throwing open one or other of the innumerable windows, doors and hatches with which the house was furnished in order to do so.

For instance, if Luigi needed the saw and the last person who was supposed to have used it was Armando, Agata would open the window of the kitchen and shriek out of it, in a voice that seemed strong enough to blow down the trees on the mountain above, "*ARMAAANDO! . . . DOVEEE LA SEGAAA?*" to which, if he was engaged in turning Stella and Bionda at a difficult place high up on the side of the plateau, he would make no reply. Whenever he was he never replied the first time she shouted as a matter of masculine principle but, finally he would shout "*LEIII!*" to the bullocks and they would eventually stop in their tracks and then at last he would cup his hands around his mouth and shout towards the house "*COSAAA?*" which in the dialect meant, literally, "THING?"

"*DOVEEE LA SEGAAA!*"

To which his invariable reply was, whatever he was asked. "*NON LO SOOOO!*" (I don't know) and Agata would throw up her hands in despair and slam the window shut and a little later she could be heard shouting to Rita and Dolores from other windows and other doors in other rooms, until the saw, or whatever it was, was finally located or else she gave up and the search, so far as she was concerned, was abandoned.

Sometimes she managed to get through to Armando, Rita, Dolores and her husband all at once, and a sort of five-part ululation would go on for some minutes in which Nero the dog, annoyed by the excessive din, would join, making it impossible for any of them to understand one another. The only one in the household of whom nothing was ever asked,

112

just as, at the early morning briefing, to whom no orders were given, was me.

At what must have been about ten o'clock, about three hours after we had consumed our *prima colazione*, the breakfast of bread and *caffè latte*, Agata would announce to all and sundry, *urbi et orbi* in the same earsplitting voice that it was time for the *merenda*, literally the picnic, and everyone dropped whatever they were doing as if it had suddenly become red-hot and untouchable and scurried, without actually running, back into the house.

By now the inhabitants of the Pian del Sotto, having shed their early morning torpor in the fresh air of the plateau, were much more lively. This was the time when they were at their best. It reminded me of the world of commerce to which I had been an unwilling recruit for a short spell before the war. Like office workers at their elevenses who throughout the morning have been nothing but subfusc figures calling one another Mr., Mrs., and Miss So-and-So, for a brief period, they, as it were, let their hair down.

Agata and the two girls were fascinated by dreams and in the kitchen there was a dog-eared book with a crude drawing of a blindfolded female seer on the cover entitled *I MIEI SOGNI*. Every morning this was laid on the table by Agata, like a sacred book and while we all ate the hot bread that she had baked in the outside oven, the rather cloying cheese which always reminded me of a foot that had gone to sleep, and drank the awful red wine which left a feeling in one's mouth as if someone had gone over it with a rasp, they used to talk about what they had dreamt the previous night and then consult the book to discover whether their visions were portents of good or evil. Luigi and Armando took no part in this. Whatever they dreamt, if they dreamt at all, they kept to themselves. As I did, they listened entranced, although pretending not to be. After a day or two I really began to envy Agata, and Rita and Dolores their capacity to have such an astonishing variety of dreams. For years now, apart from an occasional nightmare, I myself had enjoyed, if the absence of them can be said to be an agreeable state, a completely dreamless sleep. It was only now, after arriving at the Pian del Sotto, that I had begun to dream. I started to dream on the first night, and every succeeding night I dreamt the same dream: that I was picking up stones on the Pian del Sotto and it seemed to me that it lasted most of the night. The only time when I was oblivious was when Agata shrieked up the stairs "IT IS THE HOUR!"

With such a limited dream repertoire I was disposed of once and for all on the first morning.

"Stones," Agata read, having turned to the appropriate page in *I MIEI*

113

SOGNI, in which almost every conceivable and inconceivable sort of animal, vegetable, mineral, man-made object and human being dream, except those thought by the author or publisher to be indecent, was listed in alphabetical order and its significance explained. "To see stones on the ground means that your way will be hard and difficult."

"You didn't throw stones, did you?" she said.

"No, I was just picking them up and dropping them."

"That's a good thing," she said severely, as if I had any control over what I dreamt, "if you had been throwing stones it would mean that you are going to behave badly towards a certain person."

"I dreamt of *cacca*," Dolores said, proudly.

There was no need to look that up. They all knew what dreaming of *cacca* meant—money. In fact it would have been no good looking it up as it was presumably thought to be rude, although breasts were in (penises were out and so were vaginas). To dream of breasts meant that you would be devoured by illicit and morbid passions, unless they were full of milk, in which case it meant imminent maternity.

The next night Dolores dreamt of finding a wallet filled with *lire*, but this was awful. It meant that she was going to lose all the money she was going to acquire by dreaming about *cacca* and this threw her into a state of profound gloom for several days until she dreamt about a cemetery which presaged good health and happiness which restored her spirits.

I found *I MIEI SOGNI*'s interpretation of dreams rather baffling, except for my own which seemed logical enough. For instance, when Rita dreamt about ambulances it seemed that, on the principle which the book appeared to follow, that the more lugubrious the dream, the more pleasant the outcome for the dreamer would be; to dream of ambulances should ensure a state approaching bliss; when a cemetery meant good fortunes; a corpse, good business; someone moribund, the promise of long life; crying, good fortune and happiness. Yet when Agata opened the book at ambulances and read out, with gloomy relish, that they were the harbingers of scandal and enormous debts, it seemed absolutely crazy and unfair and I was not surprised that Rita, who was a gentle girl, burst into tears.

But the most ill-served of all by *I MIEI SOGNI* was the wretched Agata herself, who always dreamt of what one would have thought were completely innocuous things but all of which were thoroughly bad omens, such as birds, which meant terrible illness and death of next of kin; and abbots and priests, both of which had a thoroughly gloomy significance unless, as the book said, they were either confessing Agata, or giving her communion which meant felicity, happiness in the family and reconciliation with persons dear to one; but unfortunately, in her case, they were never doing so.

I always suspected Dolores of inventing her dreams, after having recourse to the book when no one was looking, but something happened to make me change my mind a few days after she had dreamt, or so she alleged, of *gabinetti* which the book said meant that "You have lost your direction in the darkness."

It was towards the end of the time of the *merenda* when *I MIEI SOGNI* had been put away, that those of us who were inclined to do so repaired to the *gabinetto* which was near the edge of the cliff behind the house. It was a rickety, draughty construction made of badly jointed planks and with a seat with a round hole cut in it which, as anyone who has tried it knows, is much less comfortable than an oval one. Below the seat a long shaft dug in the earth led to some unimaginable depths below. On the whole the *gabinetto*, like the ones in the *orfanotrofio*, was not a place to linger in in philosophical contemplation, but one in which to be about one's business and out again as soon as possible.

One day, just before the *merenda* ended, those of us who were still in the kitchen heard a series of muffled cries for help, *"AIUUTO! AIUUTO!"* coming from somewhere outside and we all rushed into the yard, including Agata, which was a quite exceptional thing for her to do. The cries were coming from the *gabinetto* and when the door was finally forced open it was found that the seat of the apparatus, which was riddled with wormholes and spongy with dry rot, had given way under the weight of Dolores, who was a girl who weighed all of eleven stone, precipitating her some way down the shaft where her girth caused her to become wedged in the same position in which she had been sitting when the accident occurred which was fortunate, otherwise she might never have been seen again. As it was she was only rescued with some difficulty. As a result of this disaster Armando was taken off ploughing for the rest of the morning so that he could assist Luigi in constructing another, more substantial but equally uncomfortable seat from a plank of seasoned chestnut wood and four stout stakes which Luigi had been keeping for this very purpose.

"She must have been after the *cacca*," Armando said, later, and we had a good laugh about this.

At *mezzogiorno* we all trooped back again for the midday meal which was invariably a thick vegetable soup, usually with beans and *pasta* in it and more bread and cheese and wine. Dreams were forgotten at this repast, everyone was too done in to do anything but eat, and as soon as it was over and the girls had cleared away the dishes and washed up, everyone except Agata, who was knitting one of the long, sleeveless woolly vests which I coveted, fell into a coma over the table for an hour. If it was warm enough I used to prefer to go outside, prop myself against a wall out of the wind and go to sleep until Luigi gave the signal to start work again, which must have been about half past one, by which time the effects of the meal had begun to wear off and I was beginning to feel hungry again.

The afternoon was very long—there were no breaks in it and towards four o'clock my back ached, my stones began to have a truly awful quality and I began to talk to myself in order to keep going; but at long last Agata would shout from the window "ARMAAANDO, ENRIIICO, VIIIENEI", and I would dump my last load over the cliff, take the cart up the hill and collect my sack from the place where I had hidden it at the edge of the wood, and Armando would deliver Stella and Bionda from the bondage of the plough, and we would go back together to the farmyard where the girls were already washing themselves at the trough. Then, when they had finished and the animals had drunk deeply from the trough, and Nando had fed them and made them comfortable, we used to wash too and when no one was looking I used to collect my *vaso da notte* from where I had hidden it, and climb the stairs to my little room where I changed into my own clothes and clean socks, and put on my boots again, from which I never allowed myself to be divorced except when I was in bed.

I would have liked to have shaved at this time but Signor Zanoni had warned me against doing so as he said I would not look the part if I was clean shaven, being *troppo Inglese*, as he put it, so that what I saw when I looked in a piece of broken mirror which I had found in one of the barns was something which looked like a gooseberry and I envied Armando who always had a vicious blue stubble on his face, the day after his weekly shave. Luigi, on the other hand, never seemed to grow any hair on his face at all, but he certainly didn't look English to anyone except me who was always reminded of Sergeant-Major Clegg at Sandhurst whenever I looked at him, except that unlike the sergeant-major, he never raised his voice.

It was after the evening meal that the attention of the rest of the company turned to me. If I have given the impression that I was a sort of solitary slave to whom no one else on the Pian del Sotta paid any attention then, dead or alive, I have done them all a serious injustice. I was by no means ignored. It was simply that I found myself in a very hard-working household which, at the, to me, appallingly early hour when it began to work, was as incapable of conversation as I was. At the mid-morning *merenda* the female part of it was engrossed in necromancy and at *mezzogiorno* every member of it, except Agata who had the constitution of an ox, was too fatigued to do anything but eat and snooze; and for the rest of the day we were all too dispersed and too busy with what we were doing to engage in idle conversation. I had always thought of Italian *contadini* as a race of people who sat basking in the sun before the doors of their houses while the seed which they had inserted in the earth in the course of a couple of mornings' work burgeoned without their having to do anything but watch this process taking place. I now knew differently. These people were fighting to survive in an inhospitable terrain from which the larger part of the inhabitants had either emigrated to the cities or else to the United States and South America. Rough they might be but they were courteous, too, and whenever they did talk among themselves, as when they were consulting *I MIEI SOGNI*, they rarely forgot to conduct at least a part of the conversation in Italian which I could more or less understand, as Signor Zanoni had suggested to them, so that I would not have to try to elucidate their impossibly difficult *dialetto*. By the time that I had come down from my room, having combed my hair and changed my clothes, it was always quite dark and in the kitchen a fire was burning, the only time it did, except on special occasions; and although it could not transform this large, austere room into the sort of magician's cave that Signor Zanoni's was, it at least gave it an air of homeliness and warmth which it lacked at other times.

When this last meal of the day was over, we used to sit in a half circle round the fire in our stockinged feet toasting them and talking about all sorts of subjects, except the war in which no one seemed to have any interest whatsoever, exept that it should finish.

What they all liked to do best, except for Armando who appeared to have no extra-mural interests beyond eating and sleeping and girls (he had obviously been warned off Rita and Dolores), was to talk about England and London in particular, of which they all had some knowledge but a rather distorted vision. If London had been as they imagined, it would have been a place of such infinite mystery and excitement to me that I would never have wanted to leave it.

Among themselves they spoke of London as *la citè d'la fumarassa*, the city of smoke or fog.

"There's a lot of fog in London," Luigi would state as an incontrovertible fact and it was no good saying that there was much more fog in the valley of the Po and in Milan in wintertime than there now was in London at the same season.

What they all had was the same sort of vision of the Metropolis that I had had after reading Dickens and looking at very old bound volumes of *Punch*, one in which, at midday, the streets were filled with a yellow, billowing vapour as thick as pea soup in which to open one's mouth for an instant was to be asphyxiated and in which all the other inhabitants were invisible until they suddenly loomed up like ships in a fog-bound estuary, that is all except the link boys carrying flaming torches, who escorted the more well-hipped citizens about their business and gave them some protection against the footpads who could be distinguished, if the fog ever lifted sufficiently, by the thick jerseys they wore which had horizontal, alternating black and white bands on them, the knobbly cudgels they carried and nasty little wall-eyed dogs which trotted at their heels. A London in which the sulphurous darkness was filled with the stifled cries of the lower orders, the only members of the community who could open their mouths with impunity: of old women selling lavender; coalmen in leather hats droning "coul, coul!" selling their black diamonds so that a million fires a day could be fed and produce the smoke which kept the fog going for twelve months of the year; fishwives extolling the virtues of baskets of bloaters; hawkers selling matches which had been made in factories by young women in conditions that were so dangerous that they rarely reached middle age, to which were added the sounds of the bells of muffin men, the music of hurdy-gurdies which were supported on a single pole stuck in the mud, the moaning of beggars, the noise made by the crossing-sweepers sweeping the crossings and the snorting of the horses which were harnessed to the "growlers", the hackney carriages which plied everywhere for hire.

Behind the elegant white-painted stucco façades of the rich, which is what they would have been seen to be if only one had been able to see them, lived the heavy-jowled merchants who every day went to their places of business in the City; to banks and to warehouses which had little cranes on the upper floors to haul the merchandise up to the great store rooms above their own comfortable sanctums in which they sat alone and in which yet more fires were burning while in the outer offices, thin, penurious clerks sat at high desks writing with quill pens in ledgers bound in vellum, debiting their master's customers and only rarely making a credit entry in their favour, for cases of tea by the thousand, bales of wool and cotton, cargoes of spices from the Indies, coal, iron and other more exotic minerals, precious stones, wines and spirits, most of which they never actually laid eyes on, all the traffic which engrossed the occupants of the capital of the greatest empire the world had ever known, over which the sun had shown no signs of setting, except to the most percipient, all payments, from whatever source, immediately being transmuted into the only coin minted in the only metal that was fit to be handled by those who had inherited the earth and most of its fruits, the *sterlina d'oro*, the golden sovereign.

And although all of this was what their vision of London conjured up for me after they had spoken about it as *la citè d'la fumarassa*, the city of smoke and fog, not what they knew about it themselves, they all knew about the golden sovereign, and one night when we were talking about the miraculous properties possessed by *sterlina d'oro* which neither moth nor rust could corrupt, nor mice consume, or become waste paper as bank notes could overnight, Agata went away to some secret hiding place and returned some time later with a whole handful of them, some embossed with the head of Queen Victoria, others with that of Edward Seventh and George the Fifth, and even one or two with George the Sixth on them, and on the obverse of all of them was the spirited figure of St. George on horseback killing the dragon with a lance and the horse trampling it disdainfully underfoot, a currency which it had been illegal for any inhabitant of the British Isles to possess for as long as I could remember. "They are real *sterline d'oro*, aren't they Enrico?" she asked anxiously. I said that there was no doubt they were and that they were very good things to have, especially in times like these, better than Italian lire, German marks, French francs, English pounds and even American dollars unless they, too, were all gold.

"That's good," she said. She looked happier than I had ever seen her and happier than I was ever to see her again. "There isn't a house in these mountains that hasn't got some *sterline d'oro* hidden away."

But what they really enjoyed talking about most of all was English criminals, murderers best of all. The only literature in the house besides the dream book and the one called *Barba-Nera*, the desiccated agricultural almanack which lived over the fireplace, were some old copies of a weekly magazine which was something like *La Domenica del Corriere*, the magazine which had a picture of nun being eaten by lions on the cover which had so fascinated Maria, the little mongol girl in the *ospedale Peracchi*. Some of them contained part of a series devoted to what was called *I MOSTRI CRIMINALI INGLESI*, The Monsters of English Crime, and we spent a number of happy evenings discussing them. There was Mrs. Dyer, the baby farmer, who used to drown the infants committed to her charge at Caversham Weir—I remembered Mrs. Dyer well—how could anyone forget her?—from visits to the Chamber of Horrors in the school holidays, a mad-looking pale wax figure, dressed in black bombazine, or what I imagined black bombazine to be, forever pushing the small black perambulator with which she went about her ghastly work; Crippen, they liked talking about him, because he used poison, something with which, as agriculturalists, they were acquainted, and Luigi described in detail how, in order to procure even the smallest quantity of poison to kill mice which, in this part of the world were as big as rats, from the Consorzio Agrario he had had to sign a book; and there was Mahon, the Crumbles murderer, who after having tried unsuccessfully to render down his wife in pots and pans, had travelled backwards and forwards on a local train throwing various parts of her from the windows—I had seen photographs of his handiwork because one of my friends at school had a father high up in Scotland Yard and we had been given special permission to visit the Black Museum. I remembered the occasion well because when my friend's mother had seen the photographs taken at the Crumbles she had fainted clean away.

They were all very impressed by my having seen the perambulator in the Chamber of Horrors and also the Black Museum, and this gave us the excuse for more evenings of gruesome conversation about other monsters not included in the series. But the monster they all liked best was Jack the Ripper, who was in it, because he fitted in so well with their idea of *Londra, citè d'la fumarassa* appearing out of the fog carrying a black bag to do what he was impelled to do in the dark back alleys of Houndsditch and when he had done it, vanishing into the murk from which he came, though how anyone could know, as the magazine said he did, that he carried a black bag at all, was an unexplained mystery. Feelings were very divided about the victims.

"And good riddance to them," Luigi said, stoutly. "They were *putane* weren't they?" At the mention of *putane* Armando guffawed. But the girls and Agata rounded on them, angrily. "Poor, unfortunate girls," they said. "*Putane* they might be; but who made them *putane* anyway? Evil men. And for all anyone knew they might have been mothers with children, too, and what would happen to them with their mothers dead? Much better have a *putana* for a mother than be an orphan with no mother at all."

Then, for the time being having exhausted my repertoire of crime in England, they talked of other more homely horrors, of yawning graves and white-shrouded corpses rising from them which someone they knew had seen in a churchyard not far off, of maniacs and persons with hideous disfigurements locked away in upper rooms and such, until Rita and Dolores were frightened to go up the stairs to bed and Agata had to go with them when the time came which, although it could not have been later than half past eight felt like midnight to me after my labours in the fields.

120

But in spite of the stones it was often marvellous to be working up on the Pian del Sotto: going out on to it while the morning star was still shining brilliantly in a sky that was the colour of blue-black ink; seeing the sun coming up behind Bismantova, below and far away, first illuminating the forest on the mountainside above, then flooding the plateau; sometimes rising behind dark clouds and then shining red through a hole in one of them, as if someone had opened the door of a furnace. And I liked being there when the sun was high overhead and torn white and grey clouds were racing over the mountain top from the west casting dark shadows on the pale fields, and hordes of starlings would swoop over them, and high over everything a goshawk as pale as the clouds and with wing-tips as ragged looking as they were, soared on the wind which sighed in the trees like the wind in the rigging of a sailing-ship. And I liked it, too, when the sun had gone behind the mountain and everything on the plateau was in shadow and there was a smoky blueness in the woods which were still so green in the sunlight that it was difficult to believe that autumn had come and was already well advanced.

Now the owls had taken over from the cuckoos and were hooting and there was a cool, damp smell and the bats were out in force about the house, and the sun still shone on the high peaks of the Apennines down to the south-east. And sometimes there was cloud which for days on end covered everything so thickly that I could only see a few feet in front of me and often got lost on the way with the cart to the cliff edge, and had equal difficulty in finding my way back to the field from which I had come. And sometimes it rained, and if it was not too heavy we worked with sacks over our shoulders, even the girls when they were hoeing, replacing them with dry ones when they got too wet.

The only thing I really dreaded were the days when there was such a downpour that no work could be done out of doors. Then we used to sit in the fireless room, for even then when we were all together in it, it was never lit before the evening, everyone getting more and more bored and bad-tempered, Luigi particularly, because we were wasting his time, the girls knitting socks and sweaters, Agata working away at her vest, Luigi and Armando doing absolutely nothing, and myself trying to read Boswell's *Tour of the Hebrides* which seemed absolutely meaningless on the Pian del Sotto, but every few minutes being interrupted by Dolores or Rita asking me what I was reading about now. What I would really like to have done would have been to stay in bed all day and sleep, but I thought that if I did this I would cause offence.

In the kitchen the air got stale; Armando would fiddle with the wireless which was supposed to be defunct but would sometimes deliver itself of great gusts of singing by what sounded like some gigantic tenor or bits of *Tannhäuser* before giving out some last dying squeaks and relapsing into silence. I would dearly liked to have heard the news. What on earth was going on down there in the south where the armies were? Even the *merenda* was no fun anymore when there was no work to make one look forward to it and at *mezzogiorno* great quarrels would sometimes break out between them all, and they would scream at one another in the *dialetto* with their mouths full of bread and soup, while I sat there in terror hoping that they would not decide to include me because I didn't feel like quarrelling. Something terrible had happened in the *pianura*.

Chapter Eleven

Encounter with a member of the Master Race

After I had been nearly a week at the Pian del Sotto I had still received no news from Wanda or the doctor; but on the Saturday evening the two girls went down to the village and when they returned about seven o'clock, Dolores drew from under her sweater, warm, and slightly damp, an unstamped letter addressed to a Signora Enrica, in what I immediately recognised as Wanda's impatient handwriting which always seemed to me a too slow method of communication to keep pace with her thoughts.

The letter was written in Italian and although it purported to be addressed to a Signora it was really for me.

"*Mia cara Enrica,*" it began and I experienced a feeling of intense happiness at being addressed in this way which, although it was not more than "My dear Enrica," in English, sounded much more affectionate: "I have sad news of your two old friends. They are no longer with us and my mother cries continually." (For a terrible moment I thought that they had both been executed; but the next sentence made it clear that they hadn't.) "They are now in the city and neither of them can get about as they were both accustomed to do in the past. Giorgio, the one who used to take you for rides in his motor car, has developed an illness, but you know what he is like, very imaginative. As a result of this he has left the uncomfortable lodgings, which he didn't like at all, and which he shared with your other friend, Bruno, who doesn't find them comfortable either, and now Giorgio has gone to have a check-up which could result in his having an operation, although I very much doubt if he will submit to it. In my opinion he will leave the place whenever he wants to."

Reading this I assumed that the doctor had been able to feign some complaint which required surgical treatment and had managed to have himself transferred to a hospital from which he planned to escape.

"Bruno is in a far worse situation, although his health gives no cause for alarm at present. *But I will get him out of it,*" Wanda wrote with menace, which boded no good for whoever had her father locked up. "As you know it is all the fault of that stupid; but as soon as I have overcome this problem I will try to come and see you."

123

"It is a pity," she went on, "that the little excursions which we always used to talk about are impossible at this moment. I advise you not to go too far, unaccompanied, *at your advanced age*, as these cooler, autumn days can be very treacherous, especially where you live. It is getting very late in the season to think of travelling to warmer parts which, every day, become more difficult to get to. I know that you have an impetuous nature, but do take notice of what I say to you and believe me to be your sincere, *and loving*, friend." Underlining this as she had the part about my advanced age, and signing her name with an indecipherable squiggle which she had probably learned in the bank and which came in very useful now.

While reading the letter I could feel the eyes of everyone in the room on me. It took me some time to do so and when I had finished I asked Dolores how she had come by it.

"My cousin managed to get permission to go down to Fontanellato to pray at the *santuario* for her brother who is with the Alpini in Russia—another reason, which she didn't tell me, was to buy food. While she was there a signorina got talking with her, and when she found out where my cousin lived she wrote this letter which she addressed to a Signora Enrica, but was really for you, and she asked her to take it to a certain house in the valley down by the road; but when my cousin went to the house the people said that they had never heard of anyone called Signora Enrica but that there was someone called Enrico and Signor Zanoni might know where he was to be found; and then my cousin went to him and he found out that she already knew that there was someone up at the Pian del Sotto, although she didn't know his name was Enrico; and then he told her to take the letter there and give it to Luigi, or to me, and she would have done this, but she only arrived back this afternoon and she knew that I was going down to see her this evening, anyway; so she waited."

"But how did your cousin know that there was someone up here?" I said, having been made slightly dizzy by this breathless narrative.

"She knew," Dolores said mysteriously, "and she knew that whoever it was, the letter must be for him."

"That's right," Luigi said. "Everyone knows now that someone's up here. Everyone knows everything that happens in this place. It has always been like this. If they don't see it for themselves then the birds tell them. They would have seen you when you threw the stones over the cliff."

Then with a village of the size of the one below the cliff, with at least a hundred people in it, perhaps more, they must all know that there was a stranger on the Pian del Sotto, and, by now, the news would have spread like convolvulus, only infinitely faster, outwards from the village to the

124

lonelier houses, the seeds of it carried on the wind to other villages where they would take root again and ramify until, by now, the entire region must know that I was up here.

Everyone in this room, although they showed no signs of realising it, was hopelessly compromised, and the thought that they all were, made me want to cry from sheer vexation. How much better it would have been if Luigi had told me to deposit the stones in a corner of the property, as they had been in the fields on the way up to Signor Zanoni's house, instead of pouring them over the cliff. It would have been much harder work; but it would have been well worth it. What surprised me was how calm they all were.

"Your *fidanzata* is very beautiful," said Rita, rather spitefully I thought. "Angiolina was telling us. *Alta, bionda* not a bit like us, dark, ugly things. She doesn't look as if she comes from this part of the world at all, although Angiolina says she speaks like a *Parmigiana*."

"I am *not* engaged to her," I said.

"Ha, Ha!" said Dolores. I noticed that both girls looked at me with more interest now that they knew that I had a beautiful *fidanzata* who sent me mysterious letters by devious means.

"And you're not ugly," I said. "You're very good-looking girls." Which was true.

Actually what I said was *molto bella da vedere* which was unfortunate, as it made them sound like food that looked better than it tasted. And they seized on this, happily.

"Oh, we may not be so bad to look at, although it's only you who say so, but we're not well-educated like your *fidanzata*. We can't write letters like she can." And so on. Both of them were thoroughly enjoying themselves.

I had never been very good at standing up to this peculiarly feminine form of bear-baiting but fortunately it was Agata, who was of a more practical turn of mind, who came to my rescue, although not in the way I would have wished.

"What did your intended write in the letter?" she asked. "What sort of news? Was it good or bad?"

I was in a dilemma. If I told them the truth they would become really alarmed and believe that there was an incriminating trail which led directly from Fontanellato to the Pian del Sotto. Yet it was obvious from Wanda's letter that the reason her father and the doctor had been imprisoned was that their names had been in the little book kept by that stupid. What was really bad was that so many people knew that there was a stranger among them, and now that the girls had been down to the village and had talked to Dolores's cousin, and goodness knows who else, it seemed more than likely that everyone knew that I was not an Italian fisherman who had been blown up by an Allied bomb in a raid on Genoa, but an Englishman with a desirable price on his head. What I now needed was time to think out what I ought to say but there was none. I had to reply to Agata's question immediately.

This time it was the girls who saved me. Seeing me grow red with embarrassment (I could feel myself blushing), and hesitating to reply they assumed that the contents of the letter had been of too intimate a nature to be imparted to anyone else, or pretended to, and they turned on Agata and upbraided her for having the face to ask such a question, which had seemed a perfectly reasonable one to me; at the same time giving themselves more of the sadistic pleasure which they had obtained while denigrating themselves.

"But no!" they said. "Poor boy! How can you ask him such a question? How would you have liked it if someone had asked you when you were young all the beautiful things your *fidanzato* had written to you? For shame!"

"Luigi couldn't write," Agata said.

"SHE IS NOT MY *FIDANZATA*," I said loudly for the umpteenth time, but none of them took any notice and a full-scale shouting match developed, in which everyone joined except me, about the importance of personal privacy, during which the question of what was actually in the letter was soon forgotten and no one referred to it again.

Luckily, the next day was a Sunday, when no manual work was done, apart from milking the cows and feeding the animals, not even on the Pian del Sotto, and I decided that the best thing to do would be to go away for the day, somewhere up the mountain above the house, which was something I had wanted to do even before this crisis had arisen. If I did stay at the house I would be the only person left in it for a good part of the day and I would be virtually a prisoner because, when they all went down to one or other of the villages, Nero was let off the hook, and Luigi and Armando were the only ones who knew how to put him on the chain again.

They all had different reasons for going. Agata and the girls went to attend mass, in one of the lower villages and on the way back the girls used to look out for any boys who might be about, all of whom would be deserters, living in a stage of semi-concealment rather similar to my own and like me ready to take to their heels at a moment's notice. All the other young men were still away, some having been unable to escape from their units at the Armistice, some prisoners, some still in the Balkans, and some lost in Russia, members of General Garibaldi's luckless Eighth Italian army, which had been overrun on the Don, none of whom had been heard of since December, 1942, and most of whom were never heard of again. The men did not go to mass unless they were very old. Here, in the mountains, as in the *pianura*, religion was for women; among the men it was reserved for feast days and for death. Luigi would be going to the local inn to meet his cronies, and play a noisy card game called *briscola*. And Armando would be going down to look at the girls, of whom, he told me, there was a good selection, one or two of whom, according to him, "did it". Armando told me that he would like to "do it" with Dolores.

"I'd like to screw her and screw her and screw her and screw her and screw her," he said, banging the side of one of the bullocks with a clenched fist, as if to emphasise how much he would like to do it.

"You're as bad as the English," I said. "You want to eat five times a day."

"She looks as if she does it; but she doesn't, at least not with me," he said, gloomily. "I can't understand it."

When I suggested going away for the day to Agata she seemed quite pleased. I don't think she much liked the idea of leaving me alone in the house. I might set fire to it or I might even try to unearth her cache of *sterlina d'oro*. Whatever the reasons she very willingly gave me a picnic to see me through the day; and I set off at about nine o'clock with the provisions and all the rest of my belongings in a real Italian army rucksack which Luigi had used in the first war when he was in the *Alpini* and which, although it had been slightly gnawed by rats, was still serviceable.

I looked quite smart when I set off. I had shaved and I had on my own clothes, or rather the ones that Wanda's father had given me, because Luigi said it would not look right if I met anybody in the woods wearing his ragged suit on a Sunday, although, to my mind, I looked even more conspicuous; neither like a local inhabitant, nor someone out for the day from a town.

"You can wear your old suit tomorrow when you're working on the stones again," he said, and I thought I detected a note of anxiety in his voice, as if I was perhaps planning not to return, and I was flattered to feel that although my job was a menial one I had at least managed to make myself more or less indispensable, for no one else could be spared to do it.

It was a marvellous, cloudless day, more like a day in midsummer than one getting on towards the middle of October, and it was going to be very hot. I went up across the fields in which I had worked all the week, looking at them now with a much more professional eye than when I had first arrived. How different they looked, those I had weeded of stones and Armando had ploughed and harrowed, using the trunk of a small tree,

127

and those the girls had worked on afterwards using mattocks with long prongs to break the earth up. Then I scrambled up the steep bank and took one last look at the house before entering the woods at the place where I always hid my sack of personal possessions during the day in the shallow hole which I had dug for this purpose on that first afternoon, covering it with planks and earth, just as Giovanni and his father had done when they had buried me that night down by the river.

The trees were mostly beeches but not the great tall English beeches. These were much smaller; but the bark had the same pale, luminous quality, and there were some oaks, too. These woods were nothing like the one below the Pian del Sotto, or the even worse wood below the Colle del Santo, through which Luigi had cut a path up from the river. Here there were no brambles and the ground was covered with moss.

What must have been years ago now, in the time when the immediate ancestors of these trees were alive, the *carbonari* had worked extensively over this face of the mountain and the little platforms which they had excavated from the side of it, on which they had built their fires and their huts, extended all the way up the side of it. It must have been quite long ago because any fragments of charcoal that were left, small pieces the thickness of a pencil, were buried quite deep underground; but although it was long ago, nothing grew in these clearings except weeds and grass. It was as if the soil had been sterilised by the heat, just as at some places on the Western Front where the ground had been so pulverised by high explosives that, even twenty years later it was said, no trees grew in it.

These platforms were linked with one another by paths, and as I went up through them I wondered how it was that they had not become overgrown as those in the woods below had done, until I came to places where I found stacks of wood beside the path, firewood that had been cut the previous year and had not been taken down the mountain; perhaps because the snow had come before there had been time to move it. Certainly, no wheeled vehicle could get to these places. It was only the big wooden sledges drawn by bullocks of the sort I had seen in the yard at the Pian del Sotto that could do so and it was these that kept the tunnels open.

The woods were full of fungi. I had never seen so many strange and wonderful sorts. If anything was needed to do so, they added to the magic of the place. They all seemed to be of similar, related species. The larger ones had caps up to eight or nine inches in diameter, and they were all sorts of shades of green and brown, olive, tan, chestnut and some were such a dark shade of chocolate that they were almost black. Some were sticky, as if they were coated with rubber solution, others were dry and hard but the undersides of all of them were like fine sponges with hundreds of tiny pores and most of them were a yellowish, spongy colour, except the smallest ones, which had hard, round caps like pebbles tightly crimped to the stems, so that the underparts were invisible.

The stems were thick and bulbous, like the trunks of very old oak trees which have been pollarded. Some of them had a delicious fungus smell, others scarcely any at all. The most exotic sorts were more or less the same shape as the others but they were as weird-looking as certain kinds of orchid. One had an off-white cap, was blood-red on the underside and was supported on an enormous inflamed stem which was covered with a network of red veins, like a leg that had something badly wrong with it. And when I broke the cap the flesh, which was a creamy yellow colour, changed instantly to a sinister cerulean blue and gave off a disagreeable smell. The other sort had an ordinary brown cap, but the underpart was a lurid orange and the flesh was the colour of ripe apricots; but, just like the other one, a few seconds after the flesh was exposed to the air it changed, to a greenish-blue, the colour of verdigris. This one smelled good. Looking at them, I wondered which, if any, of these strange growths were edible. I knew nothing about fungi, I was not even completely confident that I could distinguish English field mushrooms from similar looking but inedible varieties.

While I had been in the *ospedale* I had seen quite frequent references in the newspapers to persons dying in agony after consuming what was usually described as *una copiosa quantità di funghi*. In one case an entire family and its dependants had perished. Certainly, the great, greyish-white fungus with the blood-red underparts which gave off such a repulsive smell looked highly poisonous, but I only found two of these anyway, one of which I kept so that someone at the Pian del Sotto could identify it; and I gathered a few of the ones with the apricot flesh, which were more numerous. For the rest I concentrated on gathering the less colourful ones, converting my pullover into a sack in which to put them, by tying the rollneck collar with a piece of string. Soon it was full and I continued on my way.

As I climbed, the trees began to thin out and at last I came to a place where there was nothing but juniper growing. Then, quite suddenly the wood came to an end and I was out of it on what resembled a steep-sided English downland, and inclined sea of cropped grass with little islands of yews rising from it over which half a dozen hares were streaking away uphill fanning out as they went, alarmed by what must have been a rare visitor. Here I turned left and walked along the ragged coastline of the wood towards what I hoped would be the upward continuation of the steep ridge above the village, and after about a quarter of an hour I came to it.

I was on the edge of an enormous cliff which formed the entire south face of the mountain. It must have been between four and five miles long from east to west, and it swept up to what might be the summit of the mountain, or a crest on the way to it; there was no way of knowing. It was a geological phenomenon, the result of some great convulsion. It was as if a giant who had been sleeping in the depths below had suddenly woken and raised himself on his elbows in his subterranean bed, lifting the blankets of rocks above him, crumpling them as he did so and had then subsided again, leaving his knees up.

The sheer parts of this cliff were as I imagined the great precipices facing the Atlantic on the west coast of Ireland might be, Croaghaun, Slieve League, the Cliffs of Moher, cliffs I had read about but never seen, rather than something far inland in Italy. It fell away perhaps two thousand feet into a narrow valley through which a shallow river flowed over stones. On the right bank there were a couple of villages with red-tiled roofs, one of which had a campanile rising in the middle of it. Across the valley there was another mountain which formed the southern side of it. This mountain had a long, blunt ridge and was less high and less steep than the one on which I was standing, and it was partly covered with forest. Below the ridge of this other mountain was a little plateau with a lake on it which looked as if it was man-made, because it was a too perfect circle to be natural and on the outer rim of it there was a small building from which an enormous red pipe descended in one single, straight swoop to a hydro-electric station in the valley below, a concrete building of the twenties with tall windows. From the head of the valley, beyond the highest of the two villages, a road climbed to what appeared to be a sort of pass. And beyond that what must have been a further stretch of country which, in military parlance was "dead ground", out of sight, were some peaks of the main range that I had not been able to see from the Pian del Sotto because the ridge above the village and the bulk of the mountain behind blocked the view of them.

I estimated that the highest of them were probably between five and six thousand feet, and they were linked by ridges which had lesser peaks along their length which seemed to have some sort of vegetation growing on them but as the nearest of them were between six and seven miles off, it was difficult to be sure. In one or two places thin coverts of trees reached up to them, as if they were trying to draw the forests below, of which they were the highest on the cold, north face of the range up over the top of it and down the southern side into the sun.

I took off my rucksack and lay down in a grassy hollow at the edge of the cliff. The sun was hot and soon I took off my shirt and then my boots and socks. The air was filled with the humming of bees and the buzzing of insects and from somewhere further up the mountain there came the clanking of sheep bells, carried on a gentle breeze that was blowing from that direction. Then a single bell began to toll in the valley, and other more distant bells echoed it, but they soon ceased and I looked across to the distant peaks which previously had been so clearly delineated but were now beginning to shimmer and become indistinct in the haze that was enveloping them. And quite soon I fell asleep.

I woke to find a German soldier standing over me. At first, with the sun behind him he was as indistinct as the peaks had become, but then he swam into focus. He was an officer and he was wearing summer battledress and a soft cap with a long narrow peak. He had a pistol but it was still in its holster on his belt and he seemed to have forgotten that he was armed because he made no effort to draw it. Across one shoulder and hanging down over one hip in a very unmilitary way he wore a large old-fashioned civilian haversack, as if he was a member of a weekend rambling club, rather than a soldier, and in one hand he held a large, professional-looking butterfly net. He was a tall, thin, pale young man of about twenty-five with mild eyes and he appeared as surprised to see me as I was to see him, but much less alarmed than I was, virtually immobilised, lying on my back without my boots and socks on.

"*Buon giorno*," he said, courteously. His accent sounded rather like mine must, I thought. "*Che bella giornata.*"

At least up to now he seemed to have assumed that I was an Italian, but as soon as I opened my mouth he would know I wasn't. Perhaps I ought to try and push him over the cliff, after all he was standing with his back to it; but I knew that I wouldn't. It seemed awful even to think of murdering someone who had simply wished me good day and remarked on what a beautiful one it was, let alone actually doing it. If ever there was going to be an appropriate time to go on stage in the part of the mute from Genoa which I had often rehearsed but never played, this was it. I didn't answer.

"*Da dove viene, lei?*" he asked.

I just continued to look at him. I suppose I should have been making strangled noises and pointing down my throat to emphasise my muteness, but just as I couldn't bring myself to assail him, I couldn't do this either. It seemed too ridiculous. But he was not to be put off. He removed his haversack, put down his butterfly net, sat down opposite me in the hollow and said:

"*Lei, non è Italiano.*"

131

It was not a question. It was a statement of fact which did not require an answer. I decided to abandon my absurd act.

"*Si, sono Italiano.*"

He looked at me, studying me carefully: my face, my clothes and my boots which, after my accent, were my biggest give-away, although they were very battered now.

"I think that you are English," he said, finally, in English. "English, or from one of your colonies. You cannot be an English deserter; you are on the wrong side of the battle front. You do not look like a parachutist or a saboteur. You must be a prisoner of war. That is so, is it not?"

I said nothing.

"Do not be afraid," he went on. "I will not tell anyone that I have met you, I have no intention of spoiling such a spendid day either for you or for myself. They are too rare. I have only this one day of free time and it was extremely difficult to organise the transport to get here. I am anxious to collect specimens, but specimens with wings. I give you my word that no one will ever hear from me that I have seen you or your companions if you have any."

In the face of such courtesy it was useless to dissemble and it would have been downright uncouth to do so.

"Yes, I am English," I said, but it was a sacrifice to admit it. I felt as if I was pledging my freedom.

He offered me his hand. He was close enough to do so without moving. It felt strangely soft when I grasped it in my own calloused and roughened one and it looked unnaturally clean when he withdrew it.

"*Oberleutnant* Frick. Education Officer. And may I have the pleasure of your name, also?"

"Eric Newby," I said. "I'm a lieutenant in the infantry, or rather I was until I was put in the bag." I could see no point in telling him that I had been in S.B.S., not that he was likely to have heard of it. In fact I was expressly forbidden, as all prisoners were, to give anything but my name, rank and number to the enemy.

"Excuse me? In the bag?"

"Until I was captured. It's an expression."

He laughed slightly pedantically, but it was quite a pleasant sound. I expected him to ask me when and where I had been captured and was prepared to say Sicily, 1943, rather than 1942, which would have led to all sorts of complications; but he was more interested in the expression I had used.

"Excellent. In the bag, you say. I shall remember that. I have little opportunity now to learn colloquial English. With me it would be more appropriate to say 'in the net', or, 'in the bottle'; but, at least no one has put you in a prison bottle, which is what I have to do with my captives."

Although I don't think he intended it to be, I found this rather creepy, but then I was not a butterfly hunter. His English was very good, if perhaps a little stilted. I only wished that I could speak Italian a quarter as well.

He must have noticed the look of slight distaste on my face because the next thing he said was, "Don't worry, the poison is only crushed laurel leaves, a very old way, nothing modern from I.G. Farben."

Now he began delving in his haversack and brought out two bottles, wrapped in brown paper which, at first, I thought must contain the laurel with which he used to knock out his butterflies when he caught them; but, in fact, they contained beer, and he offered me one of them.

"It is really excellent beer," he said. "Or, at least, I find it so. To my taste Italian beer is not at all good. This is from Munich. Not easy to get now unfortunately. Permit me to open it for you."

It was cool and delicious. I asked him where he had come from.

"From Salsomaggiore, in the foothills," he said. "It is a spa and like all spas it is very melancholy, or at least I find them so, although we Germans are supposed to like melancholy places. It is the feeling that no one who has ever visited them has been quite well, and never will be again, that I find disagreeable. Now it is a headquarters. My job there is to give lectures on Italian culture, particularly the culture of the Renaissance, to groups of officers and any of the men who are interested. It is scarcely arduous because so few of them are."

"I must confess," he went on, "that there are some aspects of my countrymen's character that I cannot pretend to understand. I do not speak disloyally to make you feel more friendly to me but, no doubt, you, also, do not always understand your own people, but surely only Germany would employ a professor of entomology from Göttingen with only one lung, whose only interest is *lepidoptera*, to give lectures on Renaissance painting and architecture to soldiers who are engaged in destroying these things as hard as they are able. Do you not think it strange?"

"I wouldn't say that," I said, "I'm sure we do the same sort of thing and, if we don't, I'm sure the Americans do."

"Really," he said. "You surprise me. You would not say that it is strange?"

"The intention is, of course," he continued, "to make us popular with the inhabitants, but that is something we can never be. For instance, I came to that village down there by car. I suggested to the driver that he might like to accompany me up here, but he is not interested in the countryside or *lepidoptera*. Besides he told me that there is a regulation against leaving military vehicles unattended. I did not ask him to accompany me because I wanted his company but because I knew that he would not enjoy himself in that village, or any other. When we arrived at it no one would speak to us. There was scarcely anyone to speak to anyway, which was very strange because it is a Sunday. They must have thought I had come to make some kind of investigation. It might have been better if we had not been wearing guns; but it is a regulation."

I could visualise the state of panic the village must have been thrown into by their arrival, with young men running from the houses and the *stalle* and up the mountainsides, like hunted hares.

"It is not pleasant to be disliked," he said, "and it is very unpleasant to be German and to know that one is hated, because one *is* German and, because, collectively, we are wrong in what we are doing. That is why I hate this war, or one of the reasons. And of course, because of this, we shall lose it. We must. We have to."

"It's going to take you a long time to lose it at this rate," I said. "Everything seems to be going very slowly."

"It may seem so to you," he said. "But it won't be here, in Italy, that we shall be beaten. We shall hold you here, at least through this winter and perhaps we could hold you through next summer, but I do not think there will be a next summer. What is going on in Russia is more than flesh and blood can stand. We are on the retreat from Smolensk; we are retreating to the Dnieper. According to people who have just come from there we are losing more men every day than we have lost here in the Italian peninsula in an entire month. And what are you doing?" he asked.

I told him that I was on my way south towards the front. There seemed no point in telling him that I was living here. Also I was ashamed.

"If you take the advice of an enemy," he said, "you will try to pass the winter here, in these mountains. By the time you get to the battle front it will be very, very cold and very, very difficult to pass through it. Until a few days ago we all thought we would be retiring beyond the Po; but now the winter line is going to be far south of Rome. It has already been given a name. They call it the *Winterstellung*."

"Tell me one thing," I said. "Where have we got to now. I never hear any news."

"You have Termoli and Foggia on the east coast, which means that you will now be able to use bombers in close-support and you have Naples; but take my advice and wait for the spring."

I asked him where he had learned his English. He told me that he had spent several summer vacations in England before the war.

"I liked England," he said. "And the English. You do not work hard but you have the good sense not to be interested in politics. I liked very much your way of life."

He got to his feet.

"Lieutenant," he said, "it has given me great pleasure to have met you. Good luck to you and, perhaps, though I do not think it probable, we shall meet again after the war at Göttingen, or London."

"Or Philippi," I felt like saying, but didn't.

"Now if you would be so kind," he said, "please give me the empty bottle as I cannot obtain more of this beer without handing the bottles back. Bottles are in short supply."

The last I saw of him was running across the open downs with his net unfurled, in the direction from which I had come, making curious little sweeps and lunges as he pursued his prey, a tall, thin, rather ungainly figure with only one lung. I was sorry to see him go.

When I got back to the Pian del Sotto that evening everybody had already returned, except Armando, and the sole subject of conversation was the arrival at the village in the valley of *Oberleutenant* Frick and his driver and their subsequent departure from it. The bush-telegraph was working well—it was a pity that it operated in two directions, outwards as well and inwards.

As I imagined it would, the panic created by their arrival had sent all the men of military age in the area rushing off to the woods and in the time that it took someone who had a kinsman in our village to climb up by some secret path over the cliff and down to it, the *paura* had begun there and with similar results—even Armando had skedaddled—and it had been communicated to the occupants of every other village within walking distance. It was as if a stone had been thrown into a pond and the splash it had made became ripples moving outwards in concentric circles, one behind the other, as more messengers had gone out bringing the latest reports on the situation, what in our army were called "sitreps".

In the village in the valley the *paura* had begun to diminish as soon as the *Oberleutnant* had assembled his butterfly net and had begun to move out of the village on what he imagined was the way up the mountain. Officers were known to be addicted to outdoor sports, it was the one thing that officers were known to have in common, whatever their nationality, and this one was obviously a fisherman, though what he hoped to land with such a flimsy net and no rod in a river which had hardly any water in it at this season, no one knew and no one dared to ask. None of them had ever heard of butterfly hunting, or laid eyes on a butterfly hunter, so that when he asked a man and his wife who were on their way to attend mass in the village, for by this time there was no one else in sight to ask in his painstaking Italian what was the best way to the top of the mountain, they thought he must be a lunatic to want to go fishing on the top of a mountain which was over four and a half thousand feet high. And when they heard this in the village everyone was much relieved that he was only a soldier whom the war had made wrong in the head, for he was not the first to be deprived of his senses in this way. And when he returned, in what sounded like a state of euphoria, with what he had apparently described as *alcuni esemplari rari*, some rare specimens, their curiosity had got the better of their fear and he was made to display his catch before departing in an atmosphere of goodwill. For him it must have been the end of a perfect day, a German whom nobody loved.

As is usual in such cases, only the bad news that there was a German in the neighbourhood had been circulated, the fact that he was a lunatic fisherman and the later news that he was a butterfly hunter had only just got through to our village and the Pian del Sotto when I arrived, so that, unknowingly, the *Oberleutnant* had spoiled the Sunday for goodness knows how many people. And everyone at the Pian del Sotto professed surprise at the news that he was harmless, except Luigi.

"Just what I always said about Germans. They're not all bad lads," he said. And he looked at the rest of us as if we had all been labouring under some kind of delusion, of which he was the only one who had not been a victim.

"I never heard you say that," Agata said, unkindly.

"Neither did I," said Rita. "He never did."

As they seemed about to break into one of their internecine feuds, and not at this moment feeling up to it, and having decided not to mention to anyone that I was a friend of *Oberleutnant* Frick, I took the opportunity to unpack the great sweaterful of fungi which I had been lugging about with me all day and was now thoroughly sick of, and spread them on the table. Immediately, the question of whether some Germans were nice or not was forgotten.

"Don't do that! They're poisonous!" they all screamed, the first time they had ever shouted at me in the way they did at one another, when I produced the lurid variety and the other sort with the blood-red under-belly, which as a precaution, I had wrapped in paper and kept separately from the others.

"Well, you don't have to eat them," I said, with some show of spirit. "I only wanted to show them to you. I want to know what they are."

"Take them outside! They'll poison the table!"

The work of identification was carried out in the yard but although they all seemed to know something about fungi there was still a good deal of difference of opinion amongst them, about which sorts were edible. They all agreed about the ones that were poisonous—*velenoso* and those that were undoubtedly good to eat—"*mangereccio*" or "*buono*" they said, and some they were not sure about and they said "*Ma!*" which expressed grave doubt, with which opinion, now that I realised that they were actually intending to eat the specimens that passed their inspection, and that I would be eating them too, I associated myself most strongly.

In the end it emerged that the best ones were those with the blackish brown caps which they called *porcini neri*, little black pigs, and some of the paler ones which were just plain *porcini*. None of them liked the idea of eating the lurid variety and they were all agreed that the one with the white cap and the blood-red underparts, which they called *malefico*, would finish you off. I would have liked to have fed one to Nero.

"You should have brought more of the good ones and not so many of the poisonous ones," Agata said, and she wasn't joking.

"Where did you harvest them?" Luigi said when the woman had taken the ones that were *buono* into the house to prepare them. His manner was severe, that of a schoolmaster with an errant pupil. When I told him he was aghast, or pretended to be. I suspected he knew already.

"You know what that is, where you've been harvesting them?" This was the word he used, harvesting, as if they had been growing in fields like wheat. "It's old so-an-so's fungus bed (he called it *fungaia*). He'll be very angry, old so-and-so will." And so on.

"But they were all growing wild."

"Of course they were growing wild. That's the only way they do grow. They're all wild. Doesn't make any difference whether they're wild or not. He makes his living by harvesting fungus. He has to have a permission from the *commune* for that bit of forest, and he has to pay for it. No one else is allowed to touch them. When he goes up there tomorrow and finds a lot of them are gone he'll think one of us did it (and he would be right, I thought of saying, but I decided not to). They're worth a lot of money these days, fungi." And he named some fantastic price a kilo. But when Agata had fried them altogether, the *porcini* and the *porcini neri* and some other varieties, in a vast, shallow iron pan, which she told me, was only used for cooking chestnuts and fungi, I noticed that he tucked in with the rest of us. They were delicious.

While on the mountain that day where I had gone, really more than anything to commune with myself about what I should do, I had decided not to try and reach the line by walking to it but to stay where I was, at least for the moment while things were fairly quiet. It was a difficult decision to take and perhaps a selfish one so far as the people at the Pian del Sotto were concerned, but I had learned to respect Wanda's judgement in these matters and, if what *Oberleutnant* Frick had told me was true about the *Winterstellung* being stabilised south of Rome, it would be difficult to get close enough to pass through it before the snow fell, and if I did try, so far as I could see, it would mean walking down the main ridge, most of the time very high up, at least five thousand feet. To try and travel at a lower level would mean crossing perhaps hundreds of subsidiary ridges and the deep valleys in between them, most of which would be at right angles to the direction in which I would be travelling, if the country towards Bismantova, which I had seen from Signor Zanoni's orchard, was in any way typical. If only I had some maps.

I asked Luigi when the snow came.

"Here? Usually about the middle of November, sometimes earlier, sometimes later; but that's not the big snow. The big snow comes in December, towards the end of December."

"And on the mountains?"

"Always by the middle of November and often very much then on the main ridge (he called it the *crinale*). And sometimes on the top of our mountain, too. Why do you ask me this about the snow?"

"I am just interested. How do you get about when the snow comes?"

"In the big snow you must have skis. Not many of us older men have them now. Without them you have to stay where you are, except that most of the paths down to the valley are always kept open."

Then he said, "I am afraid for you when the snow comes, Enrico, because when it comes ... (*Quando viene la neve ...*)" He left the sentence unfinished. It was the first time he had ever called me by my name, and it was the last.

"Why what will happen when the snow comes?" I said, and it was suddenly as quiet in the kitchen as it had been that afternoon at the Baruffa's when Signor Baruffa had told me to go, and again I felt them all looking at me, not in an unfriendly way but as if they all knew what Luigi was going to say because it had already been discussed on some occasion when I had not been present, and were curious to see what effect his words would have on me.

"When the snow comes," he said, "if not before, wherever you are, they will come and take you away."

Chapter Twelve

The great *paura*

Now that we were all well and truly compromised, and as if they knew that it didn't really matter any more, visitors began to arrive at the Pian del Sotto, as I imagined they always had done before I came, although they never appeared when I was actually in the house; but always when I was far away working in the fields, as in a hospital when visiting hours had been laid down. They were mostly men, stocky figures all wearing felt hats like Luigi's and all equally invariably armed with the sort of umbrella that he himself carried when he went abroad, which was seldom, made of bright green oiled-cloth, huge things with cane frames and handles which looked as if they had been dipped in red ink, the products of some incredibly rural umbrella factory and as big as a commissionaire's at a Ritz. They vanished into the house and, after a while, emerged and returned from whence they came.

But as well as these commonplace visitors there were three women who came every day. They used to drift up through the woods in the afternoon dressed from head to foot in black, each carrying a wooden spindle, tapered at either end with a perforated stone at the middle of it, to the top of which the white woollen yarn which they were spinning was attached, and with the rest of the wool rolled round a distaff, a piece of wood which they carried tucked under one arm. When they reached the plateau they used to walk up and down for hours on end, spinning, quartering the fields, often passing within a few feet of me, but never speaking, not even among themselves, medieval-looking, ghostly-looking, gone into some undiscovered country of the mind to which they alone had passports and visas and from which they would probably never return; until by some, to me, imperceptible signal they used to form up in line ahead and go away. When I asked who these three weird sisters were, who gave me the creeps even more than Mrs. Dyer, the Baby Farmer of Caversham Weir in the Chamber of Horrors who was really gone, I was told that they really were sisters who had never married and were probably, because of that, *un po'strane*, a little strange, which seemed to me an understatement. I went on with my stone gathering until the stones were so few and far between that it now took about three times longer to collect a cartload than it had done originally. Personally, if the property had been mine, I would have told the stone gatherer to desist and get on with something else more important but nothing would induce me to say that I thought I had done enough. My experience of specialists and experts had been that they always made a point of holding opinions diametrically opposed to anyone else's on principle, and I had no desire to be snubbed yet again. It was Luigi's business to tell me to stop and, if necessary, I would go on picking up non-existent stones until he did. Perhaps I too was going mad.

But finally, one day, when I really thought that I should be reduced to carrying out this ridiculous threat, I found Luigi at my elbow.

"Enough," he said—"*Basta*", a word which always sounded vaguely offensive to English ears. "Bastards yourselves" we had replied sturdily to our guards when we had first heard it while being marched through the streets of Catania.

It was a memorable day, too, because everyone with the exception of Agata, downed whatever they were doing to help in removing the big rocks which I had not been able to budge myself, and a jolly hard job it was even for them I was glad to see, carrying them down to the cliff edge on a sort of stretcher and for the biggest which were too heavy for that, harnessing the bullocks to one of the sledges. But there were still some, the ones that I had compared to icebergs, which could not even be levered out of the earth with crowbars and on and around these great boulders Luigi and Nando built fires, making them red-hot and then poured water over them, or hit them with sledgehammers so that they split with a satisfying cracking noise; and I was kept busy trotting backwards and forwards to the trough for water, driving Nero the dog mad with fury each time I appeared in the yard.

When the last boulder had been broken I joined the hoeing squad which was composed of Rita and Dolores, using a *zappa*, an archaic-looking instrument with a shortish handle and two long slightly curved iron prongs like walrus teeth, which was used to break up the clods which the primitive harrow had failed to crush. The earth was heavy clay, some of it pale, the colour of putty, some of it dark and thick and incredibly adhesive, so that great clods stuck to the prongs of my *zappa* like enormous pieces of steak that had been kept too long and had gone off. The only way I could get rid of them was to whirl the *zappa* round my head, like a man throwing the hammer, until they detached themselves and flew away. The girls never got chunks of clay stuck on the *zappa* because they were more skilled in using them.

They were the biggest gas bags I have ever met in my life, talking all the time they were in the fields without intermission and including me in their conversation whenever they were on their favourite subjects which were love, marriage, love after marriage and the procreation of children, things which they didn't dare to talk about in the presence of Agata. In this way I exchanged the spiritual advantages of solitude on the Pian del Sotto for more Rabelasian pleasures.

One day they told me with a lot of giggling that there was soon going to be a dance, *un ballo*, at one of the farms just outside the village.

"Which of us are you going to take with you?" said Rita, "Dolores or me?"

Oh God, I thought, they've started again.

"If I could go, which I can't, I'd take both of you, if you'd come with me," I said.

The effect of this remark, which was dictated solely by diplomacy, was astonishing. They dropped their *zappas* and staggered about among the furrows with their hands over their mouths, uttering great gusts of laughter, until Agata hurled the window open and told them to get on with it, which they did, but it still didn't stop them carrying on this titillating interrogation and in order that they could continue it they began to hoe on either side of me and so close and in such unison that we must have looked like some song and dance act on a stage.

"Why can't you go to the ball?" Dolores said. A soppy question if ever there was one.

"Because it's dangerous."

At this Dolores whispered something in Rita's ear and they both went off into hysterics again. "All the other boys are going," Rita said when they had recovered. "Have you *paura*?" What I should have said was, "Yes, I have *paura* and so should you have." What I actually said was, "Certainly not."

"Well, if you haven't *paura* come to the ball."

"I'll have to see," I said.

It was now the middle of October. I always knew what day of the week it was but I was never sure of the date and no one in the house seemed to know either. Agata knew that the preceding Sunday, the second one in succession on which I had gone out for the day, but without this time meeting anyone or collecting any fungi, was the seventeenth after Pentecost, but no one else did, not even her daughter. The only calendar in the house was contained in the almanack over the fireplace, *Barba-Nera Lunario dell' Astronomo degli Appennini*, to which I had recourse on wet days but I discovered when I first opened it that it was already four years old and was no good for movable feasts, and was all wrong about the moon which had been full on the preceding Wednesday, which was my

141

second one at the Pian del Sotto, and was also, according to the book, the day of *S. Eduardo re d'Inghilterra confes.*, which I would have been tempted to celebrate if I had noticed it at the time.

The following day was a Friday and in the afternoon I was left alone on the plateau to carry on with the work of *zappatura*, breaking up clods with the *zappa*. Because it was a fine, warm day Rita had been taken off by her mother to help with the enormous operation which involved changing all the sheets and pillow cases in the house, and washing the dirty ones at the spring at the top end of the plateau where there was a large open cistern of water. There they walloped the linen on a sort of stone washboard. This was done every week and when the washing was finished it was hung on long lines at the edge of the cliff where it became incredibly white in the sun and wind. On this particular afternoon Dolores was not helping with the washing which she usually did; she was somewhere out of sight, working either in the house or in one of the outbuildings; Armando was ploughing, and soon after the midday meal Luigi had gone away up into the woods to decide on what trees they would cut that autumn.

Late in the afternoon, while I was hacking away with my *zappa*, I was consumed with an urgent need to visit the *gabinetto* which was a great bore, not only because it involved a longish walk but principally because it brought me within biting range of the odious Nero who seemed to bear even more murderous feelings towards me than he did to the rest of the family—and they were evil enough—probably because I was something foreign which smelled nasty to him and certainly because I used to throw the contents of the *vaso da notte* at him, which I would not have dreamt of doing if he had been nice to me in the first place. As it was, in order to reach the *gabinetto*, I always used to arm myself with a couple of carefully selected stones, one for the inward run, the other for the run-out of the yard, except when there were other members of the family present in which case they used to take over the defensive duties. Getting past Nero into the yard always reminded me of *Operation Pedestal*, I being one of the practically defenceless merchant ships, Nero a dive bomber.

On this occasion I did what I always did, pretended to make for the door of the house and as he made a rush to intercept me, foaming at the mouth (he was much too enraged to bark), I altered course to port and rushed through what was the equivalent of the Sicilian Channel, the narrows between the house and a pigsty, jumping over his chain as I did so, at the same time raising one of the stones above my head in a threatening manner and roaring at him at the top of my voice, which sufficiently impressed him with my murderous intentions to halt him long enough to let me get through and out of biting distance. And as usual, I succeeded.

When I emerged from the *gabinetto*, still prudently, clasping my stones, I was more or less at peace with the world. Nero was not. As always, he was furious at having been thwarted in his desire to tear me to pieces, and this time his rage lent him a supernatural strength. I was about thirty yards from him when, practically at the full length of his chain, he executed a fantastic leap in the air very similar to the capriole, one of the most difficult of all the evolutions performed by the horses in the Spanish Riding School at Vienna, of which I had seen photographs in a book in the *orfanotrofio*.

In doing so, he broke the running wire to which his chain was shackled and which gave him so much mobility. It parted with a twang like a breaking harp string and he landed on his stomach, unlike the horses in the Riding School, from which position he immediately regained his feet and streaked at me, as much like a rocket as a powerful mongrel dog trailing twenty feet of chain behind it could manage to be; and I took to my heels and fled in the direction from which I had come.

Yet terrified as I was of him, I was damned if I was going to take refuge in that awful *gabinetto*, and wait for him to break through the flimsy outer walls and eat me up inside it.

Having rejected it I had very little of refuge. I might have tried for the *stalle* but all the doors were shut. My best chance of survival seemed to lie in reaching a barn, about thirty-yards away in which hay was stored. This barn had a sort of lean-to construction outside it in which the hay was piled until it could be transported to the upper floor. I was doing well with Nero about fifteen yards behind me when I tripped over some large piece of disused agricultural machinery which was concealed in the grass, hurting myself dreadfully, and by the time I got up the bloody dog was almost on me; but fortunately his chain became entangled in the thing and this gave me sufficient time to reach the lean-to under which the hay rose up in a solid, sheer, unscaleable wall above me.

I was just about to turn and make a last desperate stand with the one stone which remained to me (I had dropped the other when I fell over) and with my boots as a last resource, when Dolores appeared like a chatelaine on top of it, knelt down, extended a brawny arm and hauled me up with Nero holding on to one of the turn-ups of my decrepit trousers which came away in his fangs and left him below, roaring with vexation. Although Dolores was a fantastically strong girl the effort she made threw her on her back in the hay and as I came shooting over the top with our hands locked I fell beside her, not on top of her as I would have done in a film about bucolic peasant life.

For a moment she lay there, with tears of laughter rolling down her cheeks. Then, still laughing, she turned towards me, enfolded me in her arms like a great baby in her arms and kissed me passionately.

It was an unforgettable experience, like being swallowed alive, or sucked into a vortex. It was not just one kiss, it went on and on. I felt myself going.

It was entirely spontaneous. She was obviously not expecting visitors, certainly not me, and because it was a warm evening and much hotter up in the barn where she had been working, she had taken off the tight sweater which she usually wore and was now dressed in nothing but a faded, sleeveless, navy blue vest which displayed her really superb upper works to great advantage, a short skirt and boots.

This was not the first time I had seen her in this outfit. I saw her like this almost every evening when it was fine, washing herself at the trough, together with Rita, before going inside for the evening meal, but I had always endeavoured to put her out of my mind.

This had not been as difficult as the reader might imagine. Apart from the fact that my thoughts were with Wanda, my unofficial *fidanzata*, I would not have allowed myself to even try to do what I was undoubtedly engaged in doing at this moment, if for no other reason than it would have been a gross abuse of hospitality which was being offered to me at tremendous risk and which, if it was discovered by my host and hostess and the facts were broadcast, could have a disastrous effect on the whole relationship between prisoners of war and those who were helping them. I had not even had to work this out for myself. Even before we left the *orfanotrofio* the colonel had gone to great pains to impress on us all that we must behave with the utmost punctiliousness in any dealings we had with the civilian population, and, indeed, after the prisoners made their first contact with them in the yard of the farmhouse near Fontanellato where the food and clothing depot was set up, his warning seemed superfluous. Anyone who did otherwise would have had to be possessed of a heart of stone. I myself was probably on terms of greater intimacy with Wanda than any of the other prisoners were with the girls of Fontanellato, but they were such that not even the *superiora* or her *suore* could possibly take exception to them, although I had kissed her; but even they did not know this. And at the Pian del Sotto my relationship with Rita and Dolores had been equally formal until they had begun to tease me about my *"fidanzata"*, as they insisted on calling her, and it was not only the previous day when they had begun to ask me which of them I was going to take to the dance that for a few moments I felt the atmosphere between us as we *zappa*'d away, to be charged with sexuality.

"Kiss me," she said.

I thought I had been doing so.

With all these thoughts whirling through my mind, and out again, I really kissed Dolores.

"More," she said.

She turned over until she was more or less lying on top of me which, unless I had had something like seven feet of hay under me would probably have done me an injury. Now I was drowning in long auburn hair. She smelled delicious, better than the girls in Alexandria I used to take out with their seemingly inexhaustible supply of expensive scent, a compound of herself, honest out-door sweat, which was nothing like the awful body odours of urban civilisation, wood smoke, creamy milk and clean byres, and over everything hung the sweet smell of hay and I didn't even have hay fever. The season was over. Somewhere, far off, I could hear Nero howling. What an escape I had had. Out of the frying pan into the fire.

"More," she said again. She was a great girl. In another age, when big girls were appreciated as they deserved to be, she would have been plucked from the fields to be the mistress of a king. This was the kind of girl in search of whom Saracenic pirates had put landing parties ashore and, having taken her, would have stowed her away under hatches in their galleys intact and undamaged, or more or less, to be auctioned in a Near Eastern market place and to become the principal ornament in a harem of a pasha, or even a sultan who recognised quantity and quality when he set eyes on it.

"Touch me," she said. It seemed superfluous. To me we appeared to be touching at all the points at which human beings could possibly be in contact with one another. What marvellous, strong legs she had.

"Let's go into the barn," she said, after a while. It seemed unnecessary when we were invisible to every other living thing, except for a few spiders and the doves which had come back under the eaves of the lean-to from which they had scattered in alarm and where they were now cooing sensuously, providing a sort of background music for us, where none was necessary, sunk in a couch of hay as ample and probably much more comfortable than the Great Bed of Ware.

I was spared the necessity of deciding where the next round would take place, although there was little doubt what the outcome would be, by the gong, as it were, which saved us both—in this case Agata, who had returned to the house together with Rita, burdened with washing, to find that Nero was on the loose. She, I was glad to hear, was as frightened as I had been and was now announcing the fact from within the safety of its four walls:

"AHMAANDO! EEENRICCO! DOLLORESSS! E SCAPPATO NERO!"

Although what she expected me to do about it, except take to the trees, was not clear. Even Dolores dared not turn a deaf ear to Agata. She gave me

145

one more kiss and then sat up, hitching her vest, which had got a bit disarranged, up on her shoulders. "Never mind," she said, throwing her magnificent hair back in a way which could only be described as pert, and looking like something in *La Vie Parisienne*, "You can bring me home tomorrow night, after the ball. Rita *will* be angry." And she went down over the edge of the hay like a commando scrambling on the side of an assault ship and into a landing craft, leaving me to follow and compose whatever sort of alibi I pleased.

When the time came for the girls to set off for the *ballo* the following night I still had not the slightest intention of accompanying them. Any temptation that I might have had previously to do so had been extinguished by the happenings of the previous afternoon, although there had been no difference in Dolores's behaviour towards me, nor in Rita's, which was a good sign. They were neither more nor less saucy as we *zappa*'d together and the only mention of the dance was between themselves in the *dialetto*. I think they were discussing what they should wear. I began to wonder if the events in the lean-to had never happened at all but were the product of wishful thinking or a disordered imagination, or a mixture of both.

But that evening, after supper, they both went up to change and when they returned, Dolores in a dress of flaming green, Rita in a brilliant red one, which suited her dark looks very well, both lipsticked up rather inexpertly, and with their hair arranged in an extravagant fashion, Dolores's being particularly involved and towering because she had so much of it, and they asked me if I was ready, I didn't know what to say. Armando had already gone on ahead to make his number with whoever he was taking to the dance.

I plucked up what was left of my courage, as I knew I had to, and said that I couldn't go and the reasons why which they already knew but were not interested in, and then to my surprise, Agata, who in my mind I had cast as an ugly sister who would have been glad if the whole business had collapsed, having been rather more than cool about the *ballo* up to now, said that I should go, what was the harm in it, and then when Luigi came down on her side and said that he thought that it would be safe enough ("All the other boys who are going to be there are hiding from the Germans just like you.") I had to agree, secretly pleased, although the immediate future looked extremely hazardous in more ways than one. I felt like a navigator who had left his charts behind entering a narrow strait filled with dangerous reefs.

I had already washed and shaved, too, because it was Saturday and I was wearing my own clothes. (There was time enough to explain to Luigi why it was that half the turn-up on the left leg of the trousers of the suit he had lent me was missing.) It only remained for me to take my rucksack, or rather Luigi's rucksack, which I had hung on to since that first Sunday, up to the top of the plateau and hide it; but it was a dark misty night, very wet underfoot, and when I got back to where the girls were waiting for me on the path outside the house, where Nero was making the night hideous, my boots were so thickly coated with clay that they felt as if they were soled with lead.

The girls were wearing their best coats, but they, too, wore boots and carried their dancing shoes under their arms wrapped in newspaper. Far more capable than I was of walking down the track to the Colle del Santo in the darkness, something which they had both done innumerable times, they nevertheless each put one of their arms in mine, as if to emphasise the fact that for this night at any rate they were not a couple of hardy country girls who could do anything that had to be done at the Pian del Sotto better than I could, but a pair of fragile females in need of male support and protection, and to make themselves seem even more dependant they pretended to see apparitions lurking among the trees and uttered little squeaks of terror. But not for long. After I had stumbled a few times it was they who held me up and they became as helpless with laughter as they had been when the whole business of which of them I was going to take to the dance had been discussed; and we went lurching down the hill together, making a terrible noise, like a trio of drunks.

Nevertheless, with all the laughing and joking and screaming, I began to realise that there was a difference in what was happening to my left arm which Rita was squeezing just sufficiently to show that she was there and appreciated my gallantry, but not sufficiently to encourage me to have any other thoughts about anything except keeping her upright; and my right arm which Dolores had contrived to entwine in her own so that it was like a sapling enmeshed by some giant, South American creeper. She was now enthusiastically playing a children's game called "Round and round the Garden, like a Teddy Bear", or rather the first part of it, drawing the tip of one of the fingers of her other hand round and round the palm of my own in a way which I found terribly disturbing and not evocative of the nursery at all, and at the same time chattering away innocently nineteen to the dozen with Rita which was even more rousing. I was so disturbed that my disquiet, if one can call it that, must have communicated itself to Rita and she began to give my other hand lingering squeezes which I could only describe as encouraging but, mercifully, without engaging in the operations at which Dolores was so adept and which were giving me such exquisite torments. In this state of increasing mutual excitement we descended the mountain, towards the

147

dance. At any other time I would have thought myself in heaven.

At the cross-roads at the Colle del Santo, where the shrine was—the saint would probably have fallen out of his niche if he had had any inkling of what was going through my mind—we turned right on the track which led to the village and after a few minutes came to the farmhouse from which the sound of music and laughter could be heard, although there was not a chink of light to be seen. Here, Rita banged on the door which was immediately opened and we found ourselves in the midst of the *ballo* which was already going full blast.

We were in a kitchen half as large again as the one at the Pian del Sotto and it looked even larger because most of the furniture had been removed from it. The room was brilliantly lit by a paraffin pressure-lantern. There was no fire in the hearth and there was no need of one because the number of people in the room, and the lantern which gave off an enormous glow, made it stiflingly hot.

The party consisted of about eight or nine young men and about fifteen girls, and they were all dancing, even the girls without male partners were dancing with one another. The music was provided by two elderly men sitting on a small platform made from upturned boxes working away furiously, one on a fiddle, the other with an accordion. Around the wall were a number of men and women, most of them about the same age as Luigi and Agata, and some older women, like dowagers, sitting immobile on chairs and stools. The austere room with the brilliant, hissing light, the frantic sound of the fiddle, the laughing gyrating couples and the older people disposed along the walls watching them, resembled the drawing by Phiz in *A Christmas Carol* of the dance in Mr. Fezziwig's warehouse. It was a lively, ingenuous, happy scene.

It was a great *ballo*. Nothing like the gruesome shufflings which I had learned to call dancing and to which I had grown accustomed in innumerable dark cellars in Cairo, Alexandria and Beirut, in the course of which one was expected by one's partner to talk incessantly and, if possible, wittily. Here, there was no opportunity for talking during the dances, they were too energetic, and there were no intermissions. I danced with big girls, although only one of them had anything like the unique marriage of qualities possessed by Dolores; thin girls, one or two of them mean-looking in a desirable way (Armando had arrived with one of these); normal-sized girls and small girls, some of whom were so tiny that I was so afraid of crushing their feet with my great boots that I held them at arms' length until they took offence, reminded me that they were girls and no eggshells, and drew me close to them. All, large and small, fat and thin, were marvellous dancers, better than any of the boys, better than I could ever hope to be, but they all gave me a good squeeze and expected to be squeezed back, and everyone else except the girls who were dancing together as a temporary expedient, was squeezing one another too.

When I danced with Rita she took the opportunity to holler in my ear, the only way anyone could make themselves heard in such a din, that if I would like to, I could escort her back to the Pian del Sotto after the dance (I had already danced with Dolores, which was rather like being mixed up in a whirlwind, who had also reminded me at the top of her voice that I was taking her home afterwards). Up to then with all the fun and excitement I had forgotten that I had an almost insoluble problem on my hands. Who was I going to travel with on the way back to the house? If I went with either of the two girls it would have to be Dolores who had, as it were already booked me for this purpose. Yet it was unthinkable to desert Rita in favour of one of her parents' employees. What would they say if they heard that I had left their daughter to make her own way back in the darkness. I decided that when the time came, whatever happened, the only proper course would be to take both of them together, one on one arm, the other on the other, and hope for the best. Perhaps the whole thing was an elaborate torture, a dilemma they had decided to put me into that day while they had been banging away with their *zappas* in the field, screaming with laughter at their own private jokes in the *dialetto*. Certainly the delicious time I had spent with Dolores in the hay had not been of her contriving, any more than it had been of mine and I wondered, as I whirled around the floor with them in successsion, whether Dolores had told Rita about what had happened and that they had decided to weave it into the fabric of what might very well turn out to be an involved practical joke, with Luigi and Agata and Armando all in on it and all roaring with laughter, like members of an Edwardian house party on a lawn welcoming a guest whom they had deliberately bamboozled, or a bevy of sergeants welcoming back a recruit whom they had sent out to whitewash the Last Post. Or were they both engaged in giving one another the double-cross? The combinations and permutations were almost infinite, far too numerous, anyway, to be resolved while engaged in such high jinks as we all were at this moment. And why didn't they pick on a couple of the other boys at the dance, all of whom they obviously knew, some of whom they obviously liked, and most of whom they equally obviously thoroughly enjoyed dancing with. So far as I could see there was little to choose between us. We were all equally red in the face from the heat and our exertions. It was a bit of a mystery.

On the only occasion when I stopped dancing during the evening the *padrone* of the farm and his wife introduced me to some of the grown-ups who lined the walls. Gradually, as I grasped a succession of horny male hands and the smaller but almost equally work-hardened hands of their *signoras*, looked into their friendly faces and listened to their invitations to visit their houses and drink wine with them, without anyone of them betraying even the most well-bred curiosity about who I was and where I came from, I began to realise that they only had two surnames among them; and I began to wonder what their wives' maiden names could have been before they married. Were they, too, members by birth of these two same, all-embracing clans or had they come from other villages to be married, these compact, self-sufficient, efficient-looking women.

There was wine on hand which was being dispensed in an ante-room, but the only guests who were seriously engaged in drinking it were the older men, and although some of the boys took a glass or two the majority of us drank water to assuage our raging thirsts. Drinking so much water we all had to visit the yard from time to time and when I went there myself I found a number of couples locked in fierce embrace in the drizzle, and on my way back to the house from one of these excursions I encountered Dolores, who loomed up in front of me and pinned me against a wall.

After a short interval she offered me her handkerchief to remove the lipstick which gave her mouth a pepper taste, not nearly as good as it had been in the barn.

"We'll go after the next three dances," she said.

I asked her what would happen to Rita.

"That boy with the big nose in the white pullover will look after her," she said.

But it was not to be. We went back into the room again and cut into a dance, but before it was finished I heard the word that could empty a room faster than any other, repeated again and again and again.

"*Tedeschi, Tedeschi, Tedeschi, Tedeschi.*"

The effect was of some awful kind of magic. A girl screamed. One moment the band was playing, the next there was nothing but the upturned boxes which had elevated the musicians above us. The elders moved off from the right to left through the ante-room like well-disciplined members of a theatre audience on the cry of fire. Most of the girls were already scrabbling for their coats. I still held Dolores in the attitude in which we had been on the dance floor when the music stopped. She didn't appear to be frightened, only excited, and her eyes were shining. Rita joined us. She was quite calm, too.

"Go to the wood," they said. "We'll go home. We'll be all right." And they smiled. I was proud of them, the girls from the Pian del Sotto. One or two of the others were screaming hysterically, and at the front door there was an undignified jam of boys all intent, as I was, on *sauve qui peut*. They no longer looked young and full of beans but had suddenly become shrivelled-looking and rather abject, like our guards at Fontanellato. It was not an edifying spectacle. I wondered if I appeared the same to them —after all I was more or less one of them. I only knew that although I was as intent on getting out of the house as they were I was not at all frightened. In all probability I had by now had more experience of this kind of thing than they had and unless the Germans cordoned the mountain, ruling it off in sections on the map and systematically beat each one, or used dogs, I was fairly confident that I could evade them in the woods; and I didn't think that they would ever deploy such numbers of men for such an unimportant purpose. I was really only vulnerable when in a house such as this, or if I went to sleep in the open as I had done on the day of my meeting with *Oberleutnant* Frick, which had impressed me very much.

Out in the yard I asked one of the boys who was just about to take off downhill how many *Tedeschi* there were, which was a pretty daft question to ask him because how could he know and, anyway, he had a really big *paura* and was in no mood for conversation.

"*Molti, molti,*" he said and vanished.

Molti, molti could be a brigade, a battalion, or one of those large detachments of the German Army, the equivalent of a company in the British Army, which always seemed to be under the sole command of one of their remarkable N.C.O.s who invariably seemed to be endowed with the ability and responsibility of a captain or a major; or it might be some friend of *Oberleutnant* Frick, inflamed by his lyrical descriptions of the beauty of the region, come to ask for a couple of nights' lodging, which would be nice; or there might be no one at all, which would be even nicer.

But once out on the track which led to the village there was no doubt that something pretty weird was going on in it and in some of the outlying farms also. Light was pouring from unshuttered windows which was both unusual and illegal; hoarse, outlandish voices could be heard which might by some stretch of the imagination be identified as German and along the path from the village to the house in which we had been dancing, torches were flashing, things none of the locals possessed or, if they did, never used. Whoever was wielding them would be here in a couple of minutes; and I set off for home, which was now the place where I had left my rucksack in the wood at the top end of the Pian del Sotto (Thank God that I had remembered to do so before going to the dance!); and now that it was raining I wished that I had made the hole deeper and long enough to sleep in. I knew that I would never be able to go back to the house again. Perhaps the Germans were already there.

There was no difficulty about getting to it. It would have been madness to use the path up over the Colle del Santo by which we had come down; and it was a very long way round anyway. The shortest route was across the track, over a low wooden fence and into the meadows which had been deep in grass and clover when I had first arrived at the Pian del Sotto with Signor Zanoni and had remained so until the previous week when they had been cut by a band of women armed with reaping hooks, some of whom had waved to me whenever I appeared at the edge of the cliff to discharge my loads of stones, effectively destroying any last illusions I might have that I was living in secrecy. And this was the way I went, with a hullabaloo breaking out behind me when the men with the torches reached the farm, and soon I reached the foot of the landslip where the thousands of stones lay which were a proof of my labours.

The next part was difficult; it would have been impossible if the weather had been dry. The cliff was clay, like the fields above, and when it was dry it was as hard and slippery as stone; but the face of it was scoured with gullies and now with the light rain that had been falling for some hours it was just sufficiently soft to kick steps in, and after a hard, filthy climb I reached the edge of the Pian del Sotto.

The enemy had already arrived at the house. Normally from the outside like a tomb at night, it was now illuminated by a couple of portable spotlights which also showed up a little knot of men standing in the rain who were wearing the same sort of caps with long peaks that *Oberleutnant* Frick had done. Nero was silent. Fearful for the safety of Luigi and Agata, and hoping that the Germans would not take it into their heads to shine the light along the plateau, I walked across it as quickly as I could and into the wood where my rucksack was hidden.

After what seemed a long while I saw the men pick up the lights and go off in the direction of the Colle del Santo. The next hour or two seemed an eternity. I was in anguish at what might have happened to Luigi and Agata. So far as I knew they were the only people in the area who had been sheltering an escaped prisoner and therefore the only ones who were actually liable to be shot for doing so. Perhaps they had been shot and had been left in the house as an example. The fact that Nero made no sound was particularly sinister. And I was very worried about Rita and Dolores on their way up from the Colle. They had had the intention of returning to the farm and even if they had not arrived before the raiding party had left, they would almost certainly have run into it on their way up to it from the Colle. It was also impossible to know what was going on down at the farm where the the the dance had been held, and in the village, because they were both out of sight below the cliff and I did not dare to take the risk of crossing the plateau again in order to look down on them.

What I really wanted to do was to go to the house; but this was also much too risky. The Germans might have left an ambush inside it to wait for me. There was nothing to do but stare into the rain and darkness and wait, and with the intention of doing this I put on my thick pullover, slung a sack over my shoulders and squatted down on my haunches.

I must have dozed off because the next thing I remember was being shaken awake, shivering. It was Luigi.

"Drink this," he said, handing me something which felt like a medicine bottle as if I was some elderly aunt who had come over poorly. "It's *grappa*."

I took a couple of huge swigs and felt better.

"We're all alive and we're all at the house, except Armando, and they haven't got him, and they won't," Luigi said. "This was a big rake-up. (He called it a *rastrellamento*.) There were a lot of them but nobody knows how many. They went up the ridge behind the village and then down into it from the back, and took everyone by surprise. That was the main lot. The rest came straight here, about a dozen, up over the Colle from the mill by Zanoni's place. They knew exactly what they were after, an English officer, someone must have told them, a spy.

"At first, when they didn't find you, they were very angry. They had an Italian with them who spoke their language and asked us their questions and gave them our answers, but then they began to think that whoever had given them the information must have been wrong and they became more angry with him, whoever he was, than they were with us.

"That would be good, if they shot him," he said.

"The one thing they wanted to know was why, if only four people had been sleeping in the house, there were two other beds that had been slept in. This was a difficult question for me to answer but Agata told them that Dolores, who sleeps with Rita, had had a fever and had been put to sleep in the upstairs room. They grumbled a lot and then they went away. They forgot about the other bed."

"What worried us then was what would happen if they met the girls on the road and found out that it wasn't true about Dolores having had a fever and sleeping upstairs. Luckily, they had just got to the wood above the Colle when they heard the *Tedeschi* coming down and they hid until I went and found them."

"What happened to Nero?" I said. "I didn't hear him bark."

"When the *Tedeschi* came I was in the yard. They shone their lights on my face and for a while I couldn't see anything. Nero was barking and I thought it must be you, come back from the ball, and playing some sort of joke." At this point I tried to imagine myself or the girls playing some kind of joke on Luigi with floodlights. "Then I saw that they were *Tedeschi* and Nero went for them, just as he does for everyone.

"There was one very big *Tedesco* who was in command, a sort of *sergente-maggiore* I would think, and he went towards Nero and I thought he was going to shoot him because he had a pistol in his hand; but, instead, he shouted at him in his own languge which sounds a very angry sort of language, and Nero ran away and went into his kennel and he hasn't moved from it since. I wish I knew what he said to him."

So Nero was yellow and a bully into the bargain. I, too, would have liked to have known what it was he said to him. It would have made things easier for me on the Pian del Sotto; but it was too late now. I could never go back.

"But if the *Tedeschi* knew that I was living in the house why did they bother to go to the village?" I asked.

"Because they wanted to catch our boys. They're all soldiers who ran away from their regiments after the eighth of September. They were ordered to report weeks ago; but none of them did. The *Tedeschi* were afraid that they might start a *banda* up here. That's why they wanted you, too. Luckily, almost all of them were at the ball."

From what I had seen of the boys when they were struggling to get out of the door at the farm, there was not much danger of any of them starting up a band of partisans, as least not yet. I asked him how many they had taken.

"Three, I think," he said. "Two from the village, one from the dance. They didn't get Armando."

I had never heard him talk so much the whole time I had been at the Pian del Sotto.

"While they were upstairs searching, all except one who stood over us with a machine-gun, the Italian who spoke *Tedesco* told us that it was the *segretario* of the commune who had put them up to it. He's a great Fascist, the *segretario*. It was one of his spies who found out about you. The Italian was only the clerk from the *municipio*. He was as frightened as we were. The rest I learned when I went down to the village later."

"What will happen now to the boys who weren't captured?" I said.

"They'll stay out in the woods tonight, just as you are doing, and if it's all clear tomorrow they'll go back to where they were before. Armando should be back tomorrow; but I think that it would be very dangerous for you," he said, apologetically. "You see, I have to think of the safety of the others."

I told him that I had no intention of returning. So far as I was concerned he had done enough for one war.

"I thought you might not want to," he said. "And because I was afraid that something like this might happen, I went to see a relative of ours, Agata's brother-in-law, two days ago, the day Nero broke his chain, when I was up on the mountain seeing about the wood. He's a shepherd and he's got a lot of sheep up there on the mountain and he's been living

154

up there all the summer. His name's Abramo. He'll be bringing the animals down to his place almost any time now, as soon as the weather breaks; but I told him about you and he said that if you were in trouble he would be glad to look after you for a bit. No one sees him for weeks at a time and no one ever really knows where he is because he has several huts in different places and he moves the animals about a lot. At the moment he's at a place called the Castello del Prato and you should start out early tomorrow morning for it, as soon as it's getting light. He's got plenty of food up there. Now I'll tell you how to get there. It's high up, the Castello del Prato."

He had been arranging all this for me while I had been tumbling in the hay with Dolores. I was glad that he couldn't see my face in the darkness.

The directions were easy to follow. I had to go up by the same route through the woods that I had followed the day I met *Oberleutnant* Frick, and when I got on to the open downs where the yew trees were, instead of turning left, I had to continue up over them. In this way I would eventually come out on the edge of the cliff at a place where there were some prominent rocks and a small beech wood. This was the Castello del Prato and, according to Luigi, it was about half an hour's climb from the top of the wood.

He had brought me some bread and sausage and a small flask of wine. If I needed water during the night I could get it from the spring on the edge of the wood above the house. "But watch out," he said. "There could be an ambush, though I don't think so. The *Tedeschi* were all very wet and looking forward to getting home, that's what the Italian said."

"We shall miss you," he said. "Agata and the girls have been crying and the girls wanted to come here with me but I wouldn't allow it."

It was difficult to imagine Agata crying and I felt awful being the instrument which had caused her and the girls to do so. At this moment I felt like having a good cry myself.

"Give them all my love," I said. It sounded wrong in Italian. "And thank the signora for everything."

"They thought you would like to have this," he said, fishing around in a pocket of his suit. Although I could only see him in outline and it was raining, I was sure that it was as clean and unmuddled as it always was, "The *Barba-Nera*. You always seemed to enjoy reading it. And I've brought you the clothes you worked in. I thought they might be useful."

"You've torn the trousers," he said severely. "That's a good suit, that is. How did you do it?" He sounded like my father.

"It was Nero."

"I'm going to get rid of Nero."

"Good idea, much too savage," I said.

"Savage!" he said. "Since the *Tedesco* spoke to him he hasn't moved from his kennel. I'm going to shoot him as soon as I can get a real, hard dog. I know where there is one."

This was the old Luigi I knew.

"Lucky you finished the stones before all this happened," he said. "Otherwise we would have had to have done it ourselves." He shook hands with me and went away.

Chapter Thirteen

Interlude in Cloud-Cuckoo-Land

It must have been about an hour after sunrise the following morning when I emerged from the forest on to the downs where the yew trees grew; but there was no sun and therefore no way of knowing. It was one of those days, which were becoming more frequent now, when everything was swaddled in thick, grey cloud and in the forest it lay even thicker so that going up through it I had the feeling that I was swimming in cold gruel. The forest was no longer the arcadian place it had been on that first Sunday of my day off. Now the tunnels under the trees were as dank and vaporous and foetid as the passages in a workhouse, and everything had an air of decay. The moss which had been so brilliantly green now had a dull, brownish tinge and gave off a disagreeable, sickly smell; and the fungi which had appeared so beautiful and strange with the sun slanting down on them, now seemed positively evil, the fruits of corruption, even the ones that I knew to be edible because, having eaten them, I was still alive. Now after the rain, there were fresh, and to me even more monstrous-looking growths, although, no doubt, they were edible too, enormous puff balls, which had emerged in the clearings of the charcoal burners, the size and shape of human skulls, some of them dead white as if they had been picked clean by birds on a battle field and left for ages in the sun and the rain, some darker, the colour of old ivory; and where a number of them grew together it was as if the buried dead were trying to resurrect themselves by forcing themselves, head first upwards through the earth.

Spiralling slowly up through the tunnels, passing over these long deserted platforms of the *carbonari*, I felt myself to have no past; even the time I had spent at the Pian del Sotto seemed gone beyond recall; and equally, there seemed no future either that I could look forward to with any hope or pleasure. I was on my way to meet a shepherd, a *pastore* called Abramo, who might be brave enough and kind enough to let me stay with him for a day or a week, and he probably would be, but then something would happen, as it had always done, to force me to move on;

and eventually it would end, as Luigi said it would, when the snow fell and there were no more leaves in the forests to hide beneath, and they would come and take me away. And a damn good thing it would be for everyone.

Instead of climbing the mountain to the west this morning, I should have been heading south-east towards the line and my own people. It was my duty to do so but something had happened to me during the last weeks, had crept up on me slyly without my realising it. I had become part of a stable way of life which I had no right to do, and in doing so I had lost an essential part of whatever courage and will-power I possessed previously, and of the capacity to make decisions, qualities which were essential if I was to survive. Certainly, I had already experienced some of these sombre feelings, what now seemed so long ago, that afternoon when I had left the house of the Baruffas and taken the track up the valley to Signor Zanoni's, but even then, in the depths of my despair and loneliness, there had been a small, residual flame of hope kept alive by the knowledge that there was some sort of plan of which I was at least a part.

But now two of the masters of it were in prison and the only one who was still free was engaged in trying to save them and, even if she had not been, now lacked the means to do anything. She was even more hemmed in than I was. I had been a fool and a selfish one to allow them to endanger themselves on my behalf, all the time protesting, hypocritically, against them doing so but always allowing them to go on, until two of them had paid the penalty and the other might very well do so, if she had not done so already. And when I thought of that I remembered what had happened in the hay at the Pian del Sotto, nothing that I had been brought up to think of as "really bad", but bad enough in its context, and no less heartless because it was unthinking, something which, like all the other English, I could say "sorry" for and by doing so consider myself absolved. I was no better than the man who had allowed his diary to be captured with him, who had also chased girls.

But when I came out on the downs, although I could not rid myself of this feeling of guilt which by now stemmed from so many different roots that it could never be eradicated and never be forgotten, my spirits, which could not have been lower, rose a little. The feeling of claustrophobia produced by the forest lifted, and the weariness brought on by the long night vigil fell away. The cloud was thick but there was a hugeness here on the side of the open mountain with only an occasional yew tree looming up before me, that buoyed me up and set me on my way upwards, bearing away slightly to the left so that eventually I would reach the edge of the cliff and not miss the place where the shepherd was. Soon there were no more yews and I was moving in a void with nothing visible in it except the grass immediately beneath my feet. It was as I imagined the first day of the Creation must have been when the earth was without form; but at least there was light now after darkness and as I drifted rather than walked uphill, as if I was a disembodied spirit, I felt less lost than I had done in that awful wood.

Now I came to the edge of the cliff and for the first time that day heard the clanking of sheep bells just as I had heard them coming from the same direction on that other Sunday. Here, the uniform grey nothingness of the cloud through which I had been climbing was torn apart by a violent wind that was funnelling up the gullies so that the whole face of the cliff and the trees that clung to it here seemed to be smoking, as if it was part of the rim of some immense volcano that was once again becoming active after years of lying dormant, and the forest which had grown up the side of the crater since the last eruption had taken fire and was smouldering until so much of its sap was consumed that it would explode into flame.

At first I could only hear the clanking of the sheep bells; but then after some minutes I began to hear the animals bleating. Sometimes it seemed as if they were very near but then the sound of bells and bleating receded again, and once or twice they ceased completely, as if the entire flock had plunged over the edge of the cliff; and then there was silence except for the noise of the wind which all the time was growing stronger, and I felt that I would never reach the Castello del Prato where the shepherd and his flock were supposed to be. The accession of energy that had come to me when I left the wood had passed away now and I felt weak and light-headed and once I slipped and fell and remained where I was for some time on the wet ground without any will to go on.

But then, suddenly, I was among the flock. They were tall, long-legged, black and dun-coloured creatures, nothing like our own hill sheep and, in my light-headed state, I thought at first that they were goats. Dogs were barking furiously now, somewhere close by and straight ahead, and then I heard a voice shouting at them to be silent, and unlike Nero they obeyed it.

I had arrived. It was a terribly windy place on the edge of the cliff where a little wood of dwarf beeches grew. Nearby, there was an outcrop of rocks, like a miniature tor, except that they were jagged. They formed a circle with a gently sloping amphitheatre of grass inside it, or what had been grass, but was now all churned up by the sheep, and the gaps between them had been closed with hurdles to form a large, natural pen in which the animals were folded at night. This was what Luigi had called the Castello del Prato. The Castle of the Meadow.

The shepherd was standing in the doorway of his hut which was just inside the wood. The walls were of wattle and the roof was covered with branches and turf. A fire was burning inside it and the smoke was blowing about in the doorway. He was dressed in a long, hooded robe made of black and white sheepskins with the fleece on the outside, which reached almost to his ankles, and the shoulders were so huge that, with it on from the front, he looked as if he was in a sarcophagus that had been stood on end. On his feet he wore home-made sheepskin boots with the fleece on the inside. At his feet were a couple of sheep dogs with their tongues hanging out. They were looking up at him hopefully, waiting for him to give the signal which would set them at my throat. Altogether, they were a wild, outlandish bunch.

He was a big tall man with a mottled, red face and eyes that were all bloodshot, and when I first saw him I thought he must be a heavy drinker. Perhaps he was, but the redness of his face was not due to the bottle but because it had been exposed year after year to the wind—and it was certainly windy here—and his eyes were red and watery, because of the smoke which no chimney, however well-designed, could cope with in such a place.

Then he smiled and his face was transformed under the thick, black eyebrows which had given him a lowering expression, as if he was a bull about to charge. It was like watching the sun rise after a stormy dawn. Then he came towards me and held out a great hand that was so large and hard that I felt as if I was grasping the hand of a statue, rather than that of a human being, except that he was pumping it up and down vigorously in a way that no statue could, saying at the same time, or rather bellowing against the wind in a voice that was used to annihilate distance but sounded as if it was rarely used to address other human beings, which was scarcely surprising, "You must be Enrico, the English. You can call me Abramo. I was expecting you, but not so soon. Luigi was up here and told me about you and I've been worried. I have to go down in a few days' time and there was no way of letting you know that I'd be moving. I can't leave the flock, you see. But, anyway, you're here, and welcome to my *castello* and my *palazzo*." He indicated them both with an ironic gesture of the hand.

"Well, what goes on at the Pian del Sotto?" he said. "Have you run away? I bet old Agata didn't give you much to eat. I'm married to her sister, you know, but she doesn't try anything like that with me."

I told him in a few disjointed sentences, and when I had finished he looked at me closely.

"You don't look too good," he said.

I was not feeling well at all. Standing here, outside the hut, in the streaming

160

wind, any warmth that I had gained while climbing the mountain had already gone completely. Strong as it was the wind was too damp to dry my clothes which had been wet since the previous night, and although I had a sack over my shoulders it was no protection now that it too was soaked through. I was shivering violently and my stomach felt as if it was filled with ice.

"Inside," he said. And bundled me through the door.

The interior of the hut, which he called his *baracca*, was warm and snug but the transition from the outside, which smelled far less of sheep than the interior, was too much for me. I felt everything going round, and the next thing I remember was sitting on the edge of a rough bed with my head down between my knees and being given a battered old mug half full of some colourless liquid.

"Drink," he said, and I drank.

It was as strong as the *grappa* Luigi had given me the previous night—nothing I could imagine, not even army rum, could be much stronger than that had been—but it had a different taste, something I seemed to remember having once drunk but couldn't put a name to in my present state. The strength of it, and the taste, made me throw my head back, shuddering.

"Drink it all," he said. "It'll do you good. It's good stuff (*Roba buona, fatto con grano e ginepro*, was how he described it). I make it myself with the apparatus down there," and he pointed in the direction of the edge of the cliff.

I drank it. Grain and juniper berries was what he had said. Of course, that was what it was, gin, the sort the Dutch drank; but much stronger than the Hollands in an earthenware bottle which my father kept for years at home and which nobody ever touched. I had only tried it once and disliked it. It was good now.

Then I began to feel bad again. I remember Abramo helping me to take off my wet clothes and putting me into an immensely thick shirt, then lying down on the bed which was covered with sheepskins and having more piled on top of me, and then nothing much more at all for what seemed a long time.

I must have had a temperature because I remember being wet through and Abramo changing my shirt for another of the same sort, and this happened several times and I remember asking for cold water, because I had an insatiable thirst, but he would only give me warm water, although I begged him for cold.

"Bad for your stomach, cold water," he said.

Sometimes he brought me a disagreeable, bitter infusion made with some sort of moss which he told me he gathered on the mountainside and which, like all such infusions, do the patient good because they are bitter and disagreeable. Abramo was like an alchemist. Later, when I was better, he told me he used to bathe his eyes with something he called *erba per gli occhi*, the plant for the eyes, one which had blue flowers and which, long, long afterwards I found out was something call *Euphrasia*. Abramo was one of the gentlest men I have ever met, in spite of his stony hands, and being nursed by him I felt as if I was one of his lambs. The only other thing I can remember about this time was the howling of the wind, which seemed to go on and on, and the smoke.

On the morning of the third day I woke not only better, but cured, although I felt a bit weak; and, for the first time I was able to take notice of my surroundings. It was very early but Abramo was already out, perhaps he stayed out all night guarding his sheep, I had no way of knowing, and I could see through the open door that it was a beautiful, still morning.

The *baracca* was not more than ten feet square and the two beds, one of which I was occupying, were made with the trunks of young trees and the mattresses were boughs with the leaves still on them, dead and browned by the heat of the fire. On top of them were sheepskins sewn together, some to sleep on, others to be used as covers, all of which gave off a powerful odour of sheep, which was scarcely surprising. In one corner of the hut there was a raised fireplace with a pot-hook over it from which a large copper vessel hung down over some red-hot embers. Its contents were simmering gently and from it there came a delicious smell. Above the fire there was a rudimentary chimney, made of flat stones with the joints between them filled with earth. The door was made of the same material as the walls, closely woven wattle.

Hanging on pegs above his bed was Abramo's shot-gun, a sheepskin coat similar to the one which he had been wearing and an equally long, bright green canvas coat, for wet weather, which also had a hood and a series of capes over the shoulders which, he told me, his father had acquired when he had worked as a shepherd in southern France, after the first war. Besides the fire the only illumination was provided by a candle lantern. The candles he made himself with tallow rendered from the fat of the sheep.

After a while he returned.

"You're better," he said. "I knew you would be. That's why I've got something special for you to eat," and he began ladling the contents of the pot into a couple of old army mess tins.

"I shot a hare a couple of days before you came, but I get tired of

162

eating them by myself," he said handing me one of the tins, together with a primitive wooden spoon and a slice of *polenta*.

I had never eaten anything like this stew before and I never have since. The hare had been cooked with herbs and fungi and the gravy had been made with the entrails, and was so thick that long before I got to the bottom of my can it had congealed into a delicious jelly. There was no question of requiring a second helping, each can held the best part of one and a half pints; and when I had finished he gave me an entire cheese, the size and shape of a round, two-ounce tobacco tin, which he himself had made, using the milk of the ewes. Up here, apart from salt and the maize flour, which he used to make the *polenta*, which he ate instead of bread, and roasted as a substitute for coffee, he was completely self-sufficient. He told me he didn't drink wine, it was too complicated to get it. It was bad enough now getting the grain for his illicit still, out of which he did very well, selling the drink to the local farmers.

"It's those shirts that saved you," he said, when I was admiring the great, thick shirt of cream-coloured flannel with red stitches which looked as if it had come out of a folk museum and which I was wearing.

"They belonged to my great great-grandfather. The wool came from the backs of his own sheep and my great great-grandmother spun it and wove it and then she made the shirts. I'm fifty, my father was eighty-seven when he died and my grandfather was over ninety. I don't know how old my great grandfather was when he died, all I know is these shirts are very, very old, perhaps they're the oldest shirts in the world that anyone is still wearing, and they've been worn by all the men in our family, but not every day you understand. We used them when we came home cold, and when we were in a fever. I always put one on and have a sweat when I am feeling bad. You have to sweat when you're ill, that's the way."

I was hopeless at such calculations but it seemed to me, if what Abramo said was true, and there was no reason to doubt him, that the shirts in which I had been sweating out my own fever must have been made somewhere in the latter half of the eighteenth century, almost certainly before the French Revolution. Yet the quality of the material was so extraordinary that they were in good enough condition to be not more than five years old and to last another hundred.

Later, when I got dressed, Abramo made me wrap myself in one of his sheepskin coats and left me in the sun. "You're lucky," he said, "that it's a finé day. It's been blowing a gale ever since you came. You were in the best place."

Then he told me that when he took the sheep down to their winter quarters I could go with him. His farm was somewhere on the far side of one of the ridges which led up to the summit of the mountain from the north-west, and his wife and daughters ran it during the summer when he was up on the mountain with the sheep. His only son was in Russia, with the Alpini, and, like the rest of them, had not been heard of.

"You'll be as safe with us as you will with anyone," he said, "although that's not saying much. There's no hurry. You can make up your mind in the next day or two."

But there was no need for me to make up my mind. It was done for me. Towards evening, when the sun was already beginning to sink behind the main range, something which I had not seen in all the weeks that I had lived on the mountain, a small boy arrived at the *baracca* with some mysterious news which he communicated to Abramo who in turn gave it to me.

"You are to go down to the village," he said. "An important decision has been made and I do not think that you will return, but if you do I shall be here for two days more, and my house is called La Maesta; but if you want to come tell no one at all. I will explain how to get to it."

And he did.

We set off immediately. The little boy was not more than eight years old, but he was as agile as a flea. Far too agile for me at this moment, as weak as a jelly and encumbered with my rucksack. He took me down along the edge of the cliff, hopping and skipping in front of me, and occasionally waiting for me to catch up in a way which I found rather galling, as if I was an aged relative whom he had taken out for an airing. He was a strange, very self-possessed, solemn little boy with a cropped head which looked as if it was covered in brown velvet. He never spoke.

In what must have been about a quarter of the time it had taken me to climb to the Castello, we were at the edge of the woods, where I had met *Oberleutnant* Frick. The next part was slower. It was getting dark now; and we came to a place where there were what appeared to be a series of smaller cliffs one above the other, a labyrinth without any visible tracks in it, and I was glad to see that in this difficult terrain even this super-boy had difficulty; but eventually we emerged from it on to a long, bare slope of rock which led steeply downwards away from the cliff edge and here he recovered his speed and went racing down it in front of me. Soon the rock ended and we were on scree, and he went glissading down this in much the same way as one of the Indian Army officers in the *orfanotrofio* told me that he and his men used to tear down the steep sides of the ravines on the North-West Frontier when they were withdrawing from an outlying picket in order to escape ritual mutilation by the oncoming Pathans.

Here, under the ridge, there was no wind and the smoke from the village, which was now just visible immediately below us in the dusk, sank down into the dark gulfs between the houses which were its streets and passages. And when we reached the bottom of the slope the little boy turned to me and spoke the only words he had uttered during the entire journey, except when he was talking to himself, which he did pretty incessantly when he was trying to work out what was the best way round some insurmountable rock.

"*Ecco, il paese!*" he said.

We were at the back of the village. This was the way the Germans had come down into it. The dogs were barking furiously now, just as they must have barked that night to no avail, dozens of Neros. Had Luigi really shot him? We went into it under an archway and down a narrow, cobbled alley as rough as a mountain track between tall houses and past the open doors of *stalle* from which came the smells and snuffling sounds of animals. The air in these lanes was thick with the smoke that had sunk down into them from above. It was more like the East than Europe. If London was *la cité d'la fumarassa* what did the inhabitants think this was? Finally, the little boy stopped outside a stone doorway on which I could feel but not see some sort of carving. Then he knocked twice and said "Pierino", the door opened and I followed him in.

As usual, I found myself in a kitchen, but a more ancient and splendid kitchen than any I had ever been in. The house itself was medieval; the owners people who wanted it to be like that. Sitting around a really massive table that looked as old as the house there were six men, five of whom, the ones who had their hats on, I recognised as those I had met at the dance who, between them, shared only two surnames. They were all hard, lean men. The fifth was very different. He was fat and he wore square horn-rimmed spectacles. His hair was *en brosse*, like the *maestro's*, but though he wore country clothes he didn't look like a real countryman. The effect produced by the whole lot of them looking down the long table towards me where I stood, a ruinous figure by the door, was of some sort of Selection Board; but what they were selecting it was difficult to imagine.

There were a number of wine bottles on the table and each man had a charged glass in front of him. The little boy withdrew. I was motioned to take a seat and a glass of wine was poured for me. There was no small talk. The Chairman of the Board, for that was obviously what he was, said carefully and very slowly so that I could understand, "We have been talking about you among ourselves for some days. Many of the people in this village and in the farms round about have sons and relatives who are being hunted by the Germans. Three of them were taken the other day. Some of them have sons in Russia of whom, so far, there is no news and who may never return. They feel that you are in a similar condition to that of their sons who, they hope, are being given help wherever they are, and they think that it is their duty to help you through the coming winter, which otherwise you will not survive. I speak for them because my father was born here, and they have asked me to do so. And as it has now become too dangerous to shelter you in their houses, they have decided to build you a house which no one except the people assembled in this room, our families and one other person, and he is a kinsman, will ever hear about. The work will begin at dawn tomorrow."

Chapter Fourteen

A cave of one's own

We left the house singly at half past four the following morning, after drinking acorn coffee with *grappa* in it. I had a terrible hang-over. After a marvellous dinner prepared by the elegant wife of the mysterious chairman, during which I had complimented her on the excellent mud she had produced, confusing the word for mushroom *fungo* with *fango*, which had put everyone in high good humour, the five of them had settled down to a carouse, in which I had been invited to join, as a result of which I had slept soundly in a *stalla*.

We met at the foot of the scree where I was sick and then felt better. Each of us was carrying one or more of the implements that would be needed, picks, spades, a saw, a felling axe. A mule carried the rest of the heavy gear lashed on either side of a pack saddle; crowbars, a sledge-hammer, provisions, and the most impossible thing of all for human beings to carry through a forest, two pieces of corrugated iron which had been specially bought in one of the bigger villages down in the valley.

The mule made light of the weight it was carrying, perhaps because it was a small load for a mule. Full of energy at this awful hour, it went up the screes and slabs at a good three miles an hour. Reluctantly, the Chairman of the Board had remained behind. It was obvious that he was not a fit man and would have to content himself with spinning the webs in which we were all enmeshed and contemplating the results of having spun them, just like a real chairman, behind an uncluttered desk.

By the time we reached the ridge the cocks in the village were beginning to crow and soon first light began to seep through the trees. It was a melancholy morning with a soft, penetrating rain falling. The route we followed was more or less the same one that the small boy, Pierino, had used when he had brought me down the mountain the previous evening, in reverse: except that these men knew it better than he did and avoided some of the more difficult obstacles; and quite soon we reached the place where the small cliffs were, and here we halted and I was left alone with the mule while the others went off in various directions to look for a suitable site.

Finally, one of them beckoned to the others who joined him and they stood together for some time pointing and talking until, at last, they summoned me to join them too.

"This is the place where it will be," the man who had chosen it said. He was a tall, lean, handsome man with long white hair, a nose like an eagle's beak and quick, unstudied movements, very much like those of the small boy, Pierino. It was obvious that he was the one who was in overall command of the operations in the field. His name was Francesco.

The place which had been agreed on was in one of the clefts between the cliffs and it was a good one for the purpose. No one in their senses would try to force a way through it, and if they did they would get nowhere. It was a cul-de-sac filled with trees. The only thing I could see against it was that once the leaves were gone any sort of hut standing in it would be conspicuous; but I had not taken into consideration the ingenuity of these mountain men.

First they dug out a number of trees by the roots from the bottom of the ditch. When I say "they" I have to include myself in a minor way because I, too, was allowed to work under supervision. Then they dug a trench, piling up the spoil about ten feet away from the innermost cliff and parallel to it, except at the ends where it curved in to meet it. This took much longer than they thought because while they were digging it they uncovered a perfectly enormous rock, much bigger than anything I had ever met with on the Pian del Sotto. They had a long discussion about this rock, whether or not they should abandon the site and start again somewhere else, but they decided to continue as it would be impossible to cover up the traces of their work. So they dug around it until it was almost free and then the most vigorous of them hit it with a sledgehammer many times without any result, and then they had a *merenda*, during which we ate bread and sausage and drank wine with the soft, very wetting rain falling on us. Listening to them I gathered that they had more or less decided to light a fire over it and try to split it with cold water; but they seemed to be waiting for someone else to arrive whose opinion they respected.

Then, as if he had been waiting for his cue, an old man appeared on the cliff above us and looked down rather critically on the party assembled below. He carried a long-barrelled hammer-gun, similar to Abramo's, although it was now strictly forbidden to possess any kind of firearms, and he held one of the green umbrellas over his head. He was accompanied by a long, lean, good-looking dog which had a coat which looked like tortoise-shell, and after he had drunk some wine they showed him the rock. His name was Bartolomeo.

He went over it with his hands, very slowly, almost lovingly. It must have weighed half a ton. Then, when he had finished caressing it, he called for a sledgehammer and hit it deliberately but not particularly hard and it broke into two almost equal halves. It was like magic and I would not have been surprised if a toad had emerged from it and turned into a beautiful princess who had been asleep for a million years. Even the others were impressed. There was no need to ask what this old man's profession had been. Although he looked like a man of the woods he must have spent some part of his life either working in a quarry, or as a stone-mason.

The rest was easy. He gave the two immense halves a few more light taps and they broke into movable pieces. Then he produced a smaller hammer from a bag and for the remainder of the time he was with us, except when he was making a chimney for the hut which he did by cutting a deep groove in the face of the cliff, he knapped these pieces into small blocks which he used to build a dry-stone wall on the inner side of the earthwork which had been made with the spoil from the trench.

While he was working away the rest of the party got on with their own tasks. Using the trunks of the trees which they had cut down two of them made an immensely strong framework to support the roof. To me it seemed unnecessarily robust; but at this stage I still thought that they were building a conventional hut. Then, before they put it on, they waited for the other two to finish their jobs. One was making a couple of beds inside the hut, the other was stacking a big mule-load of firewood inside it. When the beds were finished and the fuel was in they put the framework of the roof on: the upper end was embedded in the cliff, the lower end rested on the wall Bartolomeo had made on the inner side of the rampart and when this was done they wired the corrugated iron on to it and covered the whole thing with a thick layer of earth and stones and moss all the way down from the cliff to the ground so that, when it was finished, it looked from any angle like an old overgrown rock fall and it was so well-covered that when we jumped down on to it from the top of the cliff it gave off a solid sound and was completely immovable. The entrance was hidden under the roots of a beech tree which grew out of the side of the cliff, and when a piece of old sacking was draped over it, because of the angle of the wall it was completely invisible.

Late in the afternoon, when the work was almost finished, the wives of three of the men who had been building the hut arrived. On their backs they carried pack-baskets of plaited willow loaded with rice, which was priceless and had been bought on the black market, salt, cheese, bread, acorn coffee and cooking and eating utensils, enough for two persons.

"In case you want to get married, that's why they've made two beds," one of them said, and the three of them had a good laugh at this.

When all this stuff had been stowed away inside the hut the men lit a fire in the new fireplace and when he saw that it drew well and didn't smoke Bartolomeo went off with his dog without saying a word to anyone.

Then they showed me how to work the fire so that it wouldn't smoke me out, and they told me that I shouldn't light it in the daylight until the weather got really cold, except to make coffee in the early morning. They showed me how to conceal the hole at the top of the chimney with a special stone when the fire wasn't alight and they showed me where I could get water, by going through the labyrinth and then down over the cliff edge a hundred and fifty feet or so, to a place where a little spring issued from the rocks, which, they said, no one used anymore. And they told me how important it was to cover my tracks when returning to the hut—the last thing that they themselves did was to pick up every chip of wood—every small piece of wire that had been left over from the building operations, and all the match sticks they had dropped. No one threw away cigarette ends at this stage of the war.

Then we all went into the cave, for that is what I had decided to call it, and they blew up the fire and we drank some wine together. And then they told me that only they themselves or their parents or their children would visit me with supplies, and that so that I would know that they were members of one or other of these two families, they would give us a password and this would be *Brindisi*. In this way, Francesco, the man with the eagle nose, said they hoped to prevent the news that I was still in the neighbourhood from spreading. "*Ma!*" Someone said doubtfully. "*Speriamo*," they all said and the women crossed themselves.

Owls were beginning to hoot in the forest now. They picked up their instruments, the mule was already loaded, and then they wished me good luck and told me not to stay in the hut all day or I would become *triste* but to take care; and then they went away together down the mountain and I was left alone in the dwelling in which I was to pass the winter—the final refuge, and the triumphal artifact, of the men of the mountains.

The day on which I took up residence in my cave was the twenty-seventh of October, a Wednesday. And for the next week the weather was wonderful, each day seeming more beautiful than the one before, as the leaves turned, quickly now, from green to gold. They were days with the same, unforgettable loveliness that I remembered from the year before when I had been a prisoner in the barracks in Rome, and had watched the horses being put through their paces on the tan. The days were warm, and although the nights were cooler now the air still had a feeling of the south and the sky was for the most part cloudless and ablaze with stars. Only in the very early mornings was it really chilly.

In the course of them I forgot how evil the forest had seemed. It had reverted to its arcadian state, only now that the ploughing was finished and the sowing was done, it was filled with entire families out woodcutting, and the noise they made as they called to one another while they worked, and the din made by the great, loaded sledges as they crashed downhill through the tunnels, or were dragged up through them, with the drivers Olaing to encourage the beasts was positively deafening in this otherwise quiet place. For me it was a good thing that they did make a noise, otherwise I would certainly have stumbled on some of them unawares, and although they would almost certainly have been pleased to see me if I had done so, the whole point of the plan was that it had been given out that I had left the district.

In fact, it became a sort of game which helped to pass the time—to get as close to them as possible without being seen, and also avoiding the *fungaia*, whose owner I had no desire to meet. And in playing it I discovered a whole subsidiary network of very small paths which, except where they crossed them, some of them being no more than eighteen inches wide and mostly overgrown, were independent of the tunnels, so that a map of the mountain on a scale large enough to include them—and such a map never could be made—would have shown the whole of the wooded part of it covered with innumerable small veins, as well as the large main arteries.

Using these minute tracks I made long excursions through the woods, and one day I came out on a long, bare ridge of the mountain which ran north and south and from it I looked down on a large village. And I realised then that this must be the lair of the *segretario* who was so keen on catching me. I thought how excited he would have been if he had known that I was so close, although it was difficult to understand why he should be so interested in harassing a single prisoner of war.

On the way back from this excursion I heard, just below me in one of the tunnels, the voices of what seemed to be the entire party from the Pian del Sotto. For once they were not quarrelling, but talking to one another for the sheer pleasure of it; but still at the tops of their voices, and for a moment I had an insane desire to break through the few yards of vegetation which separated us and have a great re-union with them.

Every day, before I set out, I climbed down over the edge of the cliff to the spring to draw water and wash myself and shave and, once or twice, I saw a fox but I never saw any other animals except squirrels. There were not many birds in the woods now, but sometimes a woodpecker would start work somewhere nearby and it always gave me a fright when it did.

The spring was in a singularly beautiful situation below a little rocky overhang which was covered with moss and fern. The water welled up in a basin that would have been deep enough to bathe in if I had not minded spoiling it; but even if there had been another source I would not have done so. It was too lovely a place, one in which I would not have been at all surprised to meet the god Pan. Even so I never visited it more often than I needed to because the labour of clearing up every sign of my presence, which included walking backwards from it and obliterating my footprints on the muddy path as I went, was too great and was even more difficult while carrying a vessel full of water. As it was I often had to return to it because I was afraid that I had left a blob of lather, or a piece of soap on a rock, and usually I had.

And every day I received a visit from one or other of the members of the families which were sheltering me. Sometimes very shy children came; but mostly they were black-garbed grandmothers who thoroughly enjoyed this cloak and dagger work and gave the password, "Brindisi", with tremendous gusto.

Sometimes they brought me an egg or two, sometimes a sausage which I cooked over the fire which functioned marvellously with scarcely any smoke at all, and always they brought me bread and milk and very often some vegetable soup which, with some rice added to it, made a substantial evening meal. Almost always they came when it was just growing light; but I was always awake. And when I heard the word "Brindisi" uttered in conspiratorial tones, I used to get out of my sleeping bag and go to the entrance under the roots of the tree, crouching because the only place where I could stand fully upright was by the fireplace, and I used to lift the sacking and put my head out into the cool air which was so different from the frowsty air of the cave after I had spent a night in it. Then they would hand me the pot containing the soup or whatever else they had brought, and after I had handed back the pot which I had received the previous day and which I had washed, they would utter a few cheerful words of encouragement and usually, in answer to my question, say that there was "*niente di nuovo*", no news. This meant in the *comune* rather than in the world, although they sometimes said, dabbing their eyes, that there was still no news of the boys in Russia, whose grandmothers some of them were, and then they would go away down the hill, very black and respectable, with the pot concealed in a black bag made of American cloth of a sort which they all carried, even Agata when she shopped on Sundays in the village.

It was only on the last day of the month that one of them gave me the news that Genoa had been bombed. She also gave me a letter addressed to Signora Enrica, a very short letter:

Enrica Dear,
I hope to visit you one evening quite soon, although I am afraid that it will have to be a very short one, as I have very little free time from my work; but I shall let you know in advance when I am coming so please do not go away. You will be glad to know that your two old friends are now enjoying far better health.

Kisses

It ended with the same illegible signature that she had appended to her previous one.

I was very cheered by this letter, because of the good news it contained and because she had written "Enrica Dear" instead of "Dear Enrica" and "Kisses" too, and I read it many times before reluctantly putting it in the fire and watching it burn.

The next days went very slowly until finally, on the morning of the sixth of November, I received a verbal message brought by Pierino who repeated it many times in case I got it wrong, that I was to be at the charcoal burner's hut beyond the Colle del Santo on the following evening at half past six. To make sure that I got there on time he had brought me a pocket watch, the property of one of the members of the Board, and would I, he said, unwrapping it from a large pocket handkerchief, please take great care of it as it was a very old and good one.

As soon as I got the message I decided to give up going into the woods until I actually set off to meet Wanda. I had a premonition that if I continued to do so something would happen to prevent our meeting taking place. The next thirty-six hours or so until Sunday evening seemed endless. Having a watch made them pass even more slowly, although the one thing I did learn from having it was that I had been going to sleep at seven o'clock every evening. No wonder I woke early. Remaining for days inside the cave, except when I went to get water, I began to realise something of what it would be like to be immured in it for four months of winter, and I began to think about what I should do to pass the time when the snow came. The principal danger would be melancholy and lack of exercise. Somehow I had to get hold of some books to read, even if they were in Italian. I had been an idiot to jettison Boswell's *Tour to the Hebrides*, which I had buried in the woods after I left the Pian del Sotto. A Bible would be good if only one's eyes could stand the print, reading it in a cave; but how was I to get hold of any literature in what appeared to be a bookless, Bibleless community (for neither of the houses I had been in had Bibles). Perhaps I ought to write a book; the trouble was I had no desire to do so. I was more interested in trying to write poetry. I already had a couple of pencils with which I had been writing down on a small piece of paper a skeleton outline of my movements, but not naming people or places. What I needed was more paper. Only *Barba-Nera* gave me any hint on how I should comfort myself during the month of November, "*Mese dedicato al suffragio dei Defunti*" it said, which I couldn't translate properly, not knowing the meaning of *suffragio*, which sounded like something to do with votes for women. "November is vinous and wintry", it went on to say and under the heading *Lavori del Mese—Cantina:* "The only thing to do in this season is to watch over (*vigilare*) the fermentation of the wine."

On the Sunday there was heavy rain and it blew a gale. At midday I ate my evening meal, partly to relieve the tedium and partly because by now I was beginning to have a horrible feeling that the meeting with Wanda might turn out to be a carefully planned ambush, and I wanted to have a full stomach to travel on if I had to make a run for it. To cook it I had to disregard the injunction I had been given not to light a fire during the day, and I suffered for it. The fire which had worked perfectly during the fine weather was much more difficult to control when the wind was strong; and it was very strong now. It moaned in the chimney and the cave was filled with dense smoke.

By five o'clock it was beginning to get dark and I set off. I had calculated it would take me just under an hour to reach the Colle, but I had to allow for the possibility of going off course and it seemed better to be early than late, especially for an ambush. I might even arrive in time to see it being set up, although it was no night for standing around in the open. I took all my possessions with me in the rucksack, because the feeling I had that there was something wrong was very strong now. Suppose Wanda herself was a prisoner and had written under duress to suggest the meeting place— the threat to shoot her father and the doctor would be enough—and that Signor Zanoni had been put under similar pressure? (He had to be involved, even if the meeting was genuine, because he alone knew that the charcoal-burner's hut was a place that I had already been to.) It required a tortuous imagination to think this; but by this time a lot of my imaginings were beginning to be unnaturally vivid.

I left the watch behind. It was too dark in the open to tell the time by, and if I was going to be ambushed at least the owner stood some chance of getting it back. The cave seemed safe enough. If the *segretario* knew where it was he would have already arranged for me to be collected from it long ago.

Travelling through the forest at night was much more difficult than I had imagined it would be. Daylight travel had made me over confident, although I had planned the route carefully in my mind's eye—north until I picked up one of the main tunnels through the forest which I now knew well, then down it on to the Pian del Sotto, over the cliff, bear left along the base of it, then climb up to the bramble hedgerows where the track ran uphill from the Colle del Santo to Luigi's place, over the cross-roads and into the wood where the hut was.

First of all I couldn't find the tunnel, or any other, and I went so far along the side of the mountain on one of the lesser tracks that I was afraid that I had missed them, though how I could manage to do this when they all led up through the wood to the open mountain I couldn't imagine. It was difficult to think at all in the wood. Visibility was nil and the pouring rain and the swirling and clashing of the branches in the wind made it practically impossible to know whether I was on a path at all. It was like being in Chaos and when, at last, I did manage to pick up one of the tunnels I was afraid that it might be one that came out of the wood to the north of the Pian del Sotto; but I had to take a chance, there was nothing else I could do, and fortunately it was the right one.

At the bottom I crossed the plateau with the house invisible somewhere to my left, and began to descend one of the narrow gullies in the face of the cliff, but when I was about half way down I slipped and roared down the remaining fifty feet or so on my back ending up among my rocks at the bottom. I was saved from breaking my back by my rucksack which was wedged underneath me and which acted as a sort of toboggan. I was horribly shaken and incredibly dirty and wet but otherwise I was all right, and all I could think of was being in time for my appointment, even if it was an ambush, and I pushed on along the base of the cliff, past the place where the *gabinetto*, in which Dolores had come to grief, stood near the edge of it, until I judged that I should begin to climb the long easy slope which led up to the bramble hedge above the Colle.

The Colle, when I finally reached it, was no place to linger. It was utterly exposed and the wind was gusting so strongly over it that I could hardly stand. As soon as I was safely in the wood on the other side of it I left the track which led directly to the hut and made a detour so that when I got to the clearing in which it stood I would be to the right of it, instead of being directly in front of the entrance which would not be a good place to be if there was an ambush. I made a terrible lot of noise forcing my way through the undergrowth but there was not much danger of being heard on such a night.

The hut looked empty. I settled down to wait. If there was anyone inside it then whoever it was would have to give some outward sign that they were friendly. I had no intention of going in through the doorway to find out for myself. I waited for what seemed half an hour or more, but was probably not more than ten minutes, and became very cold. I found that having been without a watch for so long had destroyed my sense of time. While I waited the rain suddenly ceased, the clouds broke and a half-moon shone down into the clearing, at first partly obscured as some last ragged remnants tore across its path, and then brilliantly in a sky in which the stars were dimmed by it, a wild and wonderful night suddenly, with the wind, which was if anything stronger than ever, frenziedly tossing the branches of trees so that, in the moonlight, they looked like the manes of wild horses milling together in a round-up.

While I was taking all this in I had failed to keep an eye on the hut, and when I did look at it again I saw two figures standing outside it. The taller of the two, who was wearing a white raincoat, was undoubtedly Wanda; the shorter one looked like Signor Zanoni. And forgetting all my previous caution and precautions at the sight of them, I went towards it.

By the time I reached the hut they were already inside it. Signor Zanoni had just lit a candle lantern and was hanging it up, and Wanda was standing with her face to the entrance. Her eyes were bright, and her hair hung down to her shoulders in wet, shining coils. With her long, straight nose and regular features she looked like the Medusa. Her raincoat was soaked through and both she and Signor Zanoni were as wet as I was.

When they first saw me they looked alarmed, as they had reason to. My face was all scratched and bleeding and I was wearing Luigi's remarkable velveteen suit which was always on the point of disintegration but never actually disintegrated, and was now plastered with wet clay after my ride down the cliffside. By now I was probably rather strange-looking even when I was clean. But I had no way of knowing. I had no mirror and the pool at the spring into which I gazed, hopefully, each day while I was shaving, was too disturbed by the water welling up into it to produce any kind of steady image.

But then when she recognised me she came towards me and gave me both hands and I kissed her formally which I knew was the right thing to do with Signor Zanoni looking on, and then I did the same to him which I also knew was the right thing to do in Italy, but was something for which I always felt a certain repugnance, and still do.

"You were on time," he said taking out his watch. "It's just half past six. You haven't got long I'm sorry to say. Only half an hour. I'm going to leave you for a bit and go to the village. I'm expected there; but first let's have a drink. I think we've all earned one, especially the signorina. It was a really hard climb for her in this weather, from the road to my place and then up here through the wood." And he opened the big pack he had with him and produced a small bottle filled with *grappa*, which he uncorked and offered to her.

"Uurrgh, it's strong!" she said. "I'm not used to this stuff, but it's good."

"It's meant to be strong," he said. "Otherwise there wouldn't be any reason for making it, or any reason for drinking it."

Then he went away. And after an interval during which no words were spoken, because there was no need for words, Wanda began to tell me all the things that had happened since we had last been together.

"I'll speak in Italian," she said. "There's so little time. I have to start back to Parma tonight. There's a special bus. I had to get a permit to come on it. You have to now, especially to the mountains. The bus has to stop on the way because of the curfew, so I shan't get back to Fontanellato until tomorrow morning."

As I thought, I had read her first letter as she meant it to be read. Her father and the doctor had both been taken by the Gestapo; but the doctor had managed to simulate appendicitis which one didn't even have to be a medical man to do, but it helped him to be taken seriously by his captors and he had been removed from the prison to a hospital on the outskirts of the city where one of his colleagues had allegedly performed an operation on him and he had subsequently disappeared. I wondered why he hadn't done the job properly and died like Paul Pennyfeather in *Decline and Fall*. He could even have signed his own death certificate.

Her father's situation had been more serious.

"I said that I would get him out," she said, "and I did; but it wasn't easy. I thought and thought and then I went to see the Gestapo. I wasn't frightened because I didn't know anything about them and what went on in that house, until it was over. I was frightened then.

"I saw the big man in it. He wore civilian clothes. He looked quite angry. I told him about my father, almost everything: that he was a Slovene whose second language was German, that he had been in the Austrian Army and that we had been deported by the Italians. It wasn't difficult to give him the feeling that my father didn't care much for them without actually saying so. I did this because I knew that the Germans needed interpreters. There had been a notice in the *Gazzetta di Parma* ordering everybody between the ages of eighteen and fifty who spoke German to present themselves to the *Presidio Tedesco* in Parma, but, of course, hardly anyone had. My father was more than fifty; but I didn't think it would matter much, and it didn't. It was a

177

big risk to take because I didn't know why they wanted German speakers, and who wanted them. They might have been planning to send them to Germany; but I had to take it.

"When he heard this about my father having been in the Austrian Army and speaking German he became very friendly. Until then, I didn't realise how much the Germans despised the Fascists. He managed to make German-speaking Slovenes seem superior beings, a new feeling for people like us. It was a pity my German was so bad but he spoke good Italian. He was Austrian, from Innsbruck, and he was one of the most horrible men I have ever met."

"It was nothing to do with the Gestapo, he said. 'It was the Army which needed interpreters to help them when they were buying things. They needed someone who could help them fix a price.' This is what he said. I didn't know whether to believe him.

"In the end, he agreed to free my father so that he could do this work. But, of course, there was a condition. This is their way. There's always something more. He said that he would let him go on condition that I would report to his headquarters once a week and tell him anything that I had learned that might be of interest to them, small things but important. He told me exactly what they wanted. It was horrible, but it was lucky I went. They were going to send him to Germany the following week. It was lucky, too, that they didn't know about my cousin. He's in Dachau, or was.

"I've been going there ever since. Every Monday, and they don't forget, at least they didn't for the first two weeks. I have to tell them something which sounds interesting, but not too interesting for them to do anything about it except write it down in a book, and there can never be any names. I think they're getting tired of me. They think I'm a silly girl. Luckily, there's a new man in charge now and I don't think anyone really knows now why I keep coming to see them. I'm glad the other one went away. He asked me to go out with him."

"Good God, did you?" I said.

"Do you think I'm mad?" she said. "Do you think I want to be shot by my own people?"

"What happened about your father?" I said.

"He did one or two jobs for the Army. I must say the Gestapo told me the truth about that, at least as far as my father was concerned. All they wanted was help in buying food for an officers' mess, on the black market, of course. Then he caught a big chill on the stomach and he had to get a medical certificate. They haven't been near him since."

"Was he really ill?"

"No, of course he wasn't. He's well, or as well as anyone can be in these days. But things are becoming very difficult, not only for us, but for everybody. The bread ration is two hundred grammes a day for people like us who don't work with their hands, but as you know bread is a very important thing here. The sugar ration is two kilos, if you can get it, and that has to last from now until next March. The *pasta* ration is two thousand grammes a month. Fuel in the Plain is very, very short. All private motor-cars have been confiscated and, of course the doctor has lost his, but he can hardly grumble about that. He's lucky not to have been shot. He's somewhere in the mountains now. And the Germans took my bicycle when my father was arrested. I got it back, though. They'd taken it off to Salsomaggiore in a lorry, to the place where their *comando* is. (And that of *Oberleutnant* Frick, I thought.) So, I went there on a bus and when I saw an important-looking officer, not too young, I told him what had happened and he got hold of one of his men, a sergeant, who took me to a place where there were hundreds and hundreds of bicycles, all stolen by the Germans from people like me, and he told me to take my bicycle. Of course I couldn't see it and he told me to take any bicycle, the newer the better. It didn't matter, he said, none of the owners would ever get them back again, so I chose one like my own which was not at all new, although there were lots of beautiful ones and he said I was silly. Do you think I was silly?"

"Yes, very," I said.

"Now there are no more bicycle tyres; but luckily the one's on the bicycle I chose are good. I couldn't get on without my bicycle.

"The black market is bigger than it's ever been. Every day people are arrested at the railway station for carrying food they can't account for; but things are even worse up here. I was speaking to Signor Zanoni. People are having to make long journeys on foot, for days on end, to get what they need. The thing everyone is most short of on this side of the Apennines is salt. Over in Massa Carrara they have salt but no food."

I asked her what was happening in Italy and how the war was going. "The Fascists are back in power now," she said. "Or that's what the Germans let them think; but because they're Italians they're too clever to believe it, and that makes them behave worse. The war is not going very well. Your people are stuck between Rome and Naples; but there's a lot more bombing now, especially at Genoa. The only one's who are really attacking at the moment are the Russians. There's a big offensive in the East. And that's about all I know," she said. "I'm not very good at these things. One thing I am sure of is that I gave you the wrong advice. As you didn't want to go to Switzerland you should have gone south, which reminds me."

She produced a dog-eared picture postcard of an Alpine valley. It was of a place called Champoluc in Piedmont and it was signed by three or four people whose Christian names I recognised, even though they had been rendered into Italian. One of them was the colonel's.

"The *capitano* with the pipe took them up," she said. "They crossed from the top of the valley by something called the Col de Theodul. The next day they were in Zermatt. I'm only telling you this because I know that you're not sorry you didn't go."

"No, I'm not sorry," I said. "I'm only sorry to have been such a nuisance here."

She ignored this remark and changed the subject.

"What was it like up at the farm?" she said, in the same sort of mocking tone that the girls up there had employed.

"I hear that there were two very pretty girls. And the one I gave my letter to was very good-looking, too. Not a skeleton like me. I expect you've been enjoying yourself. Men are all the same, everywhere, especially soldiers."

"They were really nice girls," I said. "Very kind."

"Ha! Ha!" she said. "But I believe you. Am I stupid to do so?"

"I didn't think you liked the word."

"I learned it from you," she said. "Don't you remember?"

"I'm sorry," I said.

"Now you really are trying to make me angry," she said. "Why do you do it? But I won't be, there's not time. There are two other things which I must tell you before I go. The first is that you had a great friend called James in the *Orfanotrofio*. Everyone called him 'Yams' so he was re-named Giacomo. Well, the last thing the doctor managed to do before he was put in prison, the day after he took you to the mountains, was to take Giacomo. He wanted to bring him here, so that you could be together, but he wasn't very happy about making the same journey two days running, after what happened in Parma, so he took him up into the next valley, and now he's somewhere on the other side of your mountain. And he knows where you are more or less.

"The second thing is that we've heard that a British submarine took some people off from the west coast, somewhere between Rome and La Spezia. I'm going to try and find out more about it. Of course, it may not be true, but I've managed to get you some very good maps, although only enough to get to the coast, south of La Spezia; you would need dozens for the whole of it. It was difficult to get any at all because they've all been withdrawn from the shops. The Germans are afraid that they might be used by the *bande*. What I think you should try and do now is work out a route to the coast. If you could get as far as the top of the Apennines and see the country on the other side of it, it would be useful. Then, if I did get some real information, before the snow comes, you could go. But don't go down the other side now. There's hardly any food and it's getting worse every day."

"What about the *bande*?" I said. "There aren't any here, so far as I know."

"I don't know much about them," she said, "but there aren't any in this valley, and I don't think there are any in Giacomo's either. At the moment they are mostly in the big mountains, in places like Piedmont."

"Tell me, truly, what do you think the chances are?" I said.

"Of what, the submarine?"

"No, generally."

"I know you want the truth. Then I must tell you. When the snow comes, unless you can get a roof over your head, or find a *banda* that is well organised, then your chances are very, very bad."

Signor Zanoni was back, looking at his watch, looking the other way, fishing about in his big pack from which he eventually extricated a very large package done up in newspaper, and while he was doing this Wanda spoke her last words to me in English.

"He is a good man and he will do everything he can for you. Did you like his house? I was there this afternoon. That is the sort of little house I would like to have, Eric, and one day I will. He has a very good woman for a wife and she told me to tell you that they both want you to come when you can, on a Saturday night, and you can stay until Sunday evening. Now kiss me properly," she said. "That's if you want to after kissing all those other girls."

Signor Zanoni had gone outside. I kissed her. I knew it was for the last time and so did she. There was nothing to say except God bless you, which we both said. Then I embraced Signor Zanoni. He took down the lantern and extinguished it, and then they were gone, leaving me with a parcel done up in newspapers. And when they were gone, and I was left along with my parcel, I began to cry, something I had not done for as long as I could remember.

Chapter Fifteen

Journey to the end of the known world

As soon as I got back to the cave I lit a big fire and hung up my wet clothes and dried them, and while I ate some bread and sausage and drank some acorn coffee, I unpacked the parcel which Wanda had brought up from Fontanellato at great risk because, although there was nothing in it which could actually incriminate anyone by name, the contents would have been more than enough to ensure that whoever was carrying it would immediately be arrested and imprisoned if they had been stopped and made to open it.

Among the contents, some of which I have now forgotten, were a tiny compass, a pocket watch, four military maps, the Italian equivalent of our own Ordnance survey maps, on a scale of 1:25000, about two and a half inches to the mile, a pre-war tourist map of the province of Massa Carrara; a brand new Italian Army blanket; two vests sent by the *superiora*, together with a little, unsigned note of encouragement of the sort that the nuns in the convent used to enclose with our clean washing; some socks— of which I was in great need; a shirt, needles and thread, a large piece of *parmigiano*, an apfelstrudel made by Wanda's mother and, most remarkable of all, the second volume of a two-volume edition of Gibbon's *Decline and Fall of the Roman Empire*, with my own signature on the fly leaf, which I had left in the *orfanotrofio* on the ninth of September, and in which Wanda had inserted a piece of paper on which she had written the words, *Che Combinazione*!

I spent a long time over the maps. They covered all the country between the mountain and the *crinale*, the main ridge of the Apennines. They were extremely detailed and extremely difficult to read. They were executed in black and white and the general effect was rather as if a band of centipedes with inky feet had spent a day scuttling over a sheet of paper. The most complicated thing about them was the conventional signs of which there were something like a hundred and twenty, all set out at the bottom of each map, many of them such minute variants of one another that it was impossible to memorise them. There were twelve different conventional signs for twelve different sorts of trees alone.

Nevertheless, they were marvellous maps and I decided to set off as soon as I could make the necessary arrangements. There were, in fact, no arrangements to make, except to tell whoever came up the following morning that I was going, otherwise they might think that I had gone for good.

It was very fortunate for me that it was Francesco who chose to come, because it was rare for the men to do so. They had too much to do. He came on this particular morning because he had missed Signor Zanoni the previous evening when he went to the village and he wanted to find out if all had gone well.

I told him what I proposed to do and why, but without making any mention of submarines, and he immediately offered to come with me. I was tempted to let him do so but I had two very strong reasons for travelling alone. The principal one was that I had to travel in daylight and it would be dangerous for him to be seen with me. The second, which I kept to myself, was that I wanted to make the journey alone in order to prove to myself that I was not just something which had to be lugged about by other people from place to place at great personal inconvenience to themselves, something which I had been ever since the Armistice. This was very important to me and correspondingly difficult to explain to Francesco, which was why I didn't try. I told him that I would leave early the following morning, providing the weather was good enough, and that I didn't know for how long I would be away but as it only appeared to be about fifteen kilometres to the *crinale*, I expected to be back the following night.

He didn't say anything to this; but then he asked to see the maps, of which he could make very little, which was not surprising.

"I don't say that you can't do it in two days," he said, "because I have done it myself in less, when I was a younger man; but this is not an easy journey, Enrico, and you don't know the mountains. First tell me which way you are thinking of going."

I said that I had thought of going down over the edge of the cliff until I was on the eleven hundred metre contour where, according to the map, there was a mule track which continued right round the side of the mountain under the summit at this level and then continued along the side of the long ridge which extended down from it towards the south and which, eventually appeared to lead up to the *crinale*, at a point between two prominent peaks which I remembered having seen from the Castello del Prato that afternoon when I was recuperating from my chill.

If it is possible to imagine an eagle smiling, this was what Francesco contrived to do at this moment.

"And what made you think of doing that?" he enquired sardonically. I told him that I had been studying the map.

"Well, it must be very old, that map," he said. "No one's used that mule track these fifty years, certainly not in my lifetime. It doesn't go anywhere. It stops under the summit. There was a big landslide, the whole of that face of the mountain went and it took the track with it. And even if it hadn't you couldn't use it. You'd never get through the woods. They're the thickest in the Apennines, on both sides of the ridge. You wouldn't do it in a week. You'd drop dead first.

"I made this journey many, many times when I was a young man, Enrico," he said. "I know the places on the way that you must look out for and the names of them, and how long it takes, and if you will listen to me I will tell you what I know, and you can mark the way and the times on your map but you will have to be very, very careful not to go off the main ridges because there are many, many others and they all look very much the same. You can do this very easily if you're in a cloud, and then you will be lost and your map won't be much help to you then I can tell you, because in the valleys there are no landmarks as there are on the tops, and you won't be able to tell one from another. And be very careful on the *crinale*. If there's a big wind, then you must keep below it on the north side, the south is very steep and you'll be blown over the edge. It wouldn't be the first time this has happened. The other thing is lightning. If you hear thunder while you're up there, or you think a storm's coming on, don't lose a moment. You must get off it immediately, as fast as you can down the north side, and either shelter in one of the shepherd's huts or else under the rocks. If you stay on the ridge you have very little chance. It's worse than being in a bombardment. Now take your pencil and I will tell you the way as I remember it."

At this moment, if Francesco had renewed his offer to come with me I would have accepted it.

"Don't mark the first part of what I tell you now on your map," he said. "Then, if you're taken whoever it is won't know where you came from, except the top of the mountain. You might say you're an angel just come from heaven." He gave me one of his hungry, aquiline smiles.

"Now, can you see Punta Perdera? It's on the ridge that goes south towards the *crinale*, the one you wanted to go along the side of," he said, relishing the memory. "Just have a look down the cliffs on your left on the way down and remember what I told you."

After a bit I found it on the map, a sort of bulge on the otherwise narrow ridge. It had a deep gorge running down from it into the valley on the east side, the one *Oberleutnant* Frick had driven up to start his great *rastrellamento* among the *lepidoptera*. "Say half an hour down from the summit to Punta Perdera, that's two hours, altogether. It's a very open place but with trees round it. Abramo's place, La Maesta, is down in the valley on the east side. I'm only telling you how long it will take if you keep walking, not how long it will take if you stop on the way.

"There are cliffs all the time on your left and on the other side it's forest almost up to the ridge. But right on the top there are firs. They started planting them before the war as an experiment but they never finished. You have to be very careful here, all along this ridge, in case you meet a *Guardia Forestale*. If he sees you he'll take you. You can be sure of that. You must keep your eyes open all the time and be ready. Be careful on the passes—they all go from east to west across your path from one valley to another. A lot of mule drivers use them."

He went on in this way for nearly an hour. It was a brilliant, detailed re-creation of the journey to the *crinale*.

"Nine and a half, ten hours. If you have four rests of fifteen minutes say, that should be enough, otherwise you'll get cold. Eleven hours altogether," he said at the end of it.

"You had better keep my watch," he said. "You must have one for a journey like this. And take some wine. I think you have some. Whatever you do, don't drink water when you're hot, and if the weather's like it is today, don't go; but I think it'll be better tomorrow."

I told him I now had a watch of my own.

"Good," he said. "I didn't really want to lose mine (another smile). Tomorrow's Tuesday. We'll begin to worry about you on Friday, but if you don't come back we shan't come to look for you. It would do no good, we would never find you."

The outward journey was more or less as Francesco had said it would be in his itinerary. It was as if I was using a sort of Bradshaw of the mountains which kept me going whenever my strength began to fail, in case I missed my connections.

It began inauspiciously because I started an hour late, at five o'clock instead of at four, having overslept; but I made up for it in this early stage by reaching the Castello del Prato fifteen minutes earlier than the scheduled time, at five thirty.

The *baracca* was still there. Not surprising really, having been so recently abandoned; but already, it had begun to decay, unlike the one in the clearing down by the Colle del Santo which was protected from the elements, and by the following spring there would be nothing left of it but the bare frame and, like the clearings made by the *carbonari* it already had the sadness of an abandoned place. The moon was setting now and Venus was a brilliant morning star. There was no wind, the air was cold and there was a great silence, except for a faint sighing in the trees, as if they were breathing lightly and easily in their sleep, not yet ready to wake. For a moment the world seemed at peace and if ever I felt the presence of God walking in it this was the moment. If only it could have lasted forever.

At a quarter past six I reached the summit of the mountain which, sometimes, I had thought I would never reach. There was nothing much there, a cairn of stones, some rusty tins; but the dawn was beginning to break now and the sky to the east beyond Bismantova was pale and trembling as if it was alive, and the peaks on the main range were the colour of pearls, looming up more and more clearly out of the darkness which was draining away every moment that passed.

Then I went down the ridge to the south over the buoyant turf towards an open flat-topped place among the trees that was like a frying pan with a handle stretching away from me, with the sky growing brighter and brighter, and with steep cliffs falling away to the left where the landslip had been and where the mule track had been and the thick woods were, in which Francesco said that I would have been lost, and he was right.

I must have thought that I was moving faster than I really was, because it was nearly seven o'clock when I reached the Punta Perdera, the weird plateau with the fir trees growing up around it which looked like a frying pan. The sun was up now but not yet high enough to shine into it and the glow of it above the tops of the trees made the clearing so unnaturally dark. What had looked like the handle of the pan was a long ride between the trees and this was the route I had to follow along the ridge.

Chance, or instinct, made me keep to the dark side of it, although it was not more than twenty yards wide, and it was at this moment that I saw a figure coming down the ride towards me from the opposite direction on the lighter side of it. I ought to have seen him before, but his clothes blended too well with the trees. I could see now that he was wearing some sort of uniform and that he had a gun slung over his shoulder. It was too short to be a rifle. It was either a machine-pistol or a carbine.

Whoever he was he had not seen me. It would have been difficult for him to have done so against the rising sun which was brilliant now, illuminating the upper parts of the trees on his side of the ride, and I quickly went into the wood, which was full of bracken, and got down under it, close enough to the edge so that I could look out between the fronds.

He was almost abreast of me now. He was a man of about fifty, tall and thin, and very fit-looking. He was wearing a long, drab military raincoat and a peaked cap, and I could see now that it was a carbine that he had slung over his shoulder, and I lay there sweating and praying that he didn't have a dog with him. This must be one of the *Guardie Forestale* about whom both Francesco and Signor Zanoni had warned me. He moved very silently over the ground, more like a shadow than a human being, but, fortunately, his thoughts were elsewhere, and after I had

186

waited until I could see that he had reached the Punta Perdera and was going on up the mountain I, too, went rapidly on my way. If it had been ten minutes later and I had met him on the open down below the summit he would have got me.

He had given me a terrible fright and I kept on looking round to see if he was pursuing me like the Hound of Heaven but there was no sign of him, only the long, narrow ridge with the great mass of the mountain at the end of it, and I went on so fast that I was on the Passo Cornale before half past eight, wishing now that it was not such a clear, sunny day. But although there were a lot of mule droppings on it, some of them fresh, there were no people and it was the same at the Passo Mallachio, which I reached before nine o'clock, well within Francesco's schedule, going downhill gently all the time.

I was on the Passo Coletta by nine fifteen and from it I could see the whole of the south face of the mountain and I could see the place where my cave was, about half way up it towards the summit, but then things began to be difficult. The next part, uphill through the woods to a farm, La Tosa, was everything that Francesco said it would be. There was no track, or if there was I never found it. The woods were dense, the ground was rocky and full of holes and there were a lot of brambles. Because of this it was ten o'clock before I reached the farm, a gaunt, lonely building which although it had obviously only recently been abandoned, was already roofless, although the out-buildings were still intact and there was newly mown hay in the barn, which probably meant that it was the house rather than the land which had been abandoned. But there was no time to look; the fields were too far off, somewhere down the ridge to the west, and, at the moment I only had two aims, one of which was to arrive on the *crinale* on time to look over the other side of it before the sun set; the other, not to be benighted on it. It was here that I had my first rest, drank some water from the spring and refilled my water bottle which was already half empty, although it held a litre. All that day I was not hungry, only terribly thirsty.

I left again at about ten thirty and followed a track down towards the river which ran in a gorge that was so deep and narrow that although I could hear it I could never see it. Here, according to the map, I was a thousand metres above sea level, the lowest point on the entire journey, but now there was a long and murderous climb through forest to the top of a mountain called Monte Bosco in the heart of which the river rose, a climb of five hundred and fifty metres, and it was not until after twelve o'clock that I finally emerged on the screes that led to the summit.

All this time the track had run parallel to the gorge and close to the edge of it, but the gorge became more and more narrow as it got closer to the source of the river which was somewhere on the north side of the mountain, and the track bore away from it to the east to reach the summit. From it I could look down and see that the whole of the north face was hollow, like the cavity in an enormous tooth, except that it was densely packed with trees which completely hid the place where the river issued from the mountain. I thought what an impregnable, secret place in which to live it would be in the summer.

From here I moved up through a strange desiccated landscape of pale, jagged rocks and long ridges bare of vegetation which sloped up to another summit, with white screes on it which were dazzling in the strong sun. This was Campo Cocuzza. Francesco had told me this meant the bald mountain, taking off his hat to demonstrate what he meant, displaying a bald pate surrounded by a dense thatch of white hair. What I was now crossing was the Pian del Orso on which, he had told me, long ago there had been bears. No wonder they had gone away and never returned. It was an awful, desolate, windy place. And behind Campo Cocuzza was the *crinale*, the main ridge of the main range of the Apennines, with two peaks rising from it on either side of a sort of saddle which was my destination.

I was tired now and I didn't reach Campo Cocuzza until a quarter to one. The view was magnificent but I didn't care. All I wanted to do was to lie down out of the wind, which was terribly strong up here, and drink water. I wasn't at all hungry and I just lay where I was without moving, except once to put on a sweater, until a quarter to two. Then I moved on up to the *crinale* through a chaos of rocks, and finally emerged from it on to the north face at a quarter to four in the afternoon after a journey of ten and three-quarter hours, and although I felt done in I had some slight satisfaction in knowing that although I should have arrived here at three o'clock, I had beaten Francesco's schedule, which included four stops, by fifteen minutes.

The sun had already gone from the north face of the *crinale* and the wind was cold and gusting strongly. The peak to the left was over six thousand feet and I was tempted to climb it because it was absurdly easy, like climbing Box Hill, being nothing on this north side but a walk up a steepish slope entirely overgrown with myrtle with scarcely a rock to be seen; but so, equally, was the one on the right, which was only slightly less high and as I was anxious to see a pass which Francesco had mentioned as lying beyond it and one of the few which were likely to be unguarded if I did have to cross over into Massa Carrara, I set off towards it as fast as I could go. Just after four o'clock I reached the summit on all fours, which was the only way I could get to it. I had expected the wind to be strong on the top but the force of it was indescribable. If I had stood up I would have been whisked away.

It was an extraordinary evening of a sort that is commonplace in the southern oceans but rare on land. A wind of force eight or nine was blowing from the south-west out of a cloudless sky and the setting sun was drenching everything in a blinding, yellow-ochre light. The view was stupendous. I could see the Alps from the borders of Italy and France right round to what must have been the Dolomites and to the left were what I recognised from having studied the map as the Apuan Alps, where the marble quarries were, weird soaring pinnacles all yellow in the sunset. Far away there was a river which flowed below another smaller range of mountains down to the Ligurian Sea and beyond the river there was a city which must have been La Spezia, already in shadow. The *crinale* was a cliff on its southern face, falling away thousands of feet to long ridges covered with oak and beech and chestnut. Beyond the valleys which separated them there were other, lesser hills and other valleys which were as formless as the sea after a storm; but lush, friendly country in which both olives and vines must surely flourish. With its great pinnacles of rock and long mysterious vistas it was landscape by Leonardo.

But what was in the foreground, below me on the ridge itself was something much different, by a different artist or artists, working in different centuries and recording something quite different, not the splendours but the miseries of life. This was a scene by Callot, or Breughel, or Goya, someone working in the time of the great troubles which afflict the human race.

I was above the pass, the one that Francesco had told me about, which the people used carrying salt over from Massa Carrara to the *pianura* and days later re-crossed carrying food in exchange.

The way up to it from the southern side was by a path just wide enough for two laden mules to pass one another without the one on the outside being pushed over the edge. It wound up round the flanks of the mountain to the summit of which I was clinging, from some invisible combe to the col on the Pass itself where a long pole which had been stuck in the ground was oscillating in the wind. And on this path, as well as laden mules, an endless column of men and women were moving slowly upwards to it, bowed down under the weight of enormous loads. From the valley on the northern side, in which it was already twilight, another column was moving up to it, similarly laden and over it and down the other side, so that there were two ant-like columns passing one another in opposite directions. The only point of contact they had was at the col itself, which was utterly bare, except for one of those little woods of dwarf beeches which had managed to raise itself as far as the ridge and which grew just beyond the actual crossing place. Here, some of them had off-loaded their packs and were huddled on the ground with their backs to the streaming wind. The ghastly, yellow light of the sunset, the dark figures, each of whom was enduring unimaginable fatigue from the great weights they bore on their backs, some of whom had children with them who were similarly loaded, the dark birds, choughs or crows, which hung on the wind above them uttering melancholy cries which rose even above the noise of the wind, produced an unforgettably melancholy impression. After I had watched the spectacle as long as I could bear to I went back down the north side of the *crinale* with some faint inkling of what total war meant to ordinary people. I wondered what they did when night fell. Did they continue to plod on, or did they bivouac by the track under some kind of makeshift cover, or did they find shelter in some building lower down?

I went down the steep slope to the north in the gathering darkness, over an avalanche of stones, and eventually came out at the top of a great rolling meadow on the edge of which there were a couple of small, stone huts and a little labyrinth of stone pens, the *baracche* of the shepherds in their summer pastures, just as Francesco had said there would be, scattered along the mountainside at this level; but to me it seemed a miracle that I had found them.

One of the huts had a strange, primitive carving of a sheep over the lintel of the door, and in this one I decided to stay the night. Except that it was built of stone and the roof was much lower the interior arrangements were the same as in Luigi's *baracca* at the Castello del Prato. The wooden cots were in good repair and there was a fireplace and a good stock of firewood.

The most important thing was to find water before it became too dark to do so, and eventually I discovered a spring which came out from under the rocks about a hundred yards away. Then, with the door closed, I lit a fire and cooked some rice, over which I grated some of the cheese that Wanda had brought me, and when I had finished this I ate a piece of hard sausage which had been intended for my midday meal at Campo Cocuzza but which I had been too tired to swallow. As long as I kept the door shut, which was a close fit, the fire was invisible from outside, apart from some sparks from the chimney, and soon the hut was as warm as an oven. It was a bitter night outside. The wind howled in the chimney but the fire drew well and all the time that I was sitting by it I thought of those long lines of people on their Via Dolorosa.

Here, at fifteen hundred metres, that night, winter set in. By the following morning the wind had gone to the north and it battered at the door which the shepherds had made facing in this direction so that the hut would be cool on hot summer afternoons. Outside the grass was thick with frost and the spring had a glaze of ice over the pool among the rocks although the water still ran in it. Worst of all, for me, everything was enveloped in freezing cloud which reduced the visibility to not more than twenty yards. There was no question of returning to the *crinale* for another sight of the sea while this lasted; it was going to be difficult enough to find my way home.

I waited until nearly ten o'clock for the cloud to lift but if anything it got worse, and after a thin breakfast of acorn coffee and a hunk of very dry bread I set off on the return journey.

It was now, at the very beginning of it, that I made my first major error of navigation. Too lazy to climb the nine hundred feel or so to the peak on the *crinale* from which I had looked down on the Pass the previous evening, from where it would have been an easy traverse along the saddle to the ridge which would eventually take me home, I decided instead to skirt the base of the *crinale* until I reached it. And this I did, or imagined I had done when, twenty minutes later I climbed up on to it, and checked the alignment by my compass, as far as I could in such weather, and it was as it should have been at this point, approximately east-north-east.

Climbing up this ridge to the *crinale*, or what I thought was this same ridge, the previous day had taken me two hours from Campo Cocuzza, the bald mountain, and it seemed to me now, practically blindfolded by swirling cloud, that I would have to allow an equal amount of time for the downhill journey to it. I was therefore not particularly worried until close to twelve o'clock when I suddenly came down out of the murk, and found that I was not on the right ridge but on one which was more or less parallel to it to the west and divided from it by the deep, wooded gorge of the river with Monte Bosco, the mountain in the hollow core of which it rose, far away above me to my right, its upper parts hidden in the cloud, and the deserted farm of La Tosa immediately opposite me, across the valley.

Looking at the map, which up to now had been impossible because the wind would have torn it to shreds, I saw what I had failed to see when studying it in the *baracca*, that the ridge I was now on did not extend right up to the top of the *crinale* as the one I had come by had, but petered out on the side of it at about sixteen hundred metres. The previous day I had been so absorbed in reaching the top before the sun set that I had not even noticed the existence of this other ridge.

I now made another serious mistake. Instead of going back by the way I had come and then going down the proper ridge I decided to go straight down the mountain side into the gorge and then climb up the other side to

191

La Tosa by the path through the woods which I had already used the previous day. It was easy to succumb to this temptation. To go back meant at least two hours uphill and two hours down to Campo Cocuzza, if all went well; half an hour over the Pian del Orso to Monte Bosco, where I could quite easily go off course on the open ground in such thick weather, then down almost to the river bed and up again to La Tosa, perhaps two hours, six and a half hours altogether, at least four and a half of them in cloud. It would be pitch dark long before I got to La Tosa. Besides, here, a convenient track, obviously made by charcoal burners, led downhill through the forest. It was irresistible and I took it.

I entered the forest at midday. According to the map, here on the ridge, I was not more than a thousand feet above the river, perhaps less.

The track took me just far enough down into the forest to make the idea of turning back extremely unattractive; then it expired in a clearing. I decided to go straight down the side of the mountain which was at an angle of not less then seventy degrees.

The trees were some kind of oak, possibly holm oaks, and they were no more densely planted than those in the forest below the Colle del Santo, which they could scarcely be, but although there had been some brambles in that forest it was nothing compared to what was growing in this one which was one vast entanglement of bramble, and once I had embarked on what I had hoped would be a swift glissade downhill between the trees, there was no hope of turning back.

The brambles were anything up to twenty feet long and when they were twisted together in two or three strands, as they usually were, they were as unbreakable as a rope. At first I tried to cut my way through them with a knife but it was hopeless, and I soon lost it; then I tried lying on my back on my rucksack and kicking my way downhill. At first I tried to spare my clothes; but no such finesse was possible. All the time I was held at a hundred different points by brambles and to tear oneself away from one lot by brute force was only to become hung up on another, destroying Luigi's almost indestructible suit in the process. Then I tried holding the rucksack, which was an infernal nuisance, in front of me and pushing it downhill with my feet but then I felt the seat of my trousers beginning to go. At one point I found a dry watercourse full of stones which was slightly less overgrown than the rest of the hillside, but it soon ended in a vertical drop of twenty or thirty feet and I was forced to abandon it. And all the time I dared not stop, although I was drenched in sweat, because I had no idea how much progress I was making, a hundred feet, two hundred feet an hour, there was no way of knowing. I could not even get at my watch because I had carefully wrapped it up and put it inside the rucksack.

The forest was eerily silent and there was not a breath of wind. Under the trees alone it would have been dark enough; beneath them and what was really one enormous bramble bush I was in perpetual twilight. I felt as if I was entombed. If I broke a leg here no one would find my bones for years and years, perhaps never if the charcoal burners did not come again to this particular forest, and perhaps not even then, if the tracks they cut down through it passed me by. And now I remembered Francesco's words about the woods that I had listened to and then instantly forgotten, "They're the thickest in the Apennines, on both sides of the ridge. You wouldn't do it in a week. You'd drop dead first."

After what seemed many hours I could hear the river far below and I was filled with despair because I had buoyed myself with the hope that by now I must be very near the bottom; and now I began to be really afraid at the thought of being benighted in the wood, enmeshed in the brambles, unable to stand or lie down or even sit on such a slope except with my legs wrapped round a tree. Finally I could bear it no longer. I had to know the time and I succeeded in extracting the watch from the rucksack. It was nearly half past three. There was little more than half an hour of daylight left and the thought gave me renewed strength; at the same time the going became slightly easier, the sound of the river grew louder and finally I came out above it on the edge of a sheer cliff, devoid of any foot or handholds, which fell fifty feet or so to the rocks below. Upstream there was a high, unscaleable waterfall which was making all the noise. There was not much water in the stream itself.

The only way out was downstream along the edge of the cliff which was even more difficult and much more dangerous than going straight down the mountainside had been, but after a hundred yards or so I came to a less steep place where a number of rather rotten-looking, contorted juniper trees sprouted from the rocks—a piece of Chinese landscape rather than Italian—and swinging down from one to another I finally reached the river bed. I had been in the forest for four hours.

I set off downstream, floundering in the pools which were only knee deep; fortunately there were more rocks than water, otherwise it would have been impossible. I had no choice of direction. Upstream was the waterfall which was impassable, and the other bank was as steep as the one I had just descended. I expected a long and arduous journey with further falls to negotiate and having to spend the night in the gorge—anything was better than the claustrophobic horror of the bramble forest; but after a couple of hundred yards the gorge opened up revealing an enchanting vista. The cliff on both banks ran away high up the sides of the valley and the gorge became a gently sloping green vale with groves of ancient chestnut trees growing in it through which the river purled, and on the right bank a path descended through some neglected fields to an old stone farm house which was half-hidden among the trees.

I was in no state to care whether the owner of the house was a friend or foe. I splashed across the river and went up towards it and as I did so a small, wizened man who even at a distance had something somehow familiar about him, emerged from a dilapidated out-building and stood there watching me as I squelched up the path towards him, laughing in the way that I remembered so well: "Heh, Heh, Heh!"

It was the old man who, long ago now, had travelled with me in the doctor's motor car on the famous journey from the plain to the mountains.

The remainder of that day and the following one were like a dream which it is now difficult for me to believe ever happened—perhaps it didn't. That the old man existed and that he lived in the way he did is undoubtedly true, but there was something so strange about his life in this loneliest of places and so much that was unsaid by him about it, and so many questions that I might have asked him if I had been in the mood to act as an interrogator, which I wasn't, that will never be answered now because he is dead and gone. And even if I had asked them he was so very deaf, which accounted for him never answering any of the questions the doctor had asked him when we were travelling together in the motor car. As it was I had to shriek in his ear if I wanted to communicate with him in a voice that must have been audible a mile away. And because he was toothless it was difficult to understand what he said.

Seeing him now for the first time standing up, I realised how bent he was from a life spent working in the fields. He wore very baggy blue trousers, an old fawn-coloured jacket and a large cap to match which, as he had a very small head, looked as if someone had dropped a large pancake on it.

He was not at all surprised to see me and he gave no sign now, or at any other time, of having met me before. He was not even surprised by my appearance which by this time was wild and extraordinary. My suit which before had been a collection of holes, now hung in ribbons about me, one leg of my trousers had been completely shorn off below the knee and I was bleeding from innumerable long scratches on my face and hands and my one bare leg.

Then, without speaking, he indicated a stone trough in which I could wash and while I was doing so I could hear him mumbling to himself "*Vediamo un po*" ("Let's see a bit"), as if he was wondering what to do next with what was for him a rare visitor. Then he took me in to the kitchen, or rather he went into it, and I followed him anxiously, afraid that the wash in the trough might be the extent of his hospitality and that he might be going to shut the door on me. It was a huge door, with a great iron lock and a key almost a foot long, a door made of horizontal slabs of pale, silvery wood, great, thick pieces of timber that had probably been split out of one of the giant chestnuts, some of which must have been two or three hundred years old, and from which the leaves were now drifting down.

The kitchen was very dark and filled with cobwebs and an extraordinary collection of objects, almost all of them including the furniture obviously made on the premises—the table being exactly like the door but with legs on. Perhaps most remarkable of all were the mousetraps, blocks of wood with three holes in them each of which had a sort of miniature portcullis raised over the entrance until the mouse gnawed its way through a piece of thin twine to get at the bait inside when—as he now demonstrated gleefully—a spring was released and the portcullis clanged shut, decapitating the creature. And there were huge bradawls, two feet long, medieval-looking lanterns, shallow iron pans with long handles that had been beaten out by hand and wooden plates.

A very small fire was burning on the hearth, and we sat down in front of it together on two minute stools which were less than a foot above the ground for a long time while he just looked at it, occasionally making "Heh, Heh, Heh!" noises and saying to no one in particular "*Vediamo un po*", unless he was addressing an old mongrel bitch with fleas, or the cat which lay down side by side with it, like the lion with the lamb.

Then, when it was quite dark, he stirred up the fire and heated up a *polenta* made from chestnuts, of which he had an enormous store, and with it we ate some sort of bitter salad which was very good, mixed with a generous dollop of oil and vinegar which he poured from a strange, fragile glass vessel with a long spout, rather like an alchemist's retort. Then he arranged the fire again so that we would not be plunged into total darkness, talking to himself in a conversational tone all the time, not as a madman but as someone who was working out what to do next and had got into the habit of talking to himself because there was no one else to talk to. He didn't feed the animals now or at any other time while I was there, presumably they drank water from the river and shared the mice.

We were sitting on the dolls' house chairs in the semi-darkness when, without any warning and without asking me if I wanted to hear it or not, he embarked on a long story. He spoke loudly and as clearly as anyone can without any teeth, and he told it beautifully with all the different intonations of the various characters, of which there were many, all carefully enunciated. It lasted twenty minutes. He never hesitated, except

195

when he got to some amusing part of the narrative when he would stop for a moment to utter a few "Heh, Heh, Heh's!" as if he was the audience as well as the story-teller, in which I joined without having the slightest idea most of the time what I was laughing at. This was the gist of it.

"*C'era una volta*. Once upon a time," he began, "there was a man called Master Giovanni, and one day he went hunting with forty hunters. They found very little to shoot and Master Giovanni shot the only bird—but it was not like any sort of bird he had ever seen before. It had feathers of real gold, and when he got back to the palace he gave it to the King.

"Now the other hunters were jealous of Master Giovanni, and they told the King that he knew the secret of finding living things that were made of gold and they encouraged the King to order Master Giovanni to bring him a golden hen which would lay golden eggs, and this the King did, saying that if Master Giovanni did not do so he would cut off his head. Master Giovanni was very worried because he had no idea where to find a golden hen and he did not want to have his head cut off; but while he was walking in the woods feeling very miserable and trying to think where he might find a golden hen, he met an old woman who asked him why he was looking so miserable, and Master Giovanni told her the reason. 'Ask the King for a golden cage to put the golden hen in and I will find it for you,' she said.

"So Master Giovanni did what she said, asked the King for the golden cage, and the King gave him the golden cage and then the old woman told Master Giovanni where he could find the golden hen; and he did find it, and he took it to the King in the golden cage.

"The forty hunters, who were also courtiers, were very displeased at this because they had hoped that Master Giovanni would have his head cut off, and they persuaded the King to order Master Giovanni to find for him a girl with golden teeth and golden hair as a bride and this the King did, also on the same condition—that if he did not find the girl with the golden teeth and the golden hair he would have his head cut off, and Master Giovanni went away again and was very miserable.

"But that day, while he was walking by the river, he found a large fish on the bank in distress, and when Master Giovanni offered to put it back in the water the fish, in gratitude, gave him a box of powder with the word *Hell* written on it which the fish said might be very useful to Master Giovanni some day. 'All you have to do if you want to get rid of anyone, is to sprinkle some of the powder over them and they immediately burst into flames,' the fish said, and swam off.

"But Master Giovanni was still very miserable because he had still not managed to find the girl with the golden teeth and the golden hair, but by

196

good fortune he again met the old woman who had helped him to find the golden hen, and she told him to ask the King for a golden ship with a golden cannon and golden cannon balls and the best generals and captains and then sail away to Turkey where he would find the girl with the golden teeth and the golden hair.

"So the King gave him all these things, even the golden cannon and the golden cannon balls, which was not difficult now that the golden hen was laying so many golden eggs each day, and the best generals and captains, and they sailed away to Turkey and there Master Giovanni declared war on the Sultan and the guns were fired POOM, POOM! and the Sultan surrendered and gave his daughter who had golden teeth and golden hair to Master Giovanni to take back to the King as a bride.

"But, unfortunately for the King, Master Giovanni had himself fallen in love with the girl with the golden teeth and the golden hair and he decided to get rid of the King and so, when the golden ship reached home, he sprinkled the King with the magic powder which the fish had given him and the King started burning with big flames and was consumed, and Master Giovanni married the girl with the golden teeth and the golden hair and they lived happily ever after."

At the end of this story, when the King went up in flames, the old man laughed longer than I had ever heard him before, which was exactly three Heh, Heh, Heh's more than he usually allowed himself, and then embarked immediately on another story called *Il Figliolo del Re Portogallo*, but the effect of the exertions of the day were too much for me and I nodded off, waking fortunately at the very conclusion when he was saying something about someone or other calling the cook.

By now it was his time for bed. I hoped it was going to be mine, too. Nothing had been said about staying the night; but he lit one of the lanterns and led the way out of the front door to a little room which had some hay in it, illuminated it for a moment to enable me to appreciate the comfort of the place, and then went away without saying a word to me but laughing to himself as if he had played some kind of practical joke.

Here in the valley there was no wind. It was intensely dark and soft rain was falling. The only other sounds were the murmur of the river and the hooting of the owls in the woods. The old man's room was on the ground floor, next to the kitchen and the shutters were latched back from the window. Inside it there was a large black iron bedstead with a high back as solid and funereal-looking as a catafalque. The sheets and bedding were very clean. On the wall to one side of the bed there was a crucifix, a medallion of the Madonna del Rosario and various sacred postcards. The old man, made even smaller by the huge bed, was in his shirt-tails, kneeling with his head on the coverlet saying his prayers; and then I, too, went to bed in what was perhaps the loneliest house in the densest wood in the Northern Apennines.

I woke late feeling refreshed but battered, and put on my rags. The old man was nowhere to be seen but he had left me some of the chestnut *polenta*, which was a bit cloying in the morning, and some tart red wine. What I really needed was a needle and thread to attach the lower part of my trouser leg which I had managed to retrieve when it was torn off, to the upper part and, in order to try and find them I made a tour of the house.

It was larger than I had imagined it to be from the outside and in an extremity of decay, although it would be some years before it actually collapsed because the great beams which supported the roofs and floors were as strong and sound as the timbers of a newly-launched ship-of-the-line. The floors of the rooms downstairs were all cobbled as if they had been intended for the use of cows and bullocks rather than human beings, and an outside staircase led to the upper floor on which there were two crumbling chambers, one of which had a large double bedstead in it which had not been slept in for years, and a lot of old clothes hanging on pegs and dozens of old boots, one of which was occupied by a family of baby mice who dropped out of it when I picked it up and scuttled away. And there were other, smaller rooms leading off these principal ones, but the floors were too rotten to walk on and even if they had not been I was afraid that the old man might return and find me in them and be displeased.

Having failed to find a needle and thread anywhere I went and sat under one of the great chestnut trees above the river and waited for him to return. It was a beautiful day. As the previous one had been the first of winter, this, paradoxically, was the last of autumn, and as soon as it climbed high enough to do so, the sun shone down into the valley from an unclouded sky, although to the west, beyond the ridge from which I had come down into it, it was very black. From time to time a gentle breeze blew down the valley and out of the gorge, and when it did the pale golden, saw-edged leaves came floating down from the branches of the chestnut trees on to the grass in thousands. I wondered how old these trees could be. They were not nearly as tall as some of the sweet chestnuts I had seen in England but the trunks were enormously thick and their bark which had deep, spiral grooves in it, made them look like huge screws embedded in the earth.

Presently I saw the old man coming up the valley by a track which I had not noticed. He was moving at a tremendous rate, much more rapidly than I imagined such a frail, minute person could, walking in a rather crab-like manner as if he was about to move off the track to the right but never did. On his back was the old rucksack which he had had on his knees in the car, and his dog was trotting along ahead of him.

He went up past the place where I was sitting without stopping, and without paying any attention to me, although I heard him laughing, and went into the house from which he emerged after a few minutes and disappeared into an out-building. Nothing happened for about ten minutes but then clouds of smoke came billowing out of the door, as if the place was on fire. After a while they ceased and I heard a strange whirring noise as if some giant insect was in flight.

Although I did not want to disturb the old man, and was a little in awe of him, I was curious to find out what he was up to.

The place was a workshop, and everything in it, apart from his axe, was home-made, even the saw blades and the bradawls, the biggest of which were in the kitchen.

He certainly had the means to do so. At this moment he was operating a home-made forge, working the treadle furiously, heating an iron bar that was already glowing. Close by, upside down on the floor, there was a handcart, about the same size as the one I had used on the Pian del Sotto and beautifully constructed, with spoked wheels with iron tyres. It even had a braking system operated by wires which led from the brake blocks to a wooden lever on the draw bar which was fitted in such a way that if the bar was lowered to the ground the brakes would go on automatically.

At present he was making the axle and as soon as he saw me he turned over the treadling to me. It was a very ingenious sort of forge in which the wind was produced by vanes made from old tin cans revolving in a tunnel. It took a long time for him to make the axle to his satisfaction—he was like a miniature Vulcan banging away at it with various sorts of hammers, talking to himself as he worked.

The rest of the room was mostly filled with baulks of seasoned timber which had obviously been cut many years before. To make the planks for the bottom and sides of the cart he had cut a chestnut log in two and then split it down the middle, using hard wooden wedges and a maul shaped like an Indian club; then he had it into quarters, then into smaller pieces and these he had split into planks using an iron blade set in a wooden handle.

Then, when he had finished, and I had shrieked a number of questions at him which he seemed to quite enjoy answering, about the tools and how he had split the wood to make the planks he turned away and said, as always, to the world rather than to me, *"Faremo la merenda."*

And we went into the house for another dose of chestnut *polenta*.

I had decided that I must tell him that I wanted to go after the *merenda*.

But when we had just finished eating and I was about to say so he got up and said, "*Andiamo*."

By the time I had rushed to the barn and picked up my pack he was vanishing round the corner with his dog. It was just twelve o'clock.

We climbed for two and a half hours very fast through dreadful woods, filled with bramble, but the path was clear and it never faltered. Once or twice we crossed other, wider tracks used by mules, which climbed more directly to the ridge, which was above us to the right, and we crossed several streams high up near their sources. The gradient was quite easy until the last half hour when it became very steep; but at last we came out on level ground in a plantation of firs and in a few minutes more we came to a circular clearing among the trees which had a long, narrow ride leading off from it to the south along the ridge. He had brought me to the Punta Perdèra, the place where I had met the *Guardia Forestale*.

"*Vediamo un po*," he said and set off alone to spy out the land with the dog following him.

Soon he was back, laughing, and nodding to me. Presumably this meant that there was no one about.

I thanked him for all he had done, but he wasn't listening. I would have shaken his hand; but he was too remote. He just stood there waiting for me to go, and I went.

All the way up through the woods the sun had shone brightly, although away to the west, beyond the other ridge, it was raining heavily; but the clouds were moving eastwards and by the time that I reached the top of my own mountain, because that is how I now thought of it, it had begun to rain there too and this and the thought of the cave gave me an extra accession of energy, and I went down the cliff edge to the Castello del Prato in half an hour. Here I decided to have my first rest since leaving the valley three and a half hours previously; but it was already growing dark and it was miserable in the remains of Abramo's hut so I decided to go on.

As soon as I entered the labyrinth where the cave was I had a feeling that something was wrong. I waited for some time listening for voices, but I could hear nothing. As soon as I reached the cave I was sure of it. It was still there, as invisible as it had ever been; but what I had thought of as some atavistic sixth sense which I had developed during my time in the woods was nothing more than a distant whiff of woodsmoke. Here, outside the hut, it was very strong. Someone had lit a fire inside it. Smoke was pouring from the chimney.

I couldn't remain outside indefinitely in the rain. I had to find out who, if anyone, was in it. I went back through the labyrinth and left my rucksack on one of the paths I knew well which led up through the woods to the downs. If I put my head under the sacking in the doorway and found a *Guardia* or a German inside, at least I would have a chance of getting away quickly, and if I put my head in quickly without saying anything in my Anglo-Italian accent, whoever it was inside would be unlikely to shoot for fear of killing one of his own people. I was not sure where I would go if whoever it was inside turned out to be an enemy, but I knew that it would have to be either to the old man again, who had not invited me to stay, or to Abramo who had.

It was rather like diving into a swimming pool in the dark, not knowing if there was any water in it. I ducked my head under the sacking and was momentarily blinded by the fire—all I could see was the outline of a large figure sitting in front of it.

Then a voice I remembered well said, "Hullo, Eric. You've been a hell of a long time coming. Your pal from the village was getting worried. You look as if you've been trying to swim the Channel."

It was James. He had arrived just as Wanda said he might.

Chapter Sixteen

Gathering darkness

I was really pleased to see James. I was very tired of living alone. We had been close friends ever since I had been sent from Rome to the camp in the Abruzzi which was my first introduction of being a "real" prisoner of war, instead of a pampered one as a guest of a fashionable cavalry regiment and when we had both been moved to the *orfanotrofio* we had stayed together. It was James who got me the entrée to an O.K. room, although the wrong end of it. And we had planned to leave the camp together when the time came, until I fell down the stairs, after which it became impossible. I had never met anyone like James before the war and I have rarely met anyone like him since, not because he was a member of a coterie—oddly enough he wasn't—but because such people rarely leave the English countryside in which the whole of their lives are spent, and there is no doubt that figures cast in this mould will soon cease to exist as very few are now being produced.

He was very tall, very burly and had a ruddy complexion, a Roman nose, a firm mouth, a big chin and very clear blue eyes which he always directed straight at whoever he was talking to. He looked exactly like the Captain of Games in an old copy of *The Boy's Own Paper*, or Old Brooke, the Head of the House in *Tom Brown's Schooldays* and this is what he had been, Head of the House at a famous school in the Midlands where the ability to play cricket and rugby football well, and be seen to enjoy doing so, were cardinal virtues.

He loved fox hunting and his favourite books were the novels of Surtees and Sassoon's *Memoirs of a Fox-Hunting Man*. He loved England and, at this stage of the war, thought that it would be exactly the same after it was over as it had been before, except that its reputation in the world would be greatly enhanced, as I did myself. He seemed to know everyone in rural England. In the two camps we lived in together he would invariably return to our room and say, "I've just been speaking to So-and-So. His brother farms about thirty miles from our place," or "So-and-So's cousin was at my college." But what he enjoyed most at the *orfanotrofio* was talking to one of the soldiers, the one who had got me the horse (or was it mule?) who had been in the yeomanry with him and before that had been a servant with one of the big Midland Hunts, and together they used to recall the sort of days which, for both of them, had been heaven on earth.

Occasionally, we used to get on one another's nerves. Morally, he was altogether too good for me—the incident with Dolores in the hay could just not have happened to James, and I had not the slightest intention of telling him about it; and by the same token I was not quite good enough for him. Yet on the whole we got on very well.

I thought he looked very thin and rather run-down. Although he made it all sound very easy, I suspected that things had not been quite as pleasant as he made them out to be although, apart from not having lived in a cave, his experiences had been so remarkably like mine that the similarity was positively ludicrous and somehow detracted from what I had thought of as being an uncommon experience. To him it appeared less novel because there had been three or four other escaped prisoners in his neighbourhood, all of whom had lived more or less the same sort of lives, alternately hiding and working on farms—all except one who had become very strange and had taken to walking through the woods barefooted, bearing a cross made of branches, alarming the local inhabitants and his companions by his altogether too public appearances. This was one of the reasons why James had been so happy to move.

"It wouldn't have been so bad if he'd been a Catholic," he said. "The locals wouldn't have minded that. They just couldn't believe that Protestants went in for this kind of thing."

Eventually a guide had been provided to bring James over the mountains and down to the village where he had undergone a pretty stiff cross-examination by the Chairman of the Board. I was sorry that I had missed this because James's many virtues did not include any aptitude for foreign languages for which, as he once told me, he could see no future use as, once the war was over, he had no intention of ever leaving England again.

"Splendid chap," he said, speaking of the Chairman. "A bit prickly at first; but then we got talking about hill farming. I told him about my cousin's place in Perthshire and he became very friendly. In the end we had quite a party. I haven't had such a head for years. They got me up about four and his son brought me up here."

"I haven't met him," I said.

"Another good chap. Looks a bit like his father. He'd just arrived. He's a medical student in Milan. The old man looks exactly like Lord

203

Scamperdale in *Mr. Sponge*, don't you think? That picture by Leech of him sitting in front of the fire. Look, I've got it here."

James had forced me to read *Mr. Sponge's Sporting Tour* while we were in the *orfanotrofio* and much to my surprise I had thoroughly enjoyed it and now, when he opened the book at Leech's drawing of Lord Scamperdale, I realised that it was true. The Chairman was his spitting image and from now on we always referred to him as Scamperdale or Scampers. Now I told James about my journey and why I had made it.

"I don't think anything will come of this submarine thing," he said. "No more do you, and from what you say all the passes will be closed in a week or two. I made the same mistake as you did. Now we shall just have to stick it out here as long as we can. It all depends on whether the people down below in the village can get through to us with food when the snow comes. It will be awful for them when it does and they have to slog up here. We shall feel terrible about letting them do it. But even if they do get through three or four months in this hut is going to be pretty hard. We shall be just sitting here and we'll probably go to pieces; but we've got to try and keep going. We just can't fail them after all the sacrifices they've made."

Although I didn't say it I thought the best thing we could probably do so far as the people who were helping us were concerned would be to give ourselves up.

This conversation took place the following morning, before Francesco had come up to find out if I was back. After rebuking me severely for doing what he had specifically warned me against doing, which was trying to force my way through the forest, he told me something about the mysterious old man, whose name, he said, was Aurelio.

"When he was younger," he said, "he did what many of the men here did until the war came. He left the mountains and went down into the cities and about the countryside, sharpening knives with a machine. Then when he got too old to do this he went to live with his brother who had two farms, the one at La Tosa and the other the one you stayed in down by the river. The brother was married and both he and his wife were very unkind to Aurelio and worked him very hard, giving him nothing at all, except a bed to sleep in. And when the brother died, at the beginning of the war, his widow went to live in Piacenza with her sister and she couldn't sell the farms because they were too lonely and any of the young men who might have taken them were away at the war and so Aurelio stayed on. Many people think he's mad; but he's not at all. It's just being alone all the time that makes him talk to himself. He's a marvellous workman, in wood and iron. There's no one anywhere in these mountains can beat him at it. When he was young he made a bicycle entirely out of wood, the only part he didn't make was the chain. Another time he made a merry-go-round (he had to explain the word for this which was *giostra*). He made it for the children in the village. It worked by turning a big handle. It needed two people to do it and while the children went round sitting on the horses he had carved from the trunks of trees, he paid a man to play music on an accordion. He might have told you about the bicycle and the merry-go-round; but what he never tells anyone about is his aeroplane. He built an aeroplane, long, long ago, soon after the last war. It had no engine but he tried to fly in it and he launched himself in it from the top of a cliff. Fortunately, it was not a very high cliff and all he did was break a few bones but he had to be taken to hospital. People used to make jokes about it and he didn't like being laughed at, and so he never spoke of it again; but it almost flew. If he could have done sums and had known how to read and write he might have been a rich man, Aurelio. And he's a great story teller. No one knows how many stories he can remember. He's one of the last. He learned them from an old, old man who used to make a living by telling them, who had himself learned them when he was young from another story teller, who was also very old, so you see the story that you heard is very old indeed."

James and I spent twenty-two days in the cave and great parts of that time are now inseparable, one from another. The day that I returned from the *crinale* the weather broke, as it had already on the tops, and autumn was finished. It rained and rained and cold, blustering winds howled through the woods stripping the last of the leaves from the trees and with them our last protection from the eyes of our enemies, and because of this it became impossible for anyone to approach the cave with supplies during the day. And soon the *crinale* became white with snow, at first only the peaks, and then only for short periods; but the time when they were white grew longer and longer as the days went by until, one day, the whole *crinale* was white and remained so, and from that time onwards, whoever came up to the cave, at dawn or dusk, used to stand and look at it without speaking for a while and then, finally he or she would say "*E venuta la neve*", in a voice that sounded like a knell.

In spite of this we spent as much time as we could out of doors, usually in the early hours and in the late afternoon, just before dusk. We had to in order to get firewood, and the cutting of it—Francesco brought us a saw which was much less noisy than an axe—and the concealing of the stumps of the trees and the branches and logging it up sufficiently small to get it all inside and then getting the wood back to the cave without leaving any signs, and fetching water from the spring, and covering our tracks from that, and any traces left by out visitors, took up to about four hours. During these excursions we invariably got soaked through, but this was the least of our worries, because when the fire was lit the corrugated iron roof acted as a giant reflector and if we strung our clothes up close under it they dried so quickly that the only problem was to prevent them charring and becoming unusable; both James and I each lost a precious pair of socks in this way. With the fire going we were never cold; but with the wind there was always a lot of smoke and soon the cliff, the walls, our skin and our clothes, were stained a dark, indelible bronze colour. The smoke stained everything, and often it made the bunks untenable and then we lay close to the ground with our eyes streaming, just as Abramo's had done but without any of his miracle herb to soothe them. As it grew colder and we had to keep it going night and day we became obsessed by the need to keep the smoke under control and we used to have heated arguments about the best way of doing it and sometimes, when the wind was in the right quarter, we were fortunate and then the three-foot logs of oak and the twisted ones of juniper burned steadily, hour after hour, although the beautiful, silvery ashes never grew more and never grew less on the hearth.

And we read a lot, although the only way we could do so was when the fire was alight or the piece of sacking over the door was brailed up. James read the Bible and *Mr. Sponge*. I read *Barba-Nera* and the last thirty-four chapters of Gibbon which began with the Origin, Progress and Effects of the Monastic Life which, as practised in Egypt in the Fourth Century, sounded appalling:

"The actions of a monk, his words and even his thoughts, were determined by an inflexible rule, or a capricious superior: the slightest offences were corrected by disgrace or confinement, extraordinary fasts or bloody flagellation; and disobedience, murmur, or delay, were ranked in the catalogue of the most heinous crime."

"Just like the house I was in in my first year at school," James said when I read it out to him. We were constantly quoting bits of Surtees and Gibbon at one another. And James used to read out bits of the Bible, usually some bloodthirsty piece of Old Testament military history which he thought appropriate and would amuse me. He was a conventional Christian. Just as he had before the war, he used to go to church every Sunday in the *orfanotrofio*, and it would have never occurred to him not to do so. It was not just lip service to the established religion. He believed in the existence of God and the efficacy of prayer. I believed in God, and had done ever since I had been a sailor in a sailing-ship before the war; but the God I believed in was neither beneficent nor hostile. As he was everything how could he be? And if he was everything how could he be moved by prayer? If it was a question of life and death you died when the time came for you to do so, peacefully or horribly. My time had not yet come when the foot of an upper topsail had flicked me off the yard, a hundred and thirty feet above the Southern Ocean in 1939; or that night in the Bay of Catania, or the following one in the fortress where they told us that we were going to be shot; but it could be any time. It might be quite soon now.

At one time I had prayed that a bomb would not fall on the people in England I loved; but it seemed almost impertinent; better, if anything, to pray that bombs would cease to fall on anyone. To me prayer had no efficacy as a preservative, at the most it was a profession of love, a remembrance, a reminder that there had been a past and might be a future, and perhaps that was its value. At this time, whether I was right or wrong, I felt clearer in my mind about these things than I have ever done since. Another winter and I would cloud it by reading Boehm and Eckhart and enormous theosophical works in the course of which I would fall into the error of equating the act of reading with enlightenment. Now, in so far as I could decipher the eye-destroying type in the half-darkness, I read parts of the New Testament and the Book of Psalms and used the rest of the Old Testament as a sort of lucky dip, opening it each morning at random and putting my finger on a particular verse which was supposed to furnish information about the coming day; and if the prognostication was too bad, having another go; but even so the Old Testament was rarely much use at this season, most of the action, where I chanced to open it, taking place in a warmer climate, and it usually came up with counsels such as "Thus shall ye say unto the men of Jabesh-gilead: Tomorrow, by the time that the sun be hot, ye shall have help," while an icy wind howled round our habitation.

On the first Saturday morning after James appeared, we both received an invitation from Signor Zanoni to spend that night and Sunday at his house; and we went. By now I really knew the way to the *carbonari's* hut where I had met Wanda and we raced the whole way down to the house, through the forest and over the mud and rock from the cave, in just over an hour, although it was raining hard, and there, after a wonderful, unforgettable welcome, and after they had got over their initial astonishment at James's height and size, we sat in the kitchen, wrapped in blankets, eating a special *gnocchi* of potatoes which the signora had made because she knew how much I liked it, while the old aunt sat among flickering shadows in her niche by the fire.

"Eat to the bottom," the signora said, giving everybody more from the big pot, "and you will find a *sterlina d'oro*," but we never succeeded, either this time or on the other occasions on which we visited the house. Our stomachs had shrunk and the infective jaundice which had swept the camp we had been in during the winter of 1942 had not completely gone out of our systems and, occasionally, we were both overcome by a feeling of nausea when we least expected it; but in the case of the signora's *gnocchi* it was not nausea but simply that there was so much of it.

"I'll never forget these people and what they are doing for us," James said, when we left the following night to climb up back to the cave, "as long as I live."

And one night Scamperdale gave a dinner, or rather his wife did, with a lace cloth on the table and real wine glasses with stems. It was rather a taxing evening as the conversation turned on religion and I had to explain the attitude of the Church of England to Transubstantiation; but it was as a result of going to this party in my inadequate "best clothes", the thin striped trousers and black jacket that Wanda's father had given me, that one of his female relatives made me a marvellous pair of thick trousers, out of my Italian Army blanket. James was a little better off for clothes. He didn't think very much of Italian clothes, describing them as *brutta roba*, bad stuff, and he wore the kind of semi-civilian clothes of English origin that the "old" prisoners had affected in the *orfanotrofio* because, as he quite rightly said, "Doesn't matter what I wear. I'll never look like an Italian, I look more like a Goon," which was a current word for a German.

In addition to these invitations we received one of a much more unpleasant kind, which was more of a command than an invitation, and one that we felt unable to refuse, when we were visited by one of the young men who had been at the dance and two others from another village whom I had never seen before. We were not pleased at being visited in this way, because they had not come to us under the auspices of either of the two families who were looking after us and this implied that the secrecy of our cave, like most secrets in Italy, was already threadbare.

The spokesman was one of the two strangers. According to what he told us he had been a corporal in the Alpini and he looked comparatively dependable. I was much less sure of the other two. To my mind they were much too heroic and bloodthirsty. All three were armed. The two blood-thirsty ones with rather rusty 9 m.m. pistols, the corporal with a carbine which could also have done with some attention—what Sergeant-Major Clegg would have called "an idul riful", and he would have described the owner as "idul", too. Why they needed to carry weapons at all was a mystery.

The corporal, who told us that his battle name, whatever that meant, was *Il Corvo*, the Crow, said that the three of them, together with another two who had remained hidden, were proposing to attack a German petrol dump on the Via Emilia, about ten kilometres to the west of Parma and blow it up, and having heard tht we were both officers they felt that our military knowledge might be of help to them, and they wanted us to go with them. "We are the nucleus of a *banda* that will grow in numbers every day as the Allies make their victorious advance," Il Corvo said.

As he outlined the scheme all the thoroughly ridiculous defects in it became apparent. The dump was quite small, really nothing more than a staging post on the road, so that even if we succeeded in setting fire to it, its destruction could have no possible effect on the war. His ideas of how it was to be set on fire were absurd. The petrol was all stored in German army jerricans and in order to save themselves the trouble of cutting the wire and getting into the compound, a sentiment which I sympathised with, he proposed that we should dispose ourselves at various parts of the perimeter and at some given signal, although how it was to be given was not clear, we would hurl some Italian hand grenades, of which he had a small store, into the compound and then retire.

The casing of an Italian hand grenade looked as if it was made of some kind of plastic and the explosive charge was so weak that I was almost sure that it would not be enough to make a hole in a German jerrican. It was so feeble that there had been quite large numbers of people in the *orfano-trofio* who had survived the explosion of one or more of them at close quarters, whereas I had never met anyone who had come through the explosion of a German stick grenade nearby without suffering grave injury and my first impulse had been to tell Il Corvo to lay in a stock of German stick grenades; but it was obviously as difficult for him to do this as it was going to be to blow up the dump.

I told him, after having discussed the whole business with James, that he ought to try and get some proper explosives from one of the big marble quarries on the other side of the Apennines which could be brought over by one of the salt carriers but he said that this was very difficult, which was probably true (it is always easy to make suggestions, the nasty part is having to implement them).

Then we asked him if the dump was efficiently guarded and if the Germans employed dogs; but, of course, he didn't know and neither would I have done in his position; the only difference was that, in his position, I wouldn't have been thinking of carrying out such a raid at all.

We then discussed the possibility of using Molotov Cocktails and he was very keen on the idea but when I told him that we needed petrol he said that the only place we could get any was in the dump and I had a vision of us all crouching inside it and drawing off petrol from the jerricans in order to make Molotov Cocktails with which to destroy it. What was needed was some kind of delayed-action fuse which would enable us to get clear of the place before the fire started, but although I thought very hard no inspiration came to me. It was no good asking James, it had not been his business before he was captured. I was supposed to know about such things. It was all rather shaming.

The whole scheme was mad anyway. We worked out that it was fifty kilometres in a straight line from where we were to the dump—with the initiator of the scheme saddled with such an absurd nickname we found it unseemly to use the expression "as the crow flies". To reach it we would have to cross two mountains, similar to the one on which we were living, and one large river which might be in flood. Il Corvo estimated that it would take three days to reach the target which I thought was much less than the minimal possible time, and he had arranged that we would all be housed in the barn of a sympathiser, about seven kilometres away in the foothills, on the night before the operation and again on the actual evening on which it took place, after we had successfully done our work.

We managed to persuade him that it would be impossible to remain in the area after the attempt, whether it was successful or not, and that it would have to be made as soon as it grew dark so that the whole of the rest of the night could be used for the retreat to the mountains which would have to be undertaken by each man separately and each using a separate route; although he seemed to think this a very craven way of going about it.

Finally it was agreed that only one person would actually get through the wire and he would lash a grenade to a jerrican, attach a long piece of cord to the pin, run the cord out beyond the wire and then pull it out. Il Corvo liked the idea of this, but it was impossible to get him to see that two people would accomplish this mad act better than seven and with far more chance of getting away afterwards. To him it was the idea that was everything. I couldn't remember if Italian grenades had pins.

If we succeeded in carrying out this operation the Germans would lose a few thousand gallons of petrol. They would burn some villages, shoot a number of hostages, and, almost certainly, begin a series of *rastrellamenti* which would bring a number of embryonic *bande*, of which I hoped that this was not a typical example, to their knees. The time to start this sort of operation was when the Allies showed some definite sign that they were on the move. It was too early to make such an attack. At this time it was as pointless as the Charge of the Light Brigade.

But in spite of all this we decided to go with them. As James said, we had no choice. Men, women and children were risking their lives every day to keep us alive and if, when the first opportunity to strike some kind of blow, however feeble, against the enemy presented itself, we simply skulked in our cave and let Italians do it, we would be disgraced. Il Corvo was an idiot; but he was a brave one and if there were more people like him the war in Italy might have already been over.

The operation was timed to begin the following night. We had been sworn to secrecy so we could not even tell our own people about it. We fabricated a story about making another visit to the *crinale* which we were quite sure that no one believed, and the two people who heard it said that they would return the next day to make sure that we really had gone away.

We spent an awful day. To me this was much worse than *Whynot*, because it was absolutely pointless. James wrote a letter to his people and then tore it up. I didn't even begin one. It had been arranged that the rest of the *banda* would meet us at the Colle del Santo at five o'clock the following evening and there we waited in the rain growing wetter and wetter for four hours. No one came; we never saw the corporal of the Alpini with the battle name Il Corvo again, we never saw the other two, with rusty pistols either, and no one else ever referred to the operation again. We had had a very lucky escape.

In my counting of the days it rained on between sixteen and nineteen days in November and December was even worse. As James had prophesied our morale began to go down and there was one awful day when he woke to find that he had impetigo, which made him very depressed. Now he was unable to shave and he became a sorry sight, his face covered with loathsome brown crusts which I picked off for him using tweezers made from matchsticks. At the same time I developed a ghastly, dry cough, whether it was due to nerves, the wood smoke or tuberculosis I had no way of knowing. Whatever its origin it was terrible for James to have to sit all day listening to it.

"You should control yourself," he said severely, one day when he was thoroughly exasperated.

"I do try," I said. "Do you think I enjoy it?"

"I don't know," he said, and I felt like striking him; but the more I tried not to the more I coughed.

To escape from the realities of our situation we talked a lot about England and what we would do after the war. James's plans were already made. He was more than half-way to becoming a farmer. Mine were absolutely crazy. I was going to live in a little house at the end of an avenue of trees where the grass grew up to the front door, and I was going to write. I was also going to have a secondhand bookshop, like the one I had seen in Salisbury before the war. How all this was to come about without money I never explained either to myself or to James.

Then we played a game called "Lives", using the paper which I had acquired in order to write poetry (I had written one poem but it was so gloomy and defeatist that I decided to give up. "Lives" was fun. We each wrote a day in one another's lives after the war as we imagined it ought to be. We had already played this game with others more adept at it than we were, while we were locked up. Of James one of them had written:

"Three p.m. Dropped into the House. Heard the first reading of the Oakwoods (Planting and Preservation) Bill; the Pig Production Bill and the Compulsory Land Ownership Bill. Consider that the latter should be modified, so that, of all fortunes of more than ten thousand a year, at least half, and not a third, as at present, should be in land. Had a little trouble with McGovern: he asked what would become of him, as member of an industrial section of Glasgow, when that section was expunged under the Heavy Industries (Annihilation Act). I made a good, short, straight-from-the-shoulder speech, pointing out that, under the Act, he would be annihilated too. The House heard me very kindly. Felt I deserved Tea at five p.m., which I took at the House (Earl Grey, buttered toast, Patum Peperium, Tiptree Strawberry jam, Dundee Cake and Devonshire cream)." And so on.

It was a lot of nonsense, but it helped to pass the time which hung heavily now: I having come to the melancholy conclusion of the *The Decline and Fall of the Roman Empire* and not feeling sufficiently full of fight to start it again, James having finished *Mr. Sponge* for the fourth or fifth time. Very rarely we saw a newspaper but it seldom had any interesting news in it, although we did learn of the meeting of Stalin, Roosevelt and Churchill at Teheran, which seemed a long way from our cave. The Allies seemed bogged down in Italy. With such weather it was not surprising. And there were sinister advertisements, inserted by the Todt Organisation, which invited Italian workers to go to Germany where they would find a guarantee of work (there was no doubt about that), good conditions and equal social rights with German workers; and there were the usual threats and exhortations to soldiers who had been hiding since the Armistice to give themselves up. If they did, they were told, they would be sent on leave. None of them believed it. All the time I worried about Wanda. There was never any news from her.

At the end of November the rain was colossal and sometimes it was impossible for anyone to get through to the cave for days on end. Then it grew much colder and often there was thick frost, but there was one good thing, James's impetigo burnt itself out, although I still went on coughing. It was about this time that we saw Fortresses overhead, flying very high, leaving long vapour trails and mostly heading north.

Then one morning when we woke there was a strange stillness in the cave and we both remarked on it, and when we lifted the sacking we realised the reason why. The snow had come.

Four or five days passed before anyone could get to us and we became very short of food. The snow was deep and soft but on the second day it froze sufficiently hard for us to get to the spring; but that was frozen too and what was worse we had left a permanent trail to the cave for everyone to see. Now we had to melt snow in order to get water which, as anyone who has done it knows, is very slow work. Early on the morning of the fourth or fifth day, whichever it was, Scamperdale's son, the one who was a medical student, reached us on skis, the only one in the village who had them. He told us that there was bad news and that one of us would have to go down at once in order to talk with his father. It was decided that James should go because he had now lost his impetigo and my cough was very noisy. I waited for him anxiously until about an hour before sunset when he returned with three of the others, one of whom was Francesco. With them they had brought a sack of rice and about twenty loaves of bread. Francesco and the other two simply sat down in front of the fire and said nothing but "*Ma!*" from time to time. I had never seen them look so dejected.

"We have to go right away," James said, "within the hour." The *milizia* are coming for us tonight, at eight. They think we'll be in bed. The whole village has terrible *paura*. Francesco says that we'll have to go up to a place where there's some sort of shepherd's hut. You know it, apparently."

"He means the Castello del Prato," I said. "That's a hell of a place to spend a night in this weather."

"We're not going to. A guide is coming to take us across the valley. Fortunately, the snow's going on the exposed places. The wind's taking it. It's only the gullies like this that are still full of it. Any rate, that's where we're going. They say there's a *banda* forming. If we get a move on now they'll help to get the stuff up. It was awful down there," James said. "The *paura*."

213

Then far off, somewhere beyond the *crinale* to the west we heard the deep, thump, thump of bombs for the first time. They must have been big ones and a lot of them, and by some trick of acoustics the face of the cliff and the corrugated iron roof gave the sounds a resonance so that the cave actually hummed with the noise.

"That will be the railway at Pontremoli, where it comes out from the big tunnel under the mountains," Francesco said. "*Fortezze volanti*, they call them, these great planes."

"Fortresses," James said. "It must be clearer over there to be able to bomb from that height at this time of day. If only we could have a landing on the west coast, or even at Rimini. Perhaps it's beginning."

He was looking at me as he said it but I knew that he was thinking what I was thinking. "You don't believe this, any more than I do. There aren't going to be any landings. It's going to be a long job. Next March at the earliest. This *banda* we're supposed to be going to will be just like the other one, if it exists, wet. The snow has come and tonight they're coming to take us away just as people said they would; but, my God, it's good to be free, even this sort of freedom which isn't anything like what I thought freedom would be. I never want to go back into the bag, never, and I hope I never will."

Chapter Seventeen

Beginning of the end

The difficulty was to know what to take with us. Whatever it was, ultimately, it could not be more than the two of us could carry. In the end we left all the reading matter, except the Bible, and took only one small cooking pot. All the way as we crunched up the ridge a blizzard blew but, as James had said, the wind was so strong that the snow could not settle. It was terribly cold at the Castello, where the guide was waiting who was to take us down the cliff and across the valley. He was a young, shy, slight boy and his name was Alfredo. He was blue with cold.

"You must separate the loads," Francesco said. He had to shout to make himself heard above the wind. "You, Giacomo must carry your own pack and the bread, Alfredo will carry Enrico's and the cooking pot and you, Enrico, must carry the rice. It is a pity that we couldn't find a pack to put it in. It is very difficult to carry a sack if you are not used to it." Then we said goodbye, quickly. It was no place to linger.

Alfredo was very quick on his feet. He took us down through a gorge like a gillie. After a long time he stopped where there was a waterfall that had not frozen and there he lit a fire and we brewed coffee. It was nearly ten o'clock. By now the *milizia* would have made their raid on the cave. The snow had stopped, the sky was clear and the moon was about full. A freezing wind funnelled down the gorge, scattering the ashes of the fire in long trails of sparks. I was glad of the rest. The sack of rice must have weighed almost forty pounds and, as Francesco said, it was an uncomfortable load for anyone who was not used to it, especially on such steep, uneven ground.

Sometime about eleven o'clock we reached the bottom of the valley, just downstream of the village from which *Oberleutnant* Frick had set off with his butterfly hunt, and forded the river. The bottom was composed of big round stones and it was difficult to cross it when carrying so much gear. The water was bitterly cold, and the moon shone down on it through the leafless trees so that it shimmered, as it would have done in bright sunlight.

We crossed the road and began to climb steeply up the other side of the valley, stopping for about five minutes every two hours to share a cigarette with Alfredo who had a small supply of a terrible brand called *Milits* which were only issued to the armed forces. Alfredo must have been a soldier on the run too. Then we went on; but very slowly because of the big weights we were carrying. That night something happened to me on the mountain. The weight of the rice coupled with the awful cough which I had to try and repress broke something in me. It was not physical; it was simply that part of my spirit went out of me, and in the whole of my life since that night it has never been the same again.

Dawn the following morning, which was sometime around seven o'clock, found us far up along the side of the open mountain, as conspicuous as flies on a wall. The weather had changed and high grey cloud was racing overhead. We had come a long way and were now far up the valley. Here, we lay down for a bit on what looked like frozen heather and fell into a state somewhere between sleeping and waking. Then we stumbled on until we reached some woods in which we could smell smoke, and after a bit we entered a clearing occupied by *carbonari*.

It was something I shall never forget. There was a whole family of them, men, women and children, all living together in a *baracca* covered with turf and all of them were as black as night from the burning of the charcoal, and their teeth shone in their faces with an unnatural whiteness, as if they were nigger minstrels on some pre-war pier. Near by the charcoal was burning, a huge wigwam of trees which were being slowly carbonised by the fire, with earth and turf piled on them to prevent the wood from bursting into flame and being consumed.

When they saw us the *carbonari* spoke to Alfredo in some strange dialect which he could scarcely understand, inviting us into their *baracca* and when we were all crowded into it one of the men produced a greasy-looking bottle of marvellous *grappa* and gave us all a swig. They had a fire going and we all sat round it, the men, women and children, one of them a baby at its mother's breast, as black as she was. No one spoke much. We were too tired; they were too dispirited. According to Alfredo, who did manage to talk to them a little, they would leave as soon as this last lot of charcoal was ready. They had their mules, although we never saw any sign of them, perhaps they were in a village, and then they would go over into Tuscany, into the Maremma; but they were afraid because there was so little to eat there. None of them had ever remained at such an altitude so late in the season before, and they had suffered great privation. In the rudeness of their way of life, and in their general demeanour, these people were like no others I had ever met before. Their life was not so much primitive as intensely uncomfortable, far more so than our life in the cave had been, as uncomfortable as that of the Patagonian Indians, without any kind of dignity to redeem it; but these were exceptional times and, perhaps, in better weather, it would have been different.

Here, after having given us the directions so that we could reach the place where the *banda* was supposed to be, Alfredo left us and went back along the mountainside by the way we had come. He had done everything and more than anyone could have expected of him and for no reward. And now we continued on our way, James carrying the rice, I myself carrying one of the packs and one of the *carbonari*, whom Alfredo had persuaded to accompany us, the other. But when we reached the hut, a semi-ruin, it was empty except for a mangled mass of newspapers and empty tins, and the place was so filthy that we decided to push on.

Here the *carbonaro* left us, going off without a word. We wanted to thank him; but he gave us no time. We now had a really prodigious weight to carry between us but, fortunately, after we had only been walking for about a quarter of an hour, we came out on a small alpine meadow, in the middle of which there was a little, two-storeyed barn, roofed with big stone slabs. The door of the upper floor at the back was level with the meadow which here sloped very steeply, and we forced it open. It was filled with beautiful, sweet-smelling hay and we crawled into it, not caring whether we were in a safe place or not, and fell asleep at once. We were utterly done for.

The next thing I remember was somebody tugging at my foot which was towards the door and an excited voice saying "Who are you? Who are you? What are you?" again and again, and I opened my eyes to see a minute boy looking in through the open door. I answered that we were English because I was too tired to care whether we were taken or not. Then the small boy, whose name he told me was Archimede, disappeared and after discussing with James what we should do, and deciding to do nothing, we both fell asleep again.

Some time later the little boy returned leading a man of about fifty dressed in very ancient clothes by the hand because he was almost blind. And with them came a little girl who was carrying a pot of *minestra*; and while James and I consumed the contents, both eating from the same pot, the almost blind man asked us about ourselves and we told him almost everything, except the names of the people who had been sheltering us where we had come from. When we had finished, looking in our direction, but not seeing us, he said, "I, too, will give you food and shelter for as long as you wish to stay here. I have nothing to lose."

And so we remained there. With our arrival at the barn, time, which had shown itself in the past either so infinitely extended and slow-moving, as it had done during the time I spent with James in the cave, that events gave me no sensation that they were actually happening at all, or else were so compressed that they went equally unremarked, now entered one of its speeding up phases. It was as if who or whatever was shaping our ends had become impatient with the whole affair and was anxious to bring it to a conclusion.

That afternoon, because he could not see to do the work himself, the man returned again with two men from the village who made us beds in the lower part of the barn where we could light a fire by the entrance. They also cut us a supply of wood. The blind man's name was Amadeo. Every day for as long as we were there, he came up the mountain with one or other of his children, all of whom were named after eminent Ancient Greeks, bringing food and comforts but also to have long conversations with us about the outside world, about which he had a great and intelligent interest.

"Now," he would say from where he sat, "Turn me in the direction of America."

And when the direction of America was established he would draw a line in the earth on the floor and then he would begin to orientate himself to the other continents. He loved to talk for hours about outlandish places and people, places such as India where I had been and of which I was able to tell him something, although not nearly as much as he wanted to know. And James told him about England and farming there, in a way which I could never have done.

While we were living in the hut the weather was very cold, and whenever it was clear we saw the Fortresses going over, infinitely remote at thirty thousand feet or more leaving vapour trails and shining in the sun, and it was strange to think that those crews who survived the flak and the attacks of fighters, would be sitting down to eat and drink in a few hours among their own people.

It was now that I suffered a terrible misfortune. Drying my wet boots one night I left them too close to the fire and, as a result, the next morning I found that the whole of the forepart of the sole of one boot was gone, burned away. It seemed like the end; but I was to be spared a little longer. That day when Amadeo came up to the hut, this time with Pythagora, his youngest son, I told him what had happened.

"Give me the boot," he said, that was all, and he went off with it, guided by Pythagora down the hill.

That night and the whole of the next day I stayed in bed because there was nothing I could do with only one boot, but the following evening Amadeo returned bringing it with him. The repair was one of the most skilful I had ever seen. Leather for boot soles was completely unprocurable by this time, but a bootmaker in the village had carved a piece of wood to the shape of the part of the sole which was missing and grafted it on to what remained of it. He did it so well that it lasted until the end of the war and never let in a drop of water.

On Christmas Eve we were invited to go down to the village where we spent the evening and the next day as the guests of various families, including that of Amadeo and of the man who had mended my boot.

"What would you like more than anything?" a little signora said on Christmas Eve, while her children looked up wide-eyed at these strange, smoke-stained visitors from another world. It was her husband who had helped to build our beds in the barn. There was no doubt about what we would like most, either in my mind or in James's. Although we had got ourselves as clean as possible by washing in the icy spring behind the barn, what we both wanted more than anything was a hot bath.

"And you shall have it," she said. Soon she had a number of enormous vessels heating on the wood stove and another, even bigger one, over the fire. And when the water was hot she half-filled a big empty wine barrel in the cellar next door. We stripped off by turns—it was no time for false modesty—and because the barrel was too close a fit for either of us to move our arms, she and her husband took turns to scrub us and wash our hair.

On Christmas Day, after a great lunch, we were taken to the house of an engineer who was in charge of the hydro-electric works on the mountain and there, at three o'clock, to the accompaniment of awful whistlings and other atmospherics, we heard the laboured but sincere-sounding voice of the King speaking from Sandringham.

"Some of you may hear me in your aircraft, in the jungles of the Pacific or on the Italian Peaks," he said. "Wherever you may be your thoughts will be in distant places and your hearts with those you love." And although it was almost certainly not intended for people like us, the effect of what he said was too much in conjunction with all the food we had eaten and the wine we had drunk, and the people in the room witnessed the awful spectacle, something which they are unlikely ever to see again, of two Englishmen with tears running down their cheeks.

And late that evening I received a little strip of paper with only two words on it—*Baci*, Wanda. It was the best Christmas I had ever had.

We were finally taken about midday on the twenty-ninth of December. It was the coldest day so far and there was a lot of snow. James had gone off somewhere up the mountain; but I had felt too ill to go with him. I think he was glad to get away from the sound of coughing which was enough to drive anyone mad. After he had gone I went to the door to watch some Fortresses going over, and the next thing I remember was hearing a voice say "*Mani in alto!*" and I looked down and saw that there were a dozen very nasty-looking men, one or two of them in some sort of uniform, all armed to the teeth with carbines and Beretta sub-machine guns, standing in a half-circle round the door. Some even had the ridiculous little red grenades with which Il Corvo had planned to sabotage the petrol dump.

I raised my hands, thinking how lucky it was that James was away; but just then he came into view round the end of the hut. He, too, had his hands raised in the air. This was a detachment of Fascist *milizia*. I was surprised how really evil they all looked, like villains in a film. There was some kind of officer in charge of them, and we asked to speak to him and tried to get an assurance that nothing would happen to the people in the village who, we said, knew nothing about us. He told us not to worry.

"The patriotic person who denounced you lives in the village," he said. "One of the conditions that was made was that no harm would befall any of the people. Personally, I'm sorry. I would have much pleasure in burning the place to the ground and shooting the lot of them. I don't like traitors, and neither do my men."

Slowly now, we went down the mountain and around the outskirts of the village to where a number of cars and lorries were waiting and were driven away.

Epilogue

Twelve years later I returned to the Apennines with Wanda and our two children. We had finally married in the spring of 1946,* after surmounting every kind of obstacle to do so. The two of us had gone back several times, first soon after the war ended when we were working for an organisation whose job it was to assist people who had helped escaping prisoners of war. As is usual when official attempts are made to repay something with cash which was given freely at the time out of kindness of heart, a great deal of ill-will was created in this case by the Treasury, or whoever held the purse-strings, who decreed that any money that was disbursed to these people in 1946 should be at the old, pre-Armistice rate of exchange which was seventy-two liras to the pound, which by now was absolutely nothing. Most Italians, too, took exception to the official certificate which was given to them as a testimony to what they had done, and which had at the foot of it what was obviously some sort of artificial reproduction of the signature of Field-Marshal Alexander who would, undoubtedly, have been shocked if he had known what the effect would be on the recipients. It would have been better to have given nothing at all. The only thing we could do was to try and give people presents in kind instead of money, and this we sometimes contrived to do so that, eventually, someone would receive a brand new set of tyres which, in 1946, were worth a small fortune, but were still an inadequate recompense.

What would have been worth more than all this would have been if more of the prisoners who escaped in Italy had, at least, written to thank their hosts after the war was finished. Some did; many who should have known better didn't.

Now, in 1956, you could drive a jeep all the way up to Signor Zanoni's house; but the house was gone. Turning the angle of the cowshed in which I had first found him milking Bella all those years ago, we came on the ruins of it. One broken wall and a heap of stones and slates and baulks

*How we succeeded in doing so and our subsequent life together is described in *Something Wholesale*, Hodder and Stoughton, 1970.

of timber protruding from the rubble; the fireplace still standing, with the pot-hooks still hanging in it and part of the stairs which once led to the upper landing were all that was left of the house Wanda and I remembered. It had been a small house, but surely not as small as these pathetic remains suggested.

The new house rose stark and white on the ridge above. It was a three-storeyed building, and had an elegant iron balcony painted in a contemporary shade of orange. Next to it there was a huge building with ventilated windows used for the *stagionatura* of ham.

We were disappointed at the passing of the old house but the feeling soon vanished. As we always had been, we were given a royal welcome and once in the kitchen things seemed much as they always had. The signora was a bit broader in the beam, Signor Zanoni more wrinkled and a bit balder, and the children were grown-up. One was a bricklayer; another was married. Only the old aunt had died, quite blind behind her spectacles.

"The house fell down at the beginning of last year," Signor Zanoni said. "Fortunately, we were in the fields."

I asked him what had happened to make him so prosperous. Had he struck oil?

"No, Enrico," he said modestly, "I just worked hard and we have made a good thing of the *stagionatura*."

That night the signora cooked a great dinner and we had *gnocchi*. And we were invited to eat to the bottom of the pot and find the *sterlina d'oro* but, again, no one succeeded.

The next day Signor Zanoni took us up over the Colle del Santo to the village. We went by the track; the path that he had cut through the woods had grown in long ago and the hut where I had met Wanda was no more. Even the clearing had gone. On the way we went to the Pian del Sotto, but there was no one there we knew. Luigi and Agata had moved away to another farm in another province. With none of them there it was a sad place inhabited by ghosts; but Signor Pellegri, the host at the dance, and his wife were still at the farm where it had taken place.

At the village the survivors of the two great families were waiting for us, all older and much more bent. Large men whom I remembered as small boys came forward and pumped my hand, enveloping it in their great fists. One of the biggest was Pierino, the little boy who had taken me down to be interviewed by the Chairman of the Board. Only the Chairman, Scamperdale himself, the great planner, was not there. He was dead and his family were in Milan. Toasts were drunk in the wine which was as nasty as it had always been. I insisted that we should all eat at the inn in order that there should be no ill-feeling about whom we lunched with, but we would have eaten better in any of the houses. Nevertheless it was a success. Old men, without teeth, shrilled in my ear, "Well, what do you think of it now, Enrico? We've got a road, and a school. There's even a road on your mountain, and a man from Parma has dug a lake and it's full of trout. Now we have tourists. Soon, there'll be skyscrapers. You won't know us at all. Better than a cave, eh? Drink some more vino, Enrico?" and they went on to say that it was *proprio brutto vino*, which it was.

After lunch we set off to find the cave. Francesco led the way. Although he was nearer eighty than seventy-five he still had the same lean look and the very easy hillman's stride I remembered. We went up on to the ridge as quietly as we had ever done, although there was no need for quietness. In the woods there was no one cutting wood and the tunnels had all grown in. From the fields below came the growl of tractors. There were no ploughboys, like Armando, calling to their beasts any more.

On the way up I asked Francesco about the *carbonari*.

"Finished," he said. "Everyone uses methane gas for cooking now. The last *carbonari* are over the other side of the *crinale*, in the Maremma."

Francesco went on up like a hound on a strong scent and then paused on the edge of the labyrinth for a moment before suddenly going off down into one of the ditches. I could no longer remember in which part of it the cave had been. It was something I thought I would never forget. There was not much left of it when he did find it. A part of the wall which Bartolomeo, who was long dead, had built; and beneath the earth where the fireplace had been, I unearthed some charred pieces of wood, just as I once had in the clearings of the *carbonari*.

And we all sat round in the early afternoon sunshine and, from time to time someone said "*Ma!*" And I thought of all the men and women and children who had come up with food for us in all sorts of weather, bringing anything they could spare, and if they couldn't spare it they brought it just the same. They all took their courage in their hands and made the long journey up the mountain.

"We've seen some things here, my friends," Francesco said. "We and our children. Let's hope that it will never be like that again."

I knew what he meant. The partisans really began that year we were captured, 1944. There had been big fighting on what I always thought of as my mountain. We had been a sort of curtain-raiser, a little light relief before the big, epic tragedy began. Il Corvo and his friends may not have done so well at the rehearsals but it had been all right for them on the night, and all the succeeding ones of what became a very long run.

It was time to go. We had a long journey on foot in front of us. Up to the Castello del Prato, where we would not find Abramo; he had gone, the road on the mountain had been too much for him. He had retreated with his sheep to the *crinale*. Then down into the gorge where Alfredo had lit the fire that bitter night, and across the river and up the other side to the village where Amadeo, who was now completely blind and whose wife was dead, waited for us, and the man who had mended my boot and his wife, and the signora who had scrubbed our backs and her husband who had scrubbed our backs and built our beds, and many others.

Just as we were leaving Francesco took me on one side.

"There's one thing I never told you," he said. "Perhaps I should have done when you first came back, but I couldn't bring myself to. It was a matter of honour.

"You know that we are really only two families here. You remember the night you had to leave the hut in a hurry because the *milizia* were coming? Well, it was one of us who gave you away. He had helped you as much as anyone; but before the armistice he had always supported the Fascists. He thought and thought about it and then he decided that he had been wrong to abandon them because they were losing. And that's what happened. He denounced you to the *segretario*. He didn't want the reward though and he made sure that he didn't get it. Do you know how? Because he said what he had done just in time for the rest to get you out.

"It's a bit different where you're going," he went on, "but not all that much. The one who denounced you there was a woman. She did it for the same reason and she made a bargain with the militia not to burn the village or touch anyone inside it. She had to, things had become warmer then. She earned the reward; but she didn't take it either. They're always reminding her of what she did. Her life has been a misery. She was lucky not to be shot by the partisans. They kept it quiet in the village. Here, only a few know about our affair. You can meet both of them if you like; you had dinner with one of them today. He was very, very close."

"No thank you," I said, "we've all had enough of this sort of thing to last us for the rest of our lives." And I really meant it. And together with Wanda and our children and the boy who had come over the valley to guide us, we went up towards the Castello del Prato.